GLOBAL CORPORATIONS

Books by Richard Eells

CORPORATION GIVING IN A FREE SOCIETY

THE MEANING OF MODERN BUSINESS

CONCEPTUAL FOUNDATIONS OF BUSINESS (with Clarence Walton)

THE GOVERNMENT OF CORPORATIONS

THE BUSINESS SYSTEM: Readings in Ideas and Concepts (3 Volumes)
    (with Clarence Walton)

THE CORPORATION AND THE ARTS

EDUCATION AND THE BUSINESS DOLLAR (with Kenneth G. Patrick)

MAN IN THE CITY OF THE FUTURE (with Clarence Walton)

GLOBAL CORPORATIONS: The Emerging System of World Economic
    Power

GLOBAL CORPORATIONS

The Emerging System
of World Economic Power

Richard Eells

Columbia University

Introduction by George W. Ball

Revised Edition
with an Epilogue

THE FREE PRESS
A Division of Macmillan Publishing Co., Inc.
NEW YORK

Collier Macmillan Publishers
LONDON

The Free Press
A Division of Macmillan Publishing Co., Inc.
866 Third Avenue, New York, N.Y. 10022

Collier Macmillan Canada, Ltd.

Library of Congress Catalog Card Number: 75–18008

Printed in the United States of America

printing number

1   2   3   4   5   6   7   8   9   10

Original edition published by Interbook Incorporated

Library of Congress Cataloging in Publication Data

Eells, Richard Sedric Fox
    Global corporations.

    Includes bibliographical references and index.
    1.   International business enterprises.
2.   International business enterprises—Social
aspects.   I.   Title.
[HD2755.5.E44   1975]   338.8'8   75–18008
ISBN 0-02-909270-1

CONTENTS

PREFACE TO THE REVISED EDITION

When this book was written in 1971 and 1972, interest in global, or multinational, corporations was already growing. Despite the development of subsequent pessimism about the U.S. and world economies, this interest has become even more intense. Indeed, questions about the nature of these new actors on the world stage have now reached the public mind as well as that of businessmen and economists.

Two related events helped to bring this about. First, the revelations that ITT had considered giving a million dollars to prevent Dr. Allende from becoming the President of Chile; and second, the establishment by the United Nations, partly as a result of these revelations, of a Group of Eminent Persons to investigate the role of multinational corporations in the developing world and their impact on international relations.

Since these events, the attention directed at these companies has become so active and critical that David Rockefeller, in April of 1975, called for a united effort in refuting "the proliferating critics" of multinational corporations.

In view of these developments, it seemed wise to reissue this book, which was one of the first attempts to identify the total role of global corporations in the world, and to add an epilogue bringing our approach to this subject up to date. But this is all that we can do now; what the near future and the ultimate destiny of this new form of world business will be, no one can say. The many crosscutting forces in the world mean that its future will be unpredictable for a long time to come.

Richard Eells

PREFACE TO THE FIRST EDITION

Ever since my study of *The Government of Corporations* (1962), my work has dealt largely with the corporation in its global setting. The world arena of corporate action is marked by rivals for power among great institutional contenders that include not only nation-states but also many transnational institutions. The vast network of cross-border activities carried on today by transnational nonstate institutions portends a fundamental change in the international system, the emergence of a global political economy in which some nonstate transnational institutions may eventually form an integral part.

In recent years I have pursued this issue in conversations with senior staff and chief executives of small and large multinational corporations in many parts of the world: in the United States, Great Britain, the Netherlands, and Japan, where so many of the great multinational corporations are based, and in other countries of Europe; in India, New Zealand, Australia, and Southeast Asia; in smaller places, including Hong Kong, Malta, Yugoslavia, Greece, and Iran; and, of course, in the neighboring countries, Mexico and Canada.

I have discussed some of the issues raised in this book with students in my classes, especially those in the executive degree program at the Columbia Graduate School of Business, and also with many writers on corporate matters. It is primarily the probing philosophical questions about the nature of corporations that arise in these discussions which impel me to search for "the right concepts by which to conduct the analysis"; for it is only in this way, and not by merely extending familiar images of corporate enterprise into big world companies, nor by merely the piling of fact on fact, that one can make progress in an understanding of the role of multinational corporations in the world of today and tomorrow.

A grant from The Rockefeller Foundation helped to make possible much of the research for this book; I acknowledge with thanks the aid that has been extended by this distinguished foundation.

Richard Eells

GLOBAL CORPORATIONS

Introduction

Only partially aware of what they were doing, the Founding Fathers created the conditions that made possible the modern American economy by writing two key provisions into the Constitution. One prohibited the states from laying duties or imposts on imports or exports; the other delegated to the Congress the power to regulate interstate commerce—a power which the Supreme Court by a series of decisions over many years was to elaborate and expand to meet the needs of a developing continent.

Reinforcing one another, these provisions made it possible to define the market in which business could flourish by the broad boundaries of the nation rather than the constricting borders of individual states. To acclaim this as one of the major decisions of that critical year in Philadelphia involves some sterile speculative assumptions. Yet—in the absence of action of some other kind—it seems possible that, had the Constitution not contained these provisions, the United States would, in economic terms, have become little more than a kind of Germanic Federation without even a dominant Prussia to impose a *Zollverein*.

Because the individual American states were smaller in population than many of the nations of Western Europe, the nation's economy might well have suffered from arrested development. It would have been clearly impossible to build efficient industries exploiting the economies of scale within markets defined by constrictive state lines. Moreover, since economic and political fragmentation go hand in hand, one can even speculate that, if the individual states had been permitted to establish their own protected markets, the political glue that held them together might have proved inadequate.

In a very real sense, the Constitution came in the nick of time; because even by 1789 the new states were developing mercantilist habits. A farmer carting cordwood from Connecticut to New

York was stopped at the state line and made to pay duty. Another farmer, barging a load of pigs across the Hudson from New York, had to pay a tariff when his cargo reached the Jersey shore.

It was another example of where the young lawyer-politicians convened in Philadelphia reacted to a prophetic instinct. By forbidding the states to interfere with the nationwide growth of enterprise, they prepared America for the explosive expansion that accompanied the wide use of machinery. Once the Civil War had fractured old patterns, free-wheeling entrepreneurs struck out with energy and confidence to supply the burgeoning needs of an expanding nation, and, by the end of the Nineteenth Century, America was quite prepared to challenge the older industry of Europe on its own territory. Indeed we find a British writer as early as 1901 already bewailing the "American invasion." "The most serious aspect of the American industrial invasion," wrote Mr. Fred A. McKenzie, "lies in the fact that these newcomers have acquired control of every new industry created during the past fifteen years. In old trades we are hard put to it to hold our own; in the new we are scarcely making any pretense at doing so."

European industrialists had no great free market in which to expand; unlike America, the nation-states that emerged in Western Europe were not organized on a continent-wide basis. To be sure, enterprises sold their wares across national boundaries but largely in the traditional form of exports, while only a few European companies had the vigor and foresight to establish sources of production outside their home country.

It was inevitable, therefore, that American firms, with a wide continent in which to operate and maneuver, should have learned concepts of scale and magnitude far exceeding those common in European business. Meanwhile, a few American companies—particularly in the new and more dynamic sectors—had the audacity to build plants and facilities overseas. For the others, the American market provided all the challenge and opportunity required.

This abruptly changed with the Second World War. Then many Americans gained familiarity with Europe through our military involvement, while at home there was, in certain sectors, a vast expansion of production to meet wartime needs. Emerging from the war with an intact industrial plant and a new sense of scope and scale, American businessmen developed not only a wider interest in the overseas market but a greater self-confidence in expanding operations beyond the confines of their home country.

No doubt the impulse to expand around the world was also greatly stimulated by our new feeling of world mission—awareness that America was the world's most powerful nation and that we had vast responsibilities in almost every corner of the globe. And, finally, to all this was added computers and the other tools of increasingly sophisticated management that made it possible to control and direct operations thousands of miles from home base.

It was, therefore, no accident that American entrepreneurs should begin to think in global terms—not merely in terms of national markets but of the world market. No longer was it a question of producing at home and exporting overseas; new possibilities emerged for deploying the factors of production on a global scale—the opportunity to find and use materials, machines, capital and management with a new flexibility that took little account of the limits imposed by the political boundaries of nation-states which were much too confining for modern enterprise.

But just as it was inevitable that great enterprises should feel driven to organize themselves on a world scale, it was also inevitable that there would be an increasing collision between multinational corporations and nation-states. Even though created by private initiative and with no political objectives of their own, corporations that buy, sell, and produce abroad do have the power to affect the lives of peoples and of nations in a manner that necessarily challenges the prerogatives and responsibilities of political authority.

Quite likely, had national governments continued, as in the *laissez-faire* atmosphere of the Nineteenth Century, to confine their interests and activities to the advancement of empire and the protection of the lives and properties of the citizenry, this collision of competing sovereignties would have resulted in only minimal trouble. But, simultaneously with the rapid flowering of the multinational corporation, has come a vast extension and expansion of the responsibilities and activities of governments. Obviously, the degree to which governments interfere in the market place varies widely, depending on the traditions and political complexion of the particular country, but a high degree of interference is now almost universal.

3

Inevitably these two developments—the broadening of governmental responsibility and the rapid expansion of the multinational company—have resulted in a competition and, ultimately, a collision of sovereignties. How can a national government be expected to sit calmly by while a corporate management—based 5,000 miles away—is able, by its decisions, to affect the prosperity of the country over which that government presides? Who can expect local political authority, in other words, to permit absentee managements to interfere with national economic plans, create or diminish employment, and, by their decisions materially affect the foreign exchange earnings and, hence, the balance of payments of the country in question?

These questions have, of course, more relevance for small countries than for large ones, since, if the economy is both substantial and diversified, individual enterprise is unlikely to have a major impact on national policy as a whole; yet in countries medium-sized now but large by Nineteenth Century standards the effect on individual industrial sectors may still be substantial, and when the industries concerned are particularly sensitive because of considerations of national defense or even national pride, some reaction from the government in question may be expected.

Unhappily, there is little national governments can do to rectify the situation without, at the same time, seriously hobbling the effective operation of the multinational company. They can expropriate properties, restrict investments, or subject the activities of the multinational company in the country in question to multitudinous regulations, but the effect will necessarily be to interfere with the efficiency with which the multinational company conducts its operations—and hence uses the resources available to it.

Some companies have attempted to soften the reactions of national governments by corporate diplomacy—which has proved in most cases a euphemism for protective coloring. Often this has included taking local partners, listing the shares of subsidiaries on local exchanges, employing local managers, and trying to behave as though its corporate children were national companies of the host country which only distantly acknowledged their absentee parent. Efforts of this kind have been adopted with varying degrees of success, and the attempt to achieve a local identity should not be rejected out of hand, though clearly it is more suited to certain types of corporate activity than to others.

Yet, in many cases, the costs of seeking recognition as a local citizen can be excessive. The peculiar genius of the multinational company stems from its ability to view the world economy from a single point of vantage and to deploy resources without regard to national origin in response to a common set of economic standards. What makes local partners an often burdensome encumbrance is that they are, in a sense, enemies of such mobility, since their interests relate to the prosperity of the local subsidiary rather than the world enterprise as a whole. Put another way, the scope of their thinking is defined by the national economy rather than the world economy.

This fundamental difference in attitude is almost certain to produce conflicts over corporate policy affecting a wide spectrum of issues that can be reconciled only through an accommodation of interests at some cost to the full efficiency of the world company.

Conflicts, for example, are likely to occur with respect to dividend policy. A local partner may wish earnings distributed, while the management of the world company finds it more profitable to sell or abandon them. Finally, the management of a world company may find it more profitable to serve the market of a neighboring country not by production in the host country but through subsidiaries located elsewhere.

Yet, if the existence of local partners impairs the flexibility required, if the multinational corporation is to fulfill its full promise of using resources more efficiently, how does one reconcile the demands of two competing sovereignties—corporate managements and host governments? From the point of view of a host government, an absentee corporate management represents power without legitimacy, since where can one find a legitimate base for the power of corporate managements to make decisions that can affect economic life of nations to whose peoples they have no defined responsibility and to whose governments they are beholden in only a limited way?

Ever since the publication, in the early 1930's, of Berle and Means' classic study of the divorcement of control from ownership of great industrial companies, Americans have puzzled over the problem of legitimacy in the domestic context. Whence do

5

corporate managements (which are in practice frequently self-perpetuating) derive the right to make decisions affecting not only the inarticulate mass of shareholders but the economic welfare of whole communities and the pocketbooks of consumers?

This question is far from simple even in domestic terms; when translated to the level of world operations it acquires additional layers of complexity. Within our own national boundaries, an industrial corporation is kept under substantial regulation not only by state laws and regulatory agencies but by the Federal Government. For a multinational company, however, there is no overriding political authority to oversee the totality of its operations nor—and this is even more important—is there any organic arrangement to prevent national governments from interfering with the company's activities in world commerce in the same way that the United States Constitution—enforced by the Federal Judiciary—limits the power of states to interfere with a domestic company's role in interstate commerce.

In philosophical terms the problem is one of considerable intellectual interest but, if that were all that were involved, we could leave it for academic speculation. Unfortunately, it has also an acutely practical aspect: the conflict between the wide-ranging corporation that sees the whole world as its own proper arena and the outgrown concept of the nation-state that can serve as a definition of economic activity only at a substantial cost. The need to use resources efficiently makes it mandatory to find a solution that is both politically and philosophically satisfactory.

It was with this in mind that, four years ago, in a speech before a distinguished body of industrialists in London, I very tentatively put forward a proposal for the creation by a multilateral treaty of a supranational authority that would preside over the enforcement of a set of rules regulating the conduct of multinational corporations in host states while, at the same time, prescribing the limits in which host governments might interfere in the operation of such corporations. Largely as a matter of neatness—the feature was not essential to the scheme—I suggested that a corporation, wishing the protections against host governments provided by the treaty, must apply for a special charter from the supranational authority binding it to accept that authority's jurisdiction over its activities within any signatory nation except the country of its origin.

What I had in mind, of course, was that host governments might by treaty accept inhibitions vaguely suggestive of those to which state governments are subjected by the interstate commerce clause—although the exemption from interference would not be absolute but in accordance with a prescribed set of rules and exceptions. The operative standard defining the limits of interference would be the freedom needed to preserve and protect the central principle of assuring the most efficient use of world resources.

As I expected, my proposal was not received with wild enthusiasm. No one threw his black bowler in the air and there was no dancing that night on the pavements of the City. Quite clearly the time had not yet come for the idea, and there was no assurance it ever will; yet I think it possible that someday we may well have to turn to something of the kind if the multinational corporation is to realize its full social and economic potential. After all, the proposal contained no novel elements. The United States Constitution had pointed the way by limiting the power of State Governments to interfere with interstate transactions, while the Treaty of Rome had already brought about the creation of a supranational authority (the Commission of the European Economic Community) to provide supranational regulation of commerce within six member nations (now about to become ten). To be sure, the Community has not yet been able to agree on a Common Companies Law, but that would seem to be only a matter of time.

In discussing the problem with businessmen, I have sometimes heard the point made that an international incorporation seems hardly necessary since companies do very well in the United States with no federal incorporation but fifty different corporation laws. It is a point well taken and, as I suggested, though it would add to the tidiness of the solution, I do not insist on supranational incorporation. But what is clearly needed by the multinational corporation today is some overriding authority, such as the Federal Government provides in the United States, to provide ground rules limiting individual nation-states in interfering with its operations, for, so long as national governments accept no international code of restraints on their own conduct, the freedom of the mutinational corporation will be continually challenged.

That this challenge is likely to grow more, rather than less, severe seems apparent in the hardening attitude toward multinational companies found not only in the Third World but even in industrially advanced nations—an attitude that, hovering over the international landscape today, is a cloud already much larger than a man's hand. Japan has always imposed severe limits on foreign direct investment and shows few signs of true repentance. Canada is under increasing pressure to limit the operations of foreign industry; in fact, the as yet unpublished report of the Minister of National Revenue, Mr. Herb Gray, would—so it has been suggested in press leaks—set up a formal mechanism for screening efforts of foreign industry to take over Canadian companies. Recently, the so-called Colonna report prepared by the staff of the European Economic Community disclosed a school of opinion among the Eurocrats that may well be translated into serious inhibitions on the expansion of multinational companies within the Common Market.

Though still manageable, the problem is thus likely to become more critical as the expansion of world-wide enterprises generates greater counterpressures from local industry and chauvinistic politicians. Unless serious thought is given to the means of legitimatizing the operations of multinational companies within prescribed rules, national sovereignties are likely to have the last word—and it will not be a constructive one.

It was in this spirit that I put forward the suggestion to create a supranational body to administer prescribed rules, strongly urging that it not be enmeshed in the bloc-ridden machinery of the United Nations and that no effort should be wasted, in the first instance, in attempting to gain signatories outside the small circle of industrialized nations. Like the GATT the proposed treaty would be regarded primarily as a mechanism for creating a code of rules among the major trading nations, reserving the possibility that, over the years, it might provide a world charter as more and more of the less-developed countries adhered to its provisions.

It was my thesis that an international company chartered under the treaty should become, in the long run, a citizen of the world. Of course, it would continue to have a central base of operations, and its operations in its home country would be subject to local law to the extent that the organic treaty did not contain overriding regulations.

8

I had no illusions that such a company would become a citizen of the world merely by a legal laying on of hands. It would require something more than an international companies law to validate its passport; the enterprise must in fact become international. This meant, among other things, that share ownership in the parent should be more and more widely dispersed so that the company could not be regarded as the exclusive instrument of a particular nation, though I recognized that, in view of the underdeveloped state of most national capital markets even in economically advanced countries, such dispersal was not likely to occur for some years to come. Yet, over the long pull, as in more and more countries savings are effectively mobilized for investment, it is reasonable to expect that companies will acquire an increasingly denationalized character, while one may, at the time, expect a gradual internationalizing of Boards of Directors and parent company managements.

Conceived in the terms I suggested, a world companies law could not only serve a vital economic purpose, but might also have larger political implications. Freeing world business from national interference through the creation of new world instrumentalities would inevitably, over time, point up the inadequacy of our political arrangements. At least, in a small way, it might thus serve to stimulate mankind to close the gap between our archaic political structure and the visions of commerce that vault beyond confining national boundaries to fulfill the full promise of the world economy.

Unfortunately, the context in which these questions must be answered has grown more, rather than less, complicated with the revision of values that has been under way over the last few years. Macroeconomic statistics are no longer accepted as an adequate measure of national achievement; substantial qualifications are necessary. Not the least spring from those concerns now part of the new vulgate—"environment" and "ecology." So far these words imply a Pandora's box of responsibilities for nation-states, while at the same time disclosing the obsolescence of the nation-state as a unit of political responsibility; for pollution, like trade and investment, cannot be kept within national boundaries. Yet the problems of trade and pollution are inextricably intertwined since efforts to protect the environment impose additional costs on production with the unhappy result that the most polluting state may find itself in a position of relative advantage in world markets.

It is for this reason that we must in time come to devise some larger political structure in which scrutiny and regulation can extend to larger and larger geographical areas.

Within the past few years, the production of books about the multinational corporation has become a major growth industry, but most of the books have been largely descriptive in nature or concerned with the manner in which various kinds of multinational corporations operate—how they make and communicate their decisions, manage their research and development, and deal with their shareholders. Thus, very little critical attention has been paid to what seems to me the most interesting area of speculation—the role of the corporation in its organic political aspects. What does the concept mean in relation to the political structure of the world and how will two interlocking sovereignties—the managements of multinational companies and the governments of nation-states manage to resolve their contradictory objectives?

It is the special virtue of Professor Eells' study that he has not shied away from these central questions. He sees the corporation as something more than a convenient fiction by which entrepreneurs can organize to do business around the world. For him, it has both political and social implications that can in time work profound changes in the thoughts men have about the way they organize their affairs. His book should provide a powerful stimulant to a broader focus on the problem.

George W. Ball

New York City
January 7, 1972

Chapter I

THE MODERN CORPORATION
IN A NEW WORLD ROLE

While the literature on the multinational corporation is large and growing, we still lack a mature theory of the institution which places it in the context of competing political economies in the world arena. There are advocates of reform and reaction who would like to see the multinational corporation as an instrument of their own policies, but, like other great forms of collective action in the history of mankind, the corporation has a way of eluding those who seek to put it to their own exclusive uses, however noble the ideology may be which covers their mode of action. We are dealing here with the nature of an institution that is undergoing dynamic change at the same time that world politics and world economies are both merging and changing in ways that portend a new global organization of human affairs. We cannot say what the outcome of all this epochal change may be in A.D. 2000 and beyond, but we can try to place the multinational corporation in this larger dynamic process of change.

The modern corporation is one of several salient forms of collective action devised for the governance of human affairs. The Family is one of these. So is the Church, which seeks to govern man in his "vertical" relationship with divine forces. In the "horizontal" relationships among men on earth, the State in many different forms governs human affairs, notably through territorially differentiated sovereign nation-states. The Corporation is the dominant form of collective action in governing men in their productive relationships with each other and with the physical environment. The Academy is another form governing relationships concerning the discovery and uses of knowledge.

Many different types of collectivities have been devised by man for such basic purposes, but the Church, the State, the Family, the Academy, and the Corporation are five that have survived with notable success. There have been overlappings of these major types, as in the medieval Church that also strove to be a universal Empire and in the Soviet model of the modern State that tries to take over the productive function and eliminate the vertical relationship entirely. But the general trend in modern times is to differentiate the functions of Church, State, and Corporation, and to establish structural and procedural institutions appropriate to each.

It cannot be said that we have yet arrived at a stable solution of the form-and-function problem. Further differentiation and specialization are probable in the future. Some newly discovered relationships of man and his conception of himself to his total environment—as these appear in the Space Age and the New Age of Energy—are likely to turn up the need for radically new types of institutions. These new institutions will have to make their way to acceptance in competition with the older ones, and in a redistribution of functions among them all.

The multinational corporation, in this general frame of reference, can be regarded as a new institution seeking a new place in man's total environment. From the political scientist's point of view, the function of the multinational corporation may be said to be one device for the governance of man in his productive activities on a transnational and even a global basis. From a business point of view, it may be seen more narrowly as an instrument only for the profitable transnational use of owner's capital. The businessman sees business enterprise, lured on by the hope for profit, as phenomenally productive, not only in the industrialized countries where it has been responsible for pushing up the standard of living to unprecedented levels, but also potentially capable of doing so on a global basis.

Insofar as production-for-profit means the production of goods, one faces the argument that services will outdistance goods. As to the American corporation, for example, it has been said that "education, health care, and research, along with the diverse functions associated with the qualitative improvement of life in an urbanized society, promise to supplant goods production as the economy's main propulsive force."[1] Yet when one surveys the global economic situation, it hardly seems probable

1. Richard J. Barber, *The American Corporation: Its Power, Its Money, Its Politics* (Dutton, 1970), p. 291.

12

that the need for "goods production" will decline for decades to come, if ever. More likely is the prospect of heavier demand upon the corporate instrument to produce the food, the fiber, the energy resources, and all the rest that will be required to satisfy soaring expectations.

The modern corporation, in both its local and its multinational forms, is not about to be dumped into the dustbin of history as an outmoded organizational instrument. Its productional function will embrace services as well as goods and with the shift to services there will be new forms and processes in multinational corporate policy.

There is urgent need for a theory of international production that "focuses on how to obtain an optimum international allocation of resources in a world in which productive factors—especially capital—move with considerable ease among nations whose governments are by no means reconciled to the phenomenon."[2] Here we reach the key question about political and economic processes that meet and often conflict. Cross-border movement of capital and other factors of production has vastly increased during the past few decades posing a central problem for the macroeconomist: how to keep the manifold benefits accruing from extensive transnational economic intercourse while maintaining sufficient domestic freedom for each nation to pursue its legitimate economic objectives?[3] How are we to deal with the noncongruence of the transnational "domain" of a multinational corporation, on the one hand, and numerous—often jealous—national jurisdictions, on the other?

A Chilean economist argues with insight that the dependence of Latin American countries on other countries cannot be overcome without a qualitative change in their internal structures and external relations, that the internal situation in the Latin American countries is a part of the world economy, and that the underdeveloped countries "develop within the framework of a process of dependent production and reproduction" largely designed in faraway centers of monopoly capital.[4] The managers of

2. Judd Polk, "The New World Economy," *Columbia Journal of World Business*, Vol. 3, No. 1, January-February 1968, pp. 7-8.

3. Richard N. Cooper, *The Economics of Interdependence* (McGraw-Hill, 1968), Ch. 1.

4. Theotonio Dos Santos, "The Structure of Dependence," *American Economic Review*, Vol. 60, No. 2, May 1970, pp. 231-236.

the "economics of imperialism" pursue "multifaceted strategies" in an anxiety to overcome nationalistic interference with quantities and prices of raw materials shipped transnationally. The cross-border movement of factors of production, so characteristic of multinational corporate enterprise, arouses the antipathy of nationalistic critics who seek ways through domestic policy, as well as through foreign, to counter this movement, or at least its allegedly bad effects. This mobility has indeed been regarded by some economists as the essence of multinational corporate enterprise and the definitional criterion that separates it from the domestic corporate enterprise. Factor mobility is pertinent to this search, but more important are the dynamics of international politics and the resultant stresses and strains. The ignoring of factor movements in the models of international trade is now attacked as a barrier to the understanding of the stresses and strains on the international system and also of the economic viability of multinational corporations. That viability is said, for example, to depend to a large extent on economies of growth, especially where there is a large initial technological and human-capital disparity between countries.[5] Technology transfer is an important part of the factor flow,[6] and this leads to problems of international politics. Multinational corporations may, furthermore, be regarded as a substitute for the market as a method of organizing international exchange—"islands of conscious power in an ocean of unconscious cooperation"—thus raising questions of their efficiency as instruments of a political economy when they become oligopolistic decision-makers in an imperfect market.[7]

All of this goes to show how ineluctably one is led from business-enterprise considerations to political and economic theory in attempting to describe the role of the multinational corporation in the world arena.

A mature theory of the multinational corporation will treat

5. Robert E. Baldwin, "International Trade in Inputs and Outputs," *American Economic Review*, Vol. 60, pp. 430-434.

6. Jack Baranson, "Technology Transfer Through the International Firm," *American Economic Review*, Vol. 60, pp. 435-440.

7. Stephen Hymer "The Efficiency (Contradictions) of Multinational Corporations," *American Economic Review*, Vol. 60, pp. 441-448, quoting D. H. Robertson.

the interaction of what Boulding[8] calls the technological and integrative systems of the world. The multinational corporation, in these terms, would possibly be treated as a technological subsystem, while a global system of political economy, emerging under the nuclear threat, would be treated as an integrative subsystem. The multinational corporation, as a system of social and material technology, confronts the nation-state of our time; but the nation-state is itself threatened by nuclear technology, which undermines the state's capability to offer security—its first task. Gunpowder reduced the castle-keep to an insecure place; so does nuclear energy render frontiers on the map obsolescent. The multinational corporation is but one component of a technological subsystem. It may, however, offer one means of contributing to world order by becoming an integrative subsystem of the world economy.

That multinational corporations are inescapably affected by the swirl of political forces in world affairs is a truism. Less well understood is the integral role of the multinational corporation in the international system. It is not today a formal part of that system. Indeed, some observers regard the multinational corporation as little more than an ingenious corporate device for overcoming the handicaps of the international system of sovereign states.

The mutually exclusive territorial jurisdictions of states, although reasonably well suited to nationalistic purposes, seriously hamper cross-border factor mobility. But the productive instrumentalities required at this stage in man's reach for a better life on this earth necessarily include the multinational corporation, and the international system bends to this necessity. National economies—whether capitalist, socialist or mixed—probably could not shoulder the world's production and distribution tasks through state trading and other forms of public-sector economic organization at national and supranational levels, without heavy reliance on private-sector organizations of the multinational corporate type. Collectivist systems of limited nationalistic reach are incapable of producing and distributing the goods and services that will meet the mounting global expectations of peoples. The multinational corporation is a partial response to the need for

8. Kenneth Boulding, "Technology and the Love-Hate System," *Columbia Journal of World Business*, Vol. 3, pp. 41-49.

larger geographic reach, for more flexibility in organizational experimentation, for greater latitude in corporate procedure, and, above all, for more imaginative innovation in the design of corporate goals for this vast productive output.

But, there remains the stubborn fact of the "primacy of politics" in the world arena—the primary fact that the international system of sovereign states, however anachronistic it may seem to be, is the crucial element in world affairs that gives the multinational corporation its qualifying name. We have to ask ourselves whether the "multi-*national*" qualification is accurate and just, but as to the sovereignty of a multiplicity of states in the international system there can be no doubt. Sovereignty implies dominion, autonomy, freedom from external control, a claim to authoritative supremacy within a given territorial jurisdiction—these and much else besides. It is a quality now denied to business corporations which have to live within the international system.

It is a system that hardly describes the best of all possible worlds. Men aspire to a better system. What we have is inadequate, creaky, dangerous, and a barrier to the evolution of human institutions. The next step is indicated by both the universal aspirations of man and by his longing for privacies that the sovereign state ceaselessly encroaches upon. But if the state is an anachronism, it cannot be superseded until better building blocks for a new system can be created.

The quest for better ways to organize mankind goes on apace as the "organizational revolution" of our time turns up all sorts of collectivities, large and small. Some of the large-scale organizations are as threatening to liberty as the state, and the modern corporation has not escaped criticism on this point. Nor do the alternatives to nationalism necessarily point the way to a viable world-wide political economy that would avoid the divisiveness of our present international system. A world of great corporations, powerful churches, ubiquitous political parties, labor unions, and so on, without sovereign states, would have somehow to be given unity in order to reduce disorder to tolerable levels and to allow the peaceable production of the things people want. Transnational organizations of all kinds flourish and increase in number and kind because the international system of sovereign states simply does not meet human demands and aspirations; there has

16

to be a practical solution of the problem of world order that combines national and transnational, as well as public- and private-sector forms of human organization.

The multinational corporation is only one part of the practical answer to the problem of a viable world political economy. But it is a far more significant part than is generally recognized. One reason for this belated recognition is the ideological struggle that mistakenly pits corporate enterprise on the "reactionary" side against radical and revolutionary programs of the right and left. The multinational corporation today is indubitably an instrument of a capitalist economy that is under massive attack; but the zealots of Right and Left seldom pause to examine the multinational corporation as an organizational instrument that is in essence quite neutral. Another reason is that in the strong contemporary resurgence of anarchist and related doctrine there is widespread skepticism about all large-scale organizations; their power to govern men is regarded as quite as dangerous to liberty as the power of states, and there is reluctance to fly to new evils.

The most interesting reason, however, for failure to consider the multinational corporation as relevant to the creation of a world-wide political economy is one that is traceable largely to the business community itself. Preoccupied with immediate operational decisions, the managers of multinational corporations too often think only of business that has "gone international." But the multinational corporation is far more than an instrument of misnamed "international business." It is business gone *transnational* in a hampering international system. It is the modern corporation in a new phase of historic development.

This new era in the evolution of the corporation as a major social institution will in all probability see the corporate instrument drafted for global ecological service. It will help to meet the need for a better adaptation of man to his environment in the earth's biosphere. In meeting this need, the multinational corporation will seek and find a "corporate domain" that transcends the traditonal political frontiers. For this reason, it seems fair to say that the transnational dimension of the modern corporation is its natural dimension.

Confined within national political boundaries, corporate enterprise is unnaturally constricted; its market, even in large continental dimensions, as in the case of United States corporations and those which may eventually be free to roam the European Common Market, is to be contrasted with the world-wide market of the multinational corporation. The transnational reach of corporate enterprise has been possible through ingenious corporate policy that plants subsidiaries and affiliates of a corporate group in several countries. It is a policy that works almost entirely among the private sectors of the several countries and does not depend primarily upon inter-sovereign agreements. Thus it cannot properly be described as international, but rather as intercorporate (or intracorporate, as the case may be) transcending the political boundaries that mark off the territorial jurisdictions of sovereign states.

The transcendance of political frontiers by ingenious forms of transnational corporate organization does not, of course, free corporate executives from the dynamic forces of world politics. The entrance of the modern corporation into world affairs on an unprecedented scale has in fact forced both public and private policy makers to reconsider multinational corporate policy in political as well as economic terms. The goals and the strategies of large multinational corporations are now a matter of concern in most of the capitals of the world, as well as the board rooms of companies.

These policy makers cannot safely think of the world arena simply as a world marketplace, a situation for buyers and sellers. It is above all a power situation, an arena of contenders for influence and status, who include transnational firms as well as traditional sovereign actors. This concept of a world context of corporate action demands revision of some conventional modes of thought.

Chapter II

THE CORPORATION AS
MULTINATIONAL

The multinational corporation, seen in historical perspective, is the modern corporation at an advanced stage of development. The modern corporation, already recognized as one of the major social institutions of our time within the framework of certain nation-states, can now be seen as one of the major social institutions on the world scene. From this point of view, the multinational corporation appears on the scene when corporate business learns how to escape from the geographically limited confines of one nation's jurisdiction and to extend its corporate domain transnationally into other sovereign territories by means of factor mobility on a large scale.

International business in the form of marketing across political frontiers is a long established practice, but until recently, there were comparatively few companies and corporate groups whose industrial or commercial operations abroad involved plural centers of managerial responsibility. Today there are many corporations and corporate groups that operate and live under the laws and customs of numerous foreign countries as well as those of their original centers. They are not merely buyers and sellers in the world marketplace. They are multinational in that they organize productive as well as distributive centers in a number of nations.

Modern corporations, in large numbers and on an unprecedented scale, are now taking advantage of the porousness of political frontiers to set up cross-border or transnational domains of their own. This has political as well as economic implications that are receiving more and more attention in terms of the future of the international system of sovereign states and the international economy. The larger role of the multinational corporation in the world arena is elusive, however. We still cannot perceive the outlines of a possible world-wide political economy; it seems to require integration through a world order under law, ecologically sound maintenance of the earth's entire biosphere, and a mature conception of the role of corporate enterprise.

We may take a step in this direction by raising questions concerning the ultimate purpose of the corporation in its multinational form. Is the corporate domain of the multinational corporation to clash permanently—and perhaps in vain—with the sovereign claims of nation-states in the international system? Or will the international system of sovereign states give way at length to a more comprehensive and realistic world-wide political economy in which both nations and corporations will play their respective roles in harmony?

The problem can be stated partly in legalistic terms: the jurisdictional doctrines of private international law, combined with the less exclusionary national policies of states that encourage freedom of trade and the free exchange of ideas, buttressed by treaties of "friendship, commerce, and navigation" together with an increasing number of international conventions favoring transnational action by natural and corporate persons, all add up to "a relatively high degree of duty" on the part of sovereign states "to admit to their authoritative arenas both the private associations chartered by other states and the individual nationals of other states."[1]

Is the multinational corporation but one of many types of private associations that take advantage of the porousness of political frontiers to go their own way without much concern for the total problem of a world-wide political economy and its ultimate role in that political economy? Or is it a special kind of corporate entity, or corporate grouping, that deserves careful analysis in these larger terms of global social organization? What are we talking about when we focus upon the *multinational* corporation?

1. Myres S. McDougal and Associates, *Studies in World Public Order* (New Haven: Yale University Press, 1960), p. 180, citing Rabel, *The Conflict of Laws: A Comparative Study*. McDougal refers to the access of private associations and individuals to the "internal arenas" of sovereign states, as distinguished from the "inclusive arena" of an inchoate world public order.

The Problem of Definition

This is not a lexicographical question to be answered by turning to some standard dictionary or encyclopedia. The lexicographers have not come up with a standard definition of the term. Nor is this surprising in view of the recency of the term and its competitors such as "international corporation," "transnational corporation," "international enterprise," "multinational enterprise," "world enterprise," and so on. One is reminded of Ambrose Bierce's definition of the hydra: "a kind of animal that ancients catalogued under many heads." But all of these competing terms cannot be regarded as referring to one specific type of animal. There are differences of opinion about the "thing out there."

Definition, in logical precision, requires the use of both intension and extension: the term "multinational corporation" should refer to stated qualitative attributes and also to a quantitative aggregate or statistical universe of some kind. It is evident that we have a protean term in current usage. It covers a wide range of phenomena: transnational activities of diverse types and variously organized groups of firms, licensees, proprietorships, centralized and decentralized companies, and widely dispersed but wholly-owned subsidiaries. The "multi-" prefix alone refers to numbers of nations ranging from two to a score or more. Perhaps Bierce was right when he defined a dictionary as "a malevolent device for cramping the growth of a language and making it hard and inelastic." We do well to take a latitudinarian approach to the selection of terms that designate that dynamic collection of transnational phenomena now inexactly known as multinational corporate action.

On the Meaning of "Multinational"

We can assume that there is some statistical universe designated by the term "multinational corporations" and that the term "*the* multinational corporation" designates certain characteristics that distinguish the units of that statistical universe from other kinds of corporations. Semantically speaking, we are not required to assume or to prove that the designata of these verbal signs actually exist, but only that there is a definable class. We can speak of unicorns, though none may ever have existed or ever will; but we know what that verbal sign means. So it is of multi-national corporations, to which we can arbitrarily assign certain characteristics as a postulated class.

One such characteristic is indicated by the prefix "multi-." It seems to designate a business enterprise that operates in *many* different nations. The designation of "-national" is an issue to be discussed later on, but here it is assumed that the territorial units referred to are nations and that many are involved. Is the *number* really significant?

A notable fact is that this question is bypassed in terminology such as "transnational corporations" and "world enterprises." In some realms of discourse on the general subject of organized cross-border enterprise it is quite irrelevant whether one is talking about firms that operate in two countries only or those which operate in fifty, but number can become significant, especially in discourse about public policy concerning the multinational corporation.

The very multiplication of foreign jurisdictions, for example, into which expanding enterprises move has to be considered in relation to the great proliferation of sovereign states after World War I and especially since World War II. These two orders of numbers tell something about the pluralistic structure of the world arena. The theories of international economics, of international trade, of so-called international business (that is, in fact, not business between nations, but cross-border private-sector business), of international law, of international politics, are all profoundly affected by these orders of numbers.

The international system of nation-states and the system of cross-border business enterprise in which the multinational corporation plays a growing role interact in ways that may involve the function of numbers of states and firms in some specific way. There are clearly significant relationships between the numbers of units within each system and the sizes of these units. The bipolarity of the international system of nation-states since World War II, for example, reflects significant changes in recent years due to nuclear proliferation that may lead to multipolarity.

Multipolarity in the world system of multinational corporations is closely related to changes in the international system and the distribution by size in the universe of multinational corporations becomes more than an exercise in statistics—it may reveal basic changes in the world social process. The relationship between the size and numbers of multinational firms, on the one hand, and the power and numbers of nation-states, on the other, is obvious in problems of antitrust that arise in cross-border business. This can be seen especially in Europe and notably within the Common Market where many American multinational corporations have entered as an "American challenge." This entry will affect the future of federalism in Europe as well as United States policy regarding American subsidiaries abroad.

Still to be developed in social science is a comprehensive systems approach that interrelates the two systems of international politics and cross-border business, with special reference to the role of multinational corporations. Before that can be done we will need to know a good deal more than we do now about both systems. Our knowledge of the international system of nation-states and related public international organizations, inadequate as it is, outdistances at statistical and theoretical levels our knowledge of the system of cross-border business and its subsystem of multinational corporations. As to this latter subsystem, there is a paucity of hard information. The gap in knowledge is notable at the elementary level of numbers. What do we mean, to begin with, by "the multinational corporation" designated as a statistical universe?

The Test of Size

Assuming size to be a key criterion, and without regard to the numbers of countries in which the companies in this universe have productive facilities (or otherwise qualify under other criteria than size), then the *Fortune* directories of the largest industrials, commercial banks, and other types of enterprises, become helpful. These directories are not definitive for our purposes because they do not differentiate among companies on the basis of cross-border activities.

Rough indications, however, appear in such lists, which provide rankings by sales.[2] Only 133 of the top 500 industrials in

2. Jack N. Behrman, *Some Patterns in the Rise of the Multinational Enterprise*. Research Paper 18, Graduate School of Business, University of North Carolina at Chapel Hill, March 1969, pp. 47*ff.*

the world were based in the Common Market and EFTA countries of Europe in 1967, while 300 were based in the United States. In that year, only 38 non-United States companies had sales exceeding $1 billion; and while it is true that the sales of these 38 amounted to 5 per cent of total sales for the 200 non-United States largest industrials in the world, the largest of the 38 were outranked by United States companies. Thus, Royal Dutch/Shell, the top European company, was fourth in the 500 world's largest, and Unilever was ninth. British Petroleum ranked 18th, ICI 25th, VW 37th, and Renault 61st, to take a few examples. The rankings vary from year to year, but it remains true today that United States companies top the 500 list, as they do in most industrial sectors.

Size is significant not only in comparing parent companies, but also in comparing the size of affiliates in a given market with the size of their competitors. It appears, for example, that none of the European affiliates of the United States manufacturing companies listed in the top 500 for 1967 was without a nationally-owned superior in the host country, save possibly CGE in Italy and Bull-GE in France.[3] Only Ford-Germany ranked among the top European manufacturers in terms of capital employed, and it ranked 31st while Volkswagen ranked sixth.

Many of the big European industrials are essentially domestic companies or heavy exporters but without foreign-based manufacturing facilities. Without such cross-border extensions they might well be excluded from a universe of multinational corporations but not if size alone is the criterion. It may very well be that in assessing the future of the multinational corporation in the world arena, where power is an essential factor, the big so-called domestic or nationally-bound companies will loom large indeed—regardless of the absence of foreign-based affiliates. Financial power in these big companies, exerted at home and abroad, may be an essential factor in defining what one means by "multinational."

Even on these grounds, however, there is good reason to consider with some care J. N. Behrman's review, nation by nation, of the top industrials. This review leads him to the conclusion that there are "only about 40 European companies that may

3. *Id.*, p. 48.

be called 'multinational,' and many of them deserve the term only because of their operations throughout Europe,"[4] and not because of more extensive operations on other continents. There is a noticeable trend toward coordinating and centralizing operations in Europe and turning away from previous overseas expansion in some companies; this does not necessarily mean relaxation of efforts to reach world markets. For an indefinite period there could be a more rapid expansion of United States multinational companies than of the European out into the world, but what that is to mean ultimately for the entire pattern of multinational enterprises in all continents is not easily predictable. Projection depends in part upon what happens to European federation and the relationship of European political unity to corporate enterprise based there and seeking entry from other nations—notably the United States.

It depends also upon the patterns of industrial concentration in the decades ahead. At the present time there is a heavy concentration of foreign direct investment in the more technically advanced industrial sectors. It remains to be seen whether this will take new directions in the future, and what the effects will be on host governments. These governments are all potentially severe critics of the foreign control that may accompany the cross-border transfers of productive factors, and reactions of this kind could profoundly affect future political configurations of the world arena.

The Test of Integrated Operations

For some policy purposes, the best test for membership in the universe of multinational corporations is Behrman's: "the centralization of policy and the integration of key operations among the affiliates."[5] He regards it as a new form of enterprise that involves far more than cross-border financial ties, which in the world today have become extremely complex and of great concern to both private and public policy makers. They involve the effects of financial flows on the balance of payments and domestic economies; the ownership aspects of cross-border enterprise and their consequences for trade and capital formation; the

4. *Id.*, p. 53.
5. *Id.*, p. xiii.

separate treatment of various functional operations of cross-border enterprise such as trade, investment, licensing, competition and marketing, taxation, research and development—all of these matters, according to Behrman, have come to the focus of attention by policy makers. But he finds wanting due attention to a basic characteristic of the multinational enterprise: the decision processes that *coordinate* all of these diverse matters.

The oil companies were among the few industrial groups that would have fit his definition before the sixties. Today, those which would be included are mostly United States-based, although a few appear to be developing in Canada, Europe, and Japan. He expressly excludes any set of companies in which there are simply a parent and foreign affiliates; he points to the significant fact that prior to the fifties most affiliates overseas operated as though they were commercially independent of the parent despite some financial and other controls.

The power of multinational enterprises is traced in Behrman's analysis to the shift during the past decade or so from affiliate autonomy to central control in the parent, and especially to the integrated decision process. This power, one might add, is not only the power to penetrate into world markets and into the economies of nations; it is a power that needs to be assessed in terms of the multinational corporation's role in the world political arena. These further consequences are not examined in Behrman's monograph, although he does promise to consider public policy issues in a later study.

In describing the essential characteristics of the multinational enterprise (he does not call it a corporation), he emphasizes the intention of its policy makers "to treat the various national markets as though they were one—to the extent permitted by governments, at least."[6] Purely domestic companies do not do this, despite some cross-border exporting. While the domestic company is under the actual or potential control of a single government, the multinational enterprise faces several and in some cases a good many governments.

To achieve unity in the face of this political diversity, the multinational enterprise integrates strategic action in specific ways. It

6. *Id.*, p. 61.

is not enough to be an agglomeration of domestic companies held together only loosely by equity shares. What Behrman is looking for is the kind of cross-border enterprise that is coordinated by means of policy centralization as reflected in the single management center, in integrated operations, and in the pattern of ownership of affiliates. He looks for both personal and procedural techniques for achieving the centralization of authority. He looks for a single profit center. He examines those aspects of enterprise integration that deal with the location of production in appropriate market areas (rather than national markets per se), with centralized product-mix decisions, with the integration of intra-company sales at the levels of basic materials, components or semi-finished items, and finished products, with pricing patterns, with common purchasing and sourcing, with coordinated marketing, with research and development programs and especially with tightness of control in financing the enterprise.

Some real barriers to reliable knowledge of this universe are, however, indicated by Behrman. He wants to know, for example, the actual investment flows from and into each major country, how these flows were distributed by industry, the earnings and remittances related to such flows, the proportion of foreign investment in assets or sales of the industries most affected, the contribution to industrial net capital formation, the pattern of ownership of foreign-affiliated companies, and the relative size of these affiliates to domestically-owned enterprises in a given industrial sector. He found that available data did reveal substantial growth of foreign investment in the sixties, not only for direct investment by United States companies abroad, but also for companies in other nations that crossed boundaries for their direct investments abroad. Thus the United States was the major supplier of direct investments in Canada and the United Kingdom. The United Kingdom was the second largest investor in Canada; the United States had been the major supplier (45%) of foreign direct investments in France in 1964. He noted that Switzerland showed a large volume, some of which undoubtedly was from United States-owned subsidiaries there, but the Swiss publish no data on direct investments which would permit breaking out the origin of funds. These are only some of the examples Behrman cites[7] of the barriers to assessing with accuracy the growth of cross-border investments.

A factor in that growth has, of course, been the entry of new companies into the global world of business. How many companies?

Here Behrman turned first to the 1957 census of foreign investment by the United States Department of Commerce. That census estimated (by sample, not actual count) that 3,000 companies had facilities abroad. Of these, 400 had over 90 per cent of the outstanding investment. Ten years later, in 1967, the estimate ran to 4,500 United States companies; of these, it was estimated that 900 had investments aggregating over 80 per cent of the total. The top 200 companies probably had over half of the outstanding foreign direct investment.

Actual counts have been attempted. J. L. Angel's 1966 directory of American firms operating abroad recorded 14,000 affiliates of 4,200 United States parents as of 1966 in services, banking, selling, extraction and manufacturing.[8] Behrman has estimated that, as early as 1963, United States investors held over 25 per cent of the equity in approximately 18,000 foreign affiliates. Over 6,000 of these were in Europe, 1,800 in the United Kingdom, 800 in France, 700 each in Germany and Switzerland, 450 in Italy, 400 in The Netherlands, and 300 in Belgium.

Studies by J. K. Bruck and F. A. Lees indicated that 386 of the top 500 United States industrials in 1964 had foreign manufacturing facilities, but that only seven of these qualified as "multinational" if that term signified that 50 per cent or more of two of the following were overseas: total sales or earnings or assets or employment. The Bruck-Lees criteria permitted a count of 11 "multinational" companies in 1965.[9]

Behrman regards their criteria as excessively strict for purposes of classifying a company as "multinational"; it also makes "multinational" three corporations that are not industrial and

7. *Id.*, pp. 24-25.

8. J. L. Angel, *Directory of American Firms Operating in Foreign Countries*, Sixth edition (New York: World Trade Academy Press, 1966).

9. J. K. Bruck and F. A. Lees, "Foreign Content of U.S. Corporate Activities," *Financial Analysts' Journal*, September-October 1966; and "Foreign Investment, Capital Controls, and the Balance of Payments," *The Bulletin*, New York University Institute of Finance, April 1968, Appendix Table I.

not multinational in Behrman's usage of that term. He pointed to the fact that 199, or 52 per cent, of the 386 companies referred to in the Bruck-Lees studies and at least 10 per cent of their operations overseas, and of these there were seventy that were "foreign involved" to the tune of 25-50 per cent. Also, 122 were 10-24 per cent involved, while only the remaining seven were regarded as multinational. These were International Packers, International Milling, I. T. & T., United Shoe Machinery, Singer, and Colgate-Palmolive, all to be joined by Standard Oil (N.J.), Burroughs, H. H. Robertson, and H. J. Heinz by 1965.

The three in this list that Behrman excludes as not being "multinational" were: International Milling, which was in formula feeds produced in three countries; International Packers, which was in meat packing, doing its business chiefly by export and mainly from one foreign country; and Anaconda, a company of "relatively fixed" structure, whose major foreign assets were in three countries, from one of which about half the company's earnings were derived. These three companies are excluded because "multinational" implies to Behrman "many-nations" and "multiple choices" in the world-wide operations of a company.

The term multinational company is thus held to refer to "companies having sufficient alternatives in their operations abroad to require a 'multinational' mentality on the part of management—which begins to arise with 10 per cent of operations abroad; and by the time 25 per cent is foreign, the former 'domestic-international' division is on the way out in favor of a world-wide concept."[10]

Companies in the 25-50 per cent group Behrman regards as multinational or fast becoming so. These numbered (for United States companies) 70 in 1964 and 71 in 1965 in the Bruck-Lees count; four had climbed to the 50 per cent category and five from the lower category. With a loss of five from the 10-25 per cent category and a gain of twelve, there was a net increase of seven in that category, making a total of 129. Behrman figures that, if one were to take only those above 10 per cent as either multinational or on the way there, the number of United States enterprises had risen to 200 in 1965. But he emphasizes that some of these 200 were heavily "foreign" but not multinational.

10. Behrman, *op. cit.*, p. 45.

A project at Harvard under the direction of Raymond Vernon[11] has identified 170 companies as "multinational." That number compares favorably with Behrman's own estimates derived from his interviews in Europe covering some 40 European-based enterprises classifiable potentially as "multinational."

Why the smaller number for Europe, in view of its large commitments abroad? Part of the answer appears to be the greater attractiveness to the Europeans of exporting and expanding there rather than through overseas investment in manufacturing, and also the greater attraction of investing within Europe in extraction or services—including distribution—than overseas investment in manufacturing. This picture seems to be undergoing gradual change. Behrman's tables show the trend. Few companies in the United Kingdom were overseas investors, and most of this investment (as of 1965) was in extraction, agriculture, and insurance. Investing in industry was in developing countries in such traditional lines as meat freezing and food processing for local markets or the mother country. Behrman discerns few "multi-national" relationships being developed in investment of this kind. Imperial Chemical Industries and a few others in the more technologically advanced industries had moved overseas; but only quite recently was this trend observable in other major United Kingdom companies.

Elements of a Definition

The definition of the multinational corporation in terms of the integration and coordination of the decision process is greatly advanced by Behrman's work. That it does not meet the requirements of a definitive designation is evident when one examines the goals sought by enterprise managers and those values which public policy makers choose to set as corporate goals.

Here again the sly Biercian way of defining comes to mind. A goose, we are told in the *Devil's Dictionary*, is a bird that supplies

11. Professor Behrman participated in this project, financed principally by a grant from the Ford Foundation to the Harvard Business School for "study of multinational corporate groups and nation-states." See his "Multinational Enterprise & National Sovereignty," *Harvard Business Review*, March-April 1967, pp. 156*ff.*, where he speaks of "corporate families" with the parent corporation in the U.S., and of "family transactions" within the multinational corporate groups. See also, Raymond Vernon, *Sovereignty at Bay, The Multinational Spread of U.S. Enterprises* (New York & London: Basic Books, Inc., 1971).

quills for writing. Why is the multinational corporation not simply a cross-border business that supplies profits for investors? People have widely divergent views on this subject, as was shown in hearings[12] before the Joint Economic Committee of the United States Congress in 1970.

In these hearings a Canadian economist brushed aside the term "multinational corporation" as a misnomer. Melville H. Watkins, professor of economics at the University of Toronto and chief author of the Canadian Task Force Report,[13] declared that American domination of the corporate sector of Canada had reduced it to a "branch plant economy."[14] He objected to the wording of the committee's invitation to assist it in considering "the legal, social and political implications posed by the growth of the multinational corporation and the spread of direct foreign investment." He objected that "the very terminology 'multinational corporation' assumes away the most important question of all: are so-called multinational corporations in fact multinational?" They are not, he said, because "multinational corporations have an address and a nationality, rhetoric and intentions notwithstanding, and what we should be talking about here," he said, "are American corporations operating abroad."

The Canadian Task Force Report had stated that in 1963, 53 per cent of the assets of the 414 Canadian companies with assets exceeding $25 million were in companies more than 50 per cent owned by foreign enterprises. These were mostly enterprises based in the United States and the United Kingdom. There were, also, 32 per cent foreign-owned assets in smaller Canadian companies. The report had stated further that over half the assets of foreign-controlled firms in Canada in 1963 were in companies with assets exceeding $50 million and 40 per cent in those with assets over $100 million. And what happens when more subjective criteria are introduced?

12. *A Foreign Economic Policy for the 1970's, Hearings Before the Subcommittee on Foreign Economic Policy of the Joint Economic Committee*. U.S. 91st Congress, First and Second Sessions, 1969-70.

13. *Foreign Ownership and the Structure of Canadian Industry*. A report prepared for the Privy Council, Ottawa, Canada, 1968.

14. *Hearings*, cited, on July 30, 1970. The quotations here are drawn from Professor Watkins' mimeographed statement.

"Imperialistic" Enterprise

Watkins underlined "the tendency for American corporations to bring American law with them." That raised the problem of extraterritoriality, which he dubbed "legal imperialism" because it was "the tip of the iceberg of political control, of that manipulation and exploitation which is imperialism proper."

This reference is plainly to imperialism as conceived by the Marxists: their theory states that because capitalist societies are unable to find markets for their products and enough investment opportunities at home they tend to enslave even larger noncapitalist and, ultimately, even capitalist areas in order to transform them into markets for their surplus products and to open up new opportunities for investing their surplus capital.[15] In the minds of Lenin and Bukharin, imperialism was identified as the last stage of capitalism before its collapse and the onset of socialism and communism. To quote Lenin: "Imperialism is capitalism in that phase of its development in which the domination of monopolies and finance-capital has established itself; in which the export of capital has acquired very great importance; in which the division of the world among the big international trusts has begun; in which the partition of all the territory of the earth amongst the great capitalist powers has been completed."[16]

There are other kinds of imperialist theory. There is, for example, that of J. H. Hobson, whose book on *Imperialism* (1938) argued that the surpluses of capitalism ought to be used only to expand the home market—as in the increase of purchasing power and the elimination of over savings—rather than in imperialist expansion. There is also the "devil" theory of imperialism, operating on a lower intellectual level, which argues that imperialistic expansion and war are nothing but a conspiracy of evil capitalists for the purpose of private gain.

It is interesting that Watkins' testimony before the Joint Economic Committee's subcommittee suggests either that truly

---

15. Economic theories of imperialism and imperialistic policy are discussed in Hans J. Morgenthau, *Politics Among Nations*, Fourth edition (New York: Knopf, 1967), Ch. 5. See also George H. Sabine, *A History of Political Theory*, Third edition (New York: Holt, Rinehart and Winston, 1961), pp. 834*ff.*

16. V. I. Lenin, *Imperialism, the Highest State of Capitalism* (New York: International Publishers, 1933), p. 72.

multinational companies would not "create tensions and conflicts between home countries and host countries," or that there are no such companies at all since—as in the case of Canada—one simply faces "American corporations operating abroad." He spoke of the resultant "asymmetry of power that inheres in foreign direct investment," and of the futility of solving the problem "in a vacuum."

The witness declared that benefits of the "intrusion of capital, technology, managerial skills and so on" into Canada were not self-evident, and that this intrusion was less necessary than it was usually assumed to be; further, that "the only sensible alternative to foreign private ownership of the Canadian economy is Canadian public ownership, a Canadian economy owned and controlled by Canadians."

The Task Force Report was not adopted by the Canadian government. The Commons committee on external affairs and national defense announced in July, 1970 that it would recommend to parliament and the government the adoption of a long-range policy objective of at least 51 per cent share ownership by Canadians of all companies operating in Canada. Ian Wahn, chairman of the committee, stated that it rejected anti-Americanism but recognized that Canadian national interests had to be protected, and the development of Canada's economic potential had to be encouraged to the fullest possible extent.

The danger to Canada, Mr. Wahn said, was not political absorption by the United States but rather one of drift into such dependency on the United States that Canada would be unable, in practice, to adopt policies that would displease the United States; such inability might arise from fear of American reaction that would invoke circumstances unacceptable to Canadians. The Canadian government took the committee's report under advisement pending a separate cabinet study of foreign ownership.

This more sober reaction to the problem, which in the Canadian Task Force Report had taken on imperialistic implications, does not necessarily mean that this normative element in current definitions of the multinational corporation will subside. On the contrary, it may be expected to grow in propagandistic force as the debate on the subject spreads and deepens. It should be remembered that "the multinational corporation" is *terra incog-*

nita to most people even at the level of sophistication on political and economic matters.

The propagandists will try to get first into line to "educate the public" on this institution. For that reason alone it is necessary to use care in the normative aspects of definition so as not automatically—and unintentionally—to provide oil for the flames of noisy and sterile controversy. The need for clear policy guidance is too urgent and in the policy process the preparatory steps include usable definition of terms in the semantic sense of designating a universe of phenomena that are generally recognizable.

National and Transnational Orientation

For most observers, the key to a realistic definition today is the purpose of corporate management in reaching extra-national markets through cross-border organizational structures and decision processes. This essentially subjective attitude can be only partially measured objectively as in Richard Robinson's fourfold classification.[17] It is a classification that turns out to be more chronological for developmental analysis of firm-types than logical for statistical purposes, but it is useful for all that. It is based primarily on the development of managerial attitude and purpose, from a more or less limited national bias toward a global— or at least broadly regional—view of the business. Four types of firms—international, multinational, transnational, and supranational—are presented but not as necessarily successive stages in the growth of cross-boundary enterprise. The several types may well coexist.

First comes the *"international* firm" with a consolidation of operatives in a line office on the division level; its policy makers are willing to consider "all potential strategies for entering foreign markets—up to direct investment." Adopting the strategy of direct investment is evidently a characteristic mark of the second type: the *"multinational* firm." The multinational firm carries on foreign operations that are co-equal in structure and policy with its domestic operations, and its management is willing to allocate company resources without regard to national frontiers to a-

17. Sidney E. Rolfe, *The International Corporation*, Background Report for the XXIInd Congress of The International Chamber of Commerce, 1969, p. 12, citing Richard D. Robinson, *International Business Policy* (New York: Holt, Rinehart and Winston, 1964).

chieve corporate objectives. The multinational firm is "nation-
ally-based" in that decisions remain uni-national in terms of
ownership and headquarters management.

The *"transnational* firm" is managed and owned by persons
of different national origins, and as a result of this, presumably,
decisions become free of national bias.

In the *"supranational* firm" any grounds for nationalistic bias
would presumably be completely overcome because such a firm
would be "denationalized by permitting it exclusively to register
with, [be] controlled by, and pay taxes to, some international
body established by multinational convention."

This definition of "multinational firms", "nationally-biased"
in that shareholding and managerial power remained localized in
the home country but with production factors across borders,
has been said[18] to fit most of the firms considered today as
multinational. They are still identifiable as American, Dutch,
Swiss, German, Japanese, and so on. Only a few, like Shell and
Unilever, might be regarded as "transnational firms."

No legal basis for the completely "supranational firm" of
Robinson's definition exists, for even the Common Market has
yet to provide the necessary infrastructure of public administration for such a firm; the United Nations is even less likely to fill
the bill for other reasons inherent in the pattern of politics in the
world arena.

There is no evidence that Robinson's terminology has been
widely accepted in contemporary discourse, even though his
analysis is obviously a contribution of considerable value. For the
purposes of the present book, the term "multinational corporation" signifies all four types of firms under Robinson's classification, but for certain policy purposes it would be advisable to
adopt his suggested distinctions in describing different statistical
universes. Under each of his four headings one could easily distribute companies by category of business.

Corporate Autonomy

Cross-border capital flows and the extraterritorial application
of antitrust and other laws raise the question whether certain
corporations are independent of most sovereign states. The issue

18. Rolfe, *op. cit.*, p. 12.

was brought up in hearings before the Joint Economic Committee's subcommittee on a foreign economic policy for the 1970s. E. P. Neufeld, professor of economics and director of graduate studies in the Department of Political Economy, University of Toronto, Canada, discussed capital flows across the frontier from the United States. He said that the magnitude of foreign ownership, especially in equity capital, was worrying the Canadians. They were concerned, too, about the impact on Canada of United States law relating to the operation of United States subsidiary companies in Canada. The extraterritorial effects of United States legislation and "administrative initiations"—such as prohibition of trade by Canadian subsidiaries of United States companies with Communist countries and the application in Canada of United States antitrust regulations—had, he said, led an extreme left wing Canadian group to advocate a policy of nationalization of industry as the way to curb foreign ownership. A much larger group favored limits to foreign ownership in certain sectors and "the elimination of abuses that have arisen through foreign ownership."[19]

According to Professor Neufeld, "multinational firms . . . have acquired such important international dimensions in their marketing, producing, financing, research, and accounting activities, that they seem to enjoy an unusual degree of independence in their relations with particular governments." The way their profits were distributed internationally, or their capital was allocated, might not always harmonize with the results to be expected from trade and capital flows in an environment of perfect competition. The motivation for such distributions and allocations might be the vagaries of tax systems; and the suspicion might persist that individual countries are in some respects at the mercy of multinational companies.

Professor Neufeld, nevertheless, regarded the multinational firms as "an important instrument in the international transmission of technology, capital, and managerial know-how," although he did insist that the time had come "for governments to cooperate in introducing common rules of the game relating to the operations of these firms," and he called for the United States to

19. Professor Neufeld's testimony is printed in the *Hearings*, cited, Part I, pp. 24-29, December 2, 1969.

36

provide leadership in the matter. During the seventies the operation of foreign subsidiary companies would probably grow in importance—and here he included non-United States foreign subsidiary companies—calling for "a set of international rules designed to prevent the emergence of problems over which host countries are exceedingly sensitive."

Some Legal Aspects of Definition

That there are possibilities of drawing definitional lines in terms of corporate autonomy appeared in other testimony. Seymour J. Rubin,[20] former general counsel for the Agency for International Development and United States representative on the Development Assistance Committee of the Organization for Economic Cooperation and Development, questioned the words "corporation" and "company" in discussing what he preferred to call a "multinational enterprise." The context, in discussion, would generally indicate the designation of a corporate enterprise that had its ownership in one country—or perhaps, in some cases, in a number of countries—and its operations scattered, directly via subsidiaries, through various national markets. It might take the form of an American company with operating subsidiaries abroad. Another form might be a base company organized under a law of convenience—in Liechtenstein, Nassau, or Panama, for example—with subsidiaries in other countries. Companies might go abroad through means other than corporate ownership. Licensing agreements would be one example of this; in such agreements there may be little or no element of stock ownership, but control by the licensor is more or less equivalent to that which would be exercised by a parent corporation. Some of the consequences of multinational business operations, such as effective allocation of markets, may be achieved by means of simple agreement.

Possible conflicts of national sovereignty and of national policies might be affected by the mode of multinationalism, Mr. Rubin added, citing the hypothetical case of an American licensor directed by the United States Government to operate under one set of rules, e.g., as to commerce with Communist China or Cuba, while the French or Canadian licensee finds that its own

20. The testimony of Seymour J. Rubin is quoted from his mimeographed statement at the hearings before the Subcommittee on Foreign Economic Policy on July 30, 1970.

government has a different set of rules for that trade. In that case the difficulties would be the same as they would be in the case of direct ownership.

He offered a suggestion, falling perhaps "somewhere between fact and speculation," by way of defining terms. In general, one thought of the threat a multinational enterprise may pose to national sovereignty in the foreign state within whose boundaries it may exercise power of decision. One could also think of an institution whose ownership and whose interests "are so diversified among a number of nations as to be responsive not to its 'home' state—the usual problem—but to no compulsions other than its own economic interests." He thought this situation was quite unusual now, but it might not be so unusual in the future.

The American Challenge

Other implications of corporate autonomy appeared clearly in the testimony of Jean-Jacques Servan-Schreiber,[21] deputy from Lorraine in the French National Assembly, and author of *The American Challenge*. His statement to the committee began with a denial that his book had been an anti-American call to arms against the multinational corporation. (He observed that the Communist criticism, that the book was "a hymn to American capitalism," was also off the mark.) What he had tried to express, he said, was "both admiration for your economic dynamism and anxiety lest its vitality and our passivity engulf the European way of life."

He then went on to tie the multinational corporation to "certain features of the new industrial state" that had, in his opinion, aroused a growing rebellion, especially among the young. "From the radicalism of the young stems a deeply-felt conviction that a system which allows the excesses of economic competition to ride herd over social life is basically immoral." He conceded that the modern market economy, with its freedom of private initiative and the bracing energy of competition, was a most powerful tool for material progress, but it was a tool that had to be at the service of society. After centuries of poverty and servitude it was unthinkable that man be allowed "to sink back to the status of a mere object, a cog in an aimless machine of production."

21. J. J. Servan-Schreiber's testimony is in part from his mimeographed statement and in part from his oral statements at the hearings on July 30, 1970.

The essential role of politics, he declared, is the quest for human dignity, and in this search "our contemporary economy is not a Utopia." Reform without revolution—of the industrial state and of the multinational corporation's role there—is possible, he said, and it is the duty of our generation, in Europe and in America, to bring that reform about.

These remarks pointed the way to Servan-Schreiber's conception of the multinational corporation and its role in society. The crucial role of politics is to "consecrate itself to the service of man—the worker—rather than to the efficiency of production—the corporation." Business across national borders has rapidly intensified, and with this has come "the benefits of capitalism as well as the miseries of the capitalist system." Ferocious competition in business is "a locomotive of innovation, development and enrichment," and has to be given play, but the main goal of politics is to "prevent this ferociousness from hurting man himself."

Against this background, M. Servan-Schreiber noted the development of corporate activity on a global scale by firms such as IBM, Ford, Siemens, Fiat and Philips. Although they had made possible far more efficient productivity and a wholesome cross-fertilization of intelligence, talent and creativity because of "the world-wide empires they are carving out for themselves, the multinational corporations—with no political law to govern them—are also able to create a new jungle."

This "world-wide empire" designation of the verbal sign "multinational corporation" is significant of the political implications of this definition. The political implications are further evident in a question put to M. Servan-Schreiber by Senator Javits: What is to be done about the mostly American multinational corporations; are they not beneficial? Of course, they are very beneficial, was the reply, by reason of being strong, dynamic and creative; but the multinational corporation could "dominate the Common Market jungle, which has no public law."

M. Servan-Schreiber added that this was Europe's problem, namely, the inadequate federalization of authority. That federalization would have to go along with the reform of Europe's industrial system, now that a "hundred years of civil war" on that continent had at last drawn to a close. In reply to Senator Javits' question whether one could not enlist the multinational corporation in Servan-Schreiber's hopeful reforms leading to true human freedom on both sides, using this great instrument for the benefit of all, the Frenchman saw two problems: most urgently the creation of industry in Russia that would be the material base for the road to freedom there; and the reform of Europe's own industrial system.

Among the latter reforms, M. Servan-Schreiber underlined the need for "internal" reforms as well as reforms in foreign policy. The chief executives of big corporations, for example, should not be chosen without any consensus by the people they govern. Some sort of industrial democracy is required. He saw no difficulty in large compensation to corporate executives, an appropriate reward for a man's creative work. He did question the laws of inheritance, however, thus raising far-reaching legal and political implications of the verbal sign, "multinational corporation."

Labor's Point of View

The hearings included testimony by Heribert Maier,[22] director of economics in the social and political department of the International Confederation of Free Trade Unions (ICFTU). He was concerned about "the hitherto almost untrammelled freedom of the multinational companies to operate in the fields of international trade and investment" and the consequences for labor. The trade unions, he said, did not like the growing encroachment of these companies upon the sovereignty of the nation-state, especially in their disregard of national policies protecting labor. The companies, he charged, were able to make unilateral decisions affecting the earnings and job security of workers in the countries where they operate, decisions which may be motivated by considerations quite extraneous to the interest of the country concerned.

On the other hand, Mr. Maier declared that the developing countries may sometimes be actively encouraged by multinational companies to favor anti-trade union measures which permit or even assist companies to refuse to recognize trade unions and enter into bona fide collective bargaining. These companies, by conceiving profitability on a world-wide rather than a national

22. Quotations from Heribert Maier are taken from the mimeographed statement of his testimony at the hearings on July 28, 1970.

40

basis and by centralizing decision making at their international headquarters, also tended to exploit established industrial relations systems at national levels. Foreign managers, unaware of or ignoring established procedures in a nation, tend to press their own preconceived anti-trade union policies. The trade unions have difficulty in identifying the real centers of decision making in multinational companies. Threats are dangled during negotiations to shift production to other countries. Unions face difficulties in finding the profit situation of a company because of the practice of "profit smoothening" among subsidiaries distributed among many nations or because of transfers of profits to low-tax countries.

The trade unions clearly conceive of the multinational corporation as a roving quasi-sovereign entity that exploits the "jungle" that Servan-Schreiber had named: many nation-states with no overarching law to govern these roving entities and their relations with labor, with nation-states, and each other.

From labor's standpoint, the multinational corporation—concededly a superb instrument for the potential benefit of all—poses the necessity for quasi-political countermeasures. The typical trade union reaction to multinational corporate strategy is to organize bargaining power at whatever level is appropriate to the given situation and to seek to enter into coordinated bargaining at that level. Thus, M. Maier pointed to the establishment of world-wide councils representing the workers of multinational companies in all the countries where they operate—a strategy pioneered by certain international trade secretariats.

Efforts are made, for example, to harmonize the expiry dates of contracts in several countries. Negotiable areas for coordinated collective agreements in certain industries are identified. A policy of fair labor standards in international trade is advanced in order to overcome the exploitation of international labor cost differentials for boosting profits. The unions seek to have national welfare expenditures jointly determined by the governments, the trade unions, and multinational companies. They seek an "international instrument" outlining the obligations of multinational companies towards governments and trade unions, establishing rules of the game for international movement of long-term capital and enforcing international conventions guaranteeing free-

41

dom of association and the right of workers to organize and engage in collective bargaining.

The "international instrument" to which M. Maier referred would be initiated and perhaps drawn by the joint action of such bodies as the International Labor Organization, GATT, the World Bank, the IMF, the UN Trade and Development Conference, and OECD, among others.

The Multinational Corporation Defined

We may now arrive at a definition which will be viable: the multinational corporation is a cross-border or transnational business organization or aggregate of organizations that is characterized mainly by the dispersal of its managerial centers among several nations for purposes of overcoming the barriers at the political frontiers of states.

Other types of business carried on across political frontiers by nonstate entities must be considered in arriving at a comprehensive view of the emerging world political economy and the role of the modern corporation therein. The development of adequate social theory for the latter purpose depends upon the meeting of minds from several disciplines. The economist, for example, seeking a theory of international production that shows how an optimum international allocation of resources can be obtained in a world in which productive factors—especially capital—will move with ease among nations whose governments are not reconciled to the phenomenon, has much in common with the political scientist who seeks a theory of the international system that will show how a world public order can be reconciled with nationalistic interests and with those freedoms—not excluding freedom of enterprise—that are essential to "the quality of life." Both have a common interest in a theory of human "ecology" that embraces viable political and economic organizations.

All forms of business organization that transcend political frontiers are therefore relevant to the broadest approach to the future of the modern corporation in the world arena. We limit ourselves here to the multinational form as a timely point of focus, as indicated by the contemporary debate about this institution.

Chapter III

THE CORPORATE TREND IN
TIME AND SPACE

The present and future role of the multinational corporation in the world's economic and political structure and more broadly in the global social process presents a formidable problem of social analysis. One must see the multinational corporation in its historical and geographic development. The analysis demands a study of the chronological sequence of corporate developments over centuries of time, together with projections of future possibilities. It demands also an orientation that avoids fixation on parochial and national locales reaching rather for a more extensive geographic place of action.

In response to these demands, we look first at the corporate trend in time, with special attention to some historic roots of the multinational corporation. Thereafter, we seek a spatial orientation, noting especially the spread of the scene of corporate action from local, national, and regional settings outward to a global theatre of operations.

The multinational corporation is sometimes regarded as a very recent form of business enterprise without deep roots. The term itself is new, so new, in fact, that it is not treated systematically in the new *International Encyclopedia of the Social Sciences*. The multinational corporation, however, must be regarded as an historically rooted social institution, related to the political as well as the economic evolution of a world social process. Even if one looks at it only as a kind of business organization its formative forces are traceable far back into time.

The Multinational Corporation in the Economic Order

The multinational corporation stands historically in a long line of devices by which enterprises are articulated into various economic systems. It is a chapter in man's long search for ways of converting human needs into human satisfactions through economic organization.

Economic organization and economic processes are responses to persistent issues: What is to be produced? What part of the product is to be saved for further production, what part consumed for other purposes? Who are to participate in the productive process? The human responses to these issues are less durable issues than the persistent necessities.

The arrangements have been informal as well as formal, consciously contrived as well as the outcome of unplanned growth. Theories of the economic order have at times presented it as a complex of fortuitous usages and arrangements guided ideally only by some invisible hand. But the business corporation belongs to the category of arrangements that are formally contrived to serve the purposes of human controls. In one legal form or another, it is today the dominant form of business organization.

The multinational corporation, although its antecedents and its significance have to be sought elsewhere as well, can be regarded developmentally as a new form of a very old human institution: the corporation broadly conceived. Among the continuities to be noted in the history of that institution is the corporate idea used for unity of action. Another line of continuous development can be seen in corporate governance, notably the separation of ownership and control, the rise of a corps of professional managers, and the growth of managerial discretion in corporate policy making. These continuities—the corporate idea and corporate governance—connect the contemporary multinational corporation with earlier economic as well as political arrangements in the social order and help to explain its present and future role in the world social process.

Persona Ficta versus "Group Person"

The corporate idea is basically a philosopher's answer to the riddle of the One and the Many; how to conceive of unity in the face of diversity. The idea has many uses. In United States corporation law, for example, the unity of all the diversified interests that constitute a large corporate enterprise has been expressed in terms of corporate personality. The corporate person has successfully sought the protective cloak of constitutional limitations on federal and state legislative powers. But this is only a nineteenth-century twist given to the corporate idea by skillful constitutional lawyers who knew what they were doing with an idea that derives from the *societas* and the *universitas* of ancient Roman law as expounded by Justinian's lawyers and medieval legists and canonists.

The Roman law, for medieval Europe, was more than a heritage; it was a living body of actual law, practiced in courts and developed by jurists—a consistent body of vital ideas that affected the life and development of ecclesiastical, political and economic institutions. It testifies, in Vinogradoff's words, "to the latent vigor and organizing power of *ideas*, in the midst of shifting surroundings."[1] Those who have searched the history of corporate concepts throw light upon constitutive processes that relate members of society as "legal persons" and assign these "persons" the rights and duties which form their "legal personality." These "persons" may be individuals or groups.

In Gierke, there is reflected a fundamental belief in the reality of the Group-person, a belief elaborately supported by treatises on the theory of State and Corporation in classical, medieval, and modern times. This "Realism" has been shared by many over the centuries and is observable today among some pluralists. Opposed are proponents of the Fiction theory of groups, and especially of corporations.

The concept of the *persona ficta*, one outgrowth of the corporate idea, is a medieval construction. It seems to have been introduced by the canonists, notably Sinibaldo Fieschi (Pope Innocent IV, from 1243 to 1254), who was perhaps more interested in the fictitiousness than in the personality of groups. The idea that associations, secular and ecclesiastical, have a personality distinct from their members, was very old in Fieschi's time. The *univertas* of Roman law, a legal corporation, and the Roman law *societas*, a business partnership of business partners, were concepts that could and did lead to the idea of corporate personality.

The "personality" of groups may refer merely to an imposed *persona*, or mask, that provides fictitious unity behind which moves all the living complex of human members. Or "person-

---

1. Ernest Barker's "Translator's Introduction" to *Natural Law and the Theory of Society, 1500 to 1800* by Otto Gierke (Boston: Beacon Press, 1957), p. xxii.

ality" may refer to a quality resident in a real organism, either an individual human being who is a center of sentiency or a group of human beings possessing sentiency in the same way. But, the Church's lawyers clearly could not have gone that far because of the medieval ideas of mankind as a *Corpus Mysticum* and of Church and State as the soul and body, respectively, of mankind.

For Gierke, the medieval doctors failed to find the constitutive principle of the group in a natural process of growth and fell back upon the idea of divine creation. The documents did reveal "an energetic thought that human groups are organic."[2] They showed, for example, that Marsiglio of Padua tried to explain that reason, which is immanent in every community, engenders the social organism by a conscious imitation of the life-making forces of nature. But this rich vein of realistic thought about the organic life of groups stopped short of a thorough jurisprudence. Medieval doctrine was unable permanently to close off a mode of thought that the Fictionists professed that the State is merely a mechanism constructed of discrete units. That was the mechanistic doctrine that came at length to command modern juristic thought and to reduce all groups to fictional persons at most. That was the mode of thought that lay in the womb of medieval theory.

Sovereign Concession

This is perhaps an extreme view. But the wealth of group life, dependent not at all upon the State but native to the soil of free peoples, may now be threatened by a strictly mechanistic jurisprudence so dear to the early Fictionists and later on to the Austinian proponents of the concession theory of corporations— that corporate life derives solely from a sovereign concession to be a "body corporate." It was this aspect of the *persona ficta* that the Realists regarded with suspicion. They have good reason to regard it with suspicion today.

It is well to recall that Fieschi, as Pope Innocent IV, claimed —in virtue of the *plenitudo potestatis* he possessed as the vicar of Christ on earth—the right to direct authority in temporal as well as ecclesiastical matters. It was a power he claimed in such cases as the vacancy of the empire or of any kingdom, or of the

2. Otto Gierke, *Political Theories of the Middle Age*. Translated with an Introduction by Frederic William Maitland. (Cambridge University Press, 1900), p. 29.

incompetence or defect of justice in the ruler, and in all cases of sin.[3] The fictitiousness of personality in a corporate group under his watchful eye would have been important not only in the case of organizations directly related to the Church but to those of the Empire as well. Judging from his bouts with so powerful an emperor as Frederick II, one could conclude that a secular *persona ficta* might well cower before so formidable a wielder of an incipient concession theory.

The fiction theory leads naturally to a concession theory. When the Sovereign alone claims the right to create a corporation, whose personality is concededly fictitious, the corporation depends for its life on the will of the Sovereign. But managers of the modern corporation are not much concerned about this threat, at least in constitutional regimes.

In the twentieth century, at least before the rise of totalitarian dictatorships, we had become accustomed to a freedom of corporate enterprise that lends the merest lip service to the concession theory. General incorporation laws abound, together with a great ease of enterprise organization into corporate persons that move about in our vast United States continental market under established constitutional protection.

Multinational corporations move less protectedly in the world arena, where the writ of American constitutional law does not run. There is growing protest abroad that attempts to make it run—as in antitrust capital transfer controls—to govern United States multinational corporations contravenes the sovereign authority of host countries. On the other hand, there is no universal or global Sovereign competent to create and kill the corporate person. Corporate "sin," in the world arena, under the aegis of the cross-border reach of the United States sovereign arm, is not as easy to define as the sins of secular, fictitious persons of Fieschi's day. Innocent IV had authority derived from Holy Writ which was almost unquestioned in the West. Even within the United States it would be hard to find a like source for judging the sins of business corporations; a code for the world arena of corporate action is still less discoverable.

---

3. R. W. Carlyle and A. J. Carlyle, *A History of Medieval Political Theory in the West*, Vol. V, "The Political Theory of the Thirteenth Century" (Edinburgh and London: William Blackwood and Sons, 1928), p. 332.

In England, the attorney-general could once descend upon a town or a guild with his *Quo Warranto*, demanding proof that its right to act as "a body corporate and politic" was lawfully grounded in sovereign consent. Such sovereign demands on the business corporation of today are theoretically possible but in practice rare. Yet it requires no great flight of the imagination to think of new and exacting codes of behavior for corporations—and especially multinational corporations—that will underline the fictitiousness and the transciency of corporate persons.

Apologists for free enterprise may insist, with Gierkeian Realism, on the natural necessity for corporate enterprise at home and abroad, and confute the fiction and concession theories of corporateness. Unless the sovereign state is about to pass into the limbo of useless and forgotten institutions, this kind of plea may prove to be of little avail. That could happen if more exacting codes of corporate behavior receive stern ecological content, for example, or other social imperatives that transcend traditional political geography.

The corporate idea, as a contribution to unity in large enterprises, is so tough and venerable that it makes little difference today whether the corporate "person" is viewed as fictitious or real. Indeed, it may be argued that it makes little difference, as a matter of sociological theory and of the daily life of a firm, whether it is viewed as a person or not. Corporation theory may emphasize other aspects of the large business enterprise that seem far more significant. Organization and systems theories, for example, have little or nothing to say about the corporate idea. Aside from the usefulness of corporate personality to lawyers, what good, it may be asked, is the attempt to discover the unity of a group either in a *persona ficta* or a "real" group-person?

Unity via Contract

Unity may be thought of as founded in contract, and in contractual relations alone. The corporation may be considered as a contract, or a series of contracts: a contract between the sovereign state and the corporation; between the corporation members or shareholders, who bind themselves to seek a common purpose; and between the shareholders among themselves. Actually, the sovereign state cannot permit the contracting away of limitations on its power to govern; nor would an allegedly sovereign corporation ever likely concede that its organizational unity springs from and necessarily depends upon a sovereign state's concession. In law and in practice, the powers of a corporation—the charter of its governance by directors—derive from legislative action. That is of course to use "powers" in the strictly legal sense of authority to act; corporation law sets both the powers and limitations on powers of those who govern corporate affairs.

In another sense of the term, "power to govern" means *capability* to command. That capability will hardly be described in statute books. The search for its source leads to the analysis of participation in the making of decisions, or in Bertrand Russell's phrase "the production of intended effects." Power, conceived of as a kind of influence, has to be seen—in realistic terms—as control over value practices and patterns.

Earlier Corporations

In English law, the early corporations were towns, guilds, hospitals, and colleges, as well as cathedral chapters and orders. The law of corporations, as conceived by Kyd and Blackstone, would seem to have little relevance at first glance to our modern law of companies and corporations; but the idea of a juristic person, which had arisen on the continent in other circumstances, was thereby carried into company law in England—and later on into corporation law in the United States—with remarkable consequences for modern corporate enterprise.

In United States constitutional law, the word "person" in the Fifth and Fourteenth Amendments is operative as a substantial bar to federal and state encroachments on corporate enterprise; it does not refer alone to natural persons. Foreign corporations are not excluded from this protection, although United States law still permits states of the Union to impose conditions for entry to do business within their borders. As applied to corporations created in a state—such as Delaware—seeking to do business in, say, New York, the judicial bar to "unconstitutional conditions" has been a significant factor in opening up a continental market for corporate enterprise in the United States. In all the industrial countries there are legal forms for doing business collectively that guarantee security and continuity for the corporate entity. The *société anonyme*, the *Aktiengesellschaft*, the *sociedad anónima*—these and other forms of corporate organization were all worked out and in operation long before the multinational corporation appeared.

The modern business corporation, like its predecessors, has arisen in response to the demands of a social environment that has changed constantly. Even in antiquity, there was a vast difference between the trading associations of merchants at Kanes, two centuries before the fall of the old Hittite Kingdom and over eighteen centuries before the Christian era, and the complex agreements of the highly developed industrial organization of Attica just before the Macedonian conquest. The legal and social forms controlling the predominantly agrarian economic activities of Europe and England in the Middle Ages contrast with those which developed during the Industrial Revolution. The bonds of unity required for business enterprise in one era may not suffice for another, and those of even so recent a period as the nineteenth century require radical revision for the postwar conditions of the last third of the twentieth.

The multinational corporation is a response to new demands. The demands are global in their reach. When goods are produced through the efforts of many men working together as a group, but separated by political frontiers in many parts of the world, there must be some new and enduring bond of unity that expresses a common purpose which will be readily understood not only by those within the group but also by those who have business relations with the group. The multinational corporation of today is an attempt to provide that form of expression.

Long before the corporate idea was fully developed for business purposes in a legal sense, men were organizing cross-border companies to do what sovereigns alone could not do. The Muscovy Company,[4] for example, was an early joint-stock company that began in the middle of the sixteenth century with a subscribed capital of upwards of £6,000 under the leadership of Sebastian Cabot for the outfitting of three ships. The company's

---

4. See Arthur Stone Dewing, *The Financial Policy of Corporations*, Fifth edition (New York: Ronald Press, 1953), Vol. I, pp. 20*ff.*, and John P. Davis, *Corporations* (1905), Ch. IV, in the Capricorn Books Edition, New York, 1961, edited by Abram Chayes.

charter, granted by Philip and Mary in 1554, noted that certain nobles and others had "already fitted out ships for discoveries northward, northwestward and northeastward [to lands] not as yet frequented by subjects of any other Christian monarch" in amity with England. These persons were now designated, for further voyages and adventures, as "The Merchants Adventureres for the Discovery of Lands, Territories, Isles and Seigniories unknown, and not by the Seas and Navigations, before this late Adventure and Enterprise by Sea or Navigation, commonly frequented." This company name was somewhat shortened in 1566 to the "Fellowship of English Merchants for Discovery of New Trades." This came to be known more briefly as the Russia or Muscovy Company. The geographical reference, as in the case of similar ventures such as the Levant, Morocco, and Turkey Companies, indicated the exercise of considerable governmental powers in the area.

Sebastian Cabot was authorized by the Crown to act as "governor" throughout his lifetime, while four others, of the most "sad, discreet and honest of the fellowship" were to be consuls, and twenty-four others were to be assistants. These had not only the power to admit new members and to make laws for the government of their members and their trade, but also to punish interlopers who might offend against the privileges of the Company. The members of the Company had the exclusive right to trade in the described territories, to license or refuse to license others to trade there, and to seize ships and goods of unlicensed intruders. They made agreements with the Czar of Russia which not only gave them exclusive trading privileges, but also full power to govern all the English in Russia. They were a law unto themselves in this respect; in the fining and imprisonment of offenders they could call upon the Czar's officers, his prisons, and his instruments of torture.

The Russia Company thus became a transnational organization with functionally, as well as geographically, defined jurisdiction. As time went on, the Company moved beyond the Czar's dominions into Armenia, Media, Hyrcania, Persia, and the lands tributary to the Caspian Sea. No English subject was to trade to these areas without the "order, agreement, consent, or ratification" of the Company, on pain of the usual forfeiture. Why this remarkable grant of powers? There were "sundry subjects of the realm," perceiving that "divers Russian wares and merchandise" were now imported by the Russia Company, "after all their great charge and travel," who for their own "peculiar gain [sought] utterly to decay the trade" of the Russia Company, contrary to its charter and "in great disorder, traded into the dominions of Russia . . . to the great detriment of this commonwealth." The Russia Company was obviously an arm of the English government as well as a "regulated-exclusive" business enterprise, to use Davis's term. It was at the start a business venture, and thus to be distinguished from Stora Kopperberg of Sweden, which is sometimes incorrectly called the world's oldest corporate enterprise; the Swedish company was established by royal charter in 1347 as little more than a department of the sovereign authority.

The granting of a charter to the Russia Company had been preceded by a voyage in which the adventurers demonstrated their own initiative and, at their own expense, the possibility of developing a trade to Russia. Similarly, the Levant Company was the reward of an enterprising group of English adventurers who, according to the language of the Crown, had "at their own great costs and charges, found out and opened a trade to Turkey." It was a time when England enjoyed no settled relations with nations whose trade had not been "discovered." After "discovery" by these companies, not only trade but also general diplomatic relations were carried on by them or at their initiative. The Levant Company, for example, made direct appointments of English political representatives to Turkey. Queen Elizabeth's costly presents to the Czar were paid for by the Russia Company, and these gifts were made with privileges in mind on both sides. Trading privileges were often granted at the start through capitulations directly conceded by the Czar and other sovereigns to the companies, and not by means of treaties.

For unity of action the corporate form was required, both for the effectiveness of the venture and for its continuity regardless of the mortality of the men in the association. Subscriptions or membership could be transferred and passed to others by inheritance, while the "societie or company" itself, as indicated by its charter, enjoyed a continuing existence. Modern industrial states provide for this continuity of organization in their general incorporation laws where the concession theory prevails, and where no sovereign concession is required for voluntary creation by a corporate enterprise by tacit consent.

One must distinguish between the older concepts of "international business"—in the form of marketing products abroad or of buying and owning foreign companies' stocks and bonds for the purpose of dividend and interest payments as return on the investment—and foreign operations based on direct foreign investment coupled with a high degree of managerial control centered somewhere and focusing on certain aspects of enterprise policy. It is only the latter kind of contemporary realization of the corporate idea that leads toward the multinational corporation.

The Case of Unilever

Unilever is an outstanding example of bridging the gap between sovereign states by creating a new transnational corporate unity. It is a group of companies that were brought together in 1929 by a merger of the Margarine Union and Lever Brothers Limited.

The background of each of these merging groups is interesting. The Margarine Union had been formed in 1927 from merging a number of European firms with interests in various branches of the oils and fats industry. The most important of these were Van den Berghs and Jurgens, Dutch margarine makers in business throughout Europe and elsewhere. These two firms, 50 years earlier, had exported butter from the Netherlands to the United Kingdom. By 1872, rising standards of living in the United Kingdom had brought the demand for butter beyond the capacity of contemporary sources of supply. Margarine had been invented by Mège-Mouriès of France and Van den Berghs and Jurgens were competitors in meeting the new demands for margarine, particularly in the industrial populations of large towns in the United Kingdom and Germany. They shared a major supply problem in raw materials, and, in acquiring oil-milling enterprises, they ran into conflict with soapmakers, especially Lever Brothers Limited, started in 1885 by W. H. Lever (who became Lord Leverhulme in

1917). After nearly sixty years of rivalry, conditions of business in the margarine trade after World War I led Van den Berghs and Jurgens to amalgamate in 1927.

In the meantime, Lever Brothers Limited had developed into a multinational corporation of substantial proportions. W. H. Lever had in the beginning—responding to rising standards of living among the English working-class people—applied large-scale manufacturing methods to the promotion of a branded specialty, Sunlight Soap. Before that it had been a bulk trade. After an enormous success in this enterprise, Lever began to pay attention to overseas markets, especially those—as in the United States—where standards of living were rising. By the time he died in 1925, Lever's firm was in business all over the world.

In response to the raw materials problem, Lever Brothers had created its own sources of supply in the Solomon Islands from 1906 onwards, and in the Congo from 1911. It had gone into the African merchants' trade in 1910 and had bought the Niger Company in 1920. Lord Leverhulme had private interests in the food trades, especially fish shops (MacFisheries), canned goods (Angus, Watson, Pelling Stanley), and sausages and ice-cream (Walls); in 1922-23 these interests were sold to Lever Brothers Limited. They became the foundation of Unilever's business in food products, including Batchelors (canners) and Birds Eye frozen foods in the United Kingdom and many food companies in other countries.

Unilever Limited (English) is linked with Unilever N.V. (Dutch) by a common Board of Directors, and by an equalization agreement covering the payment of dividends and the division of assets on liquidation. The Board functions as a central control in several ways. In the first place, the 24 directors are executives, heads of departments with functional or regional responsibilities, and are remunerated as managers in "N.V." and "Limited". The chairman of N.V. is a vice-chairman of Limited, while the chairman of Limited is a vice-president of N.V. Then there is a Special Committee, composed of the chairman of N.V., the chairman of Limited and a second vice-chairman of Limited, with much power and with efficiency due to their continuous personal association. Effective centralizing of control is possible through the Annual Operating Plan.

This AOP has been described by George Cole, chairman of Limited, as a reciprocal arrangement.[5] Unilever at the top draws up an annual plan and hands it down to some 500 operating companies; but at the same time these companies send up theirs. Commenting on this reciprocity, Cole has quoted the verse:

Along these lines from toe to crown
Ideas flow up and vetoes down.

He hoped that was not true of Unilever. "There's the upping and downing—obviously one-way traffic would be crazy." As far as you possibly can, you must plan *upwards*. Each unit—each company—draws up an annual plan, which covers the year ahead and looks forward to the one after that. Most of the companies also have less detailed plans for the years ahead of that.

The plan for each company gives its estimate of its prospective sales, margins, advertising, and other expenses, together with an estimate of the following year's profit or loss. This plan will then be discussed with people at the top of the regional groups and production groups.

This short-term planning is organized on continuous and well-established lines. Forecasts on the major macroeconomic variables such as national income, general prices and population, are provided by the central service departments, which are one of the three categories of command (the others being groups arranged on regional lines for coordinating policies on a world basis and for products). When the AOP comes to the parent Board for general review and decision, it becomes a yardstick to measure a particular company's activities as well as the activities of Unilever as a whole, but the door is open thereafter to necessary modifications.

Matters considered at headquarters in relation to the AOP cover expansion of output of this or that product, shutting a facility down here and building a new plant there, buying a new company, moving into competition with other companies, and moving into this or that market. Changes in policies of governments that might entail grave consequences for a company are among the most urgent matters.

As Cole put it in an interview: "The Government in a certain country looks as if it may soon get rather wobbly. You have

5. *The Observer* (London), Weekly Review, January 6, 1963.

considerable interests in that country: men, women, families, plant, materials. How are you going to be affected? You are continually looking out—not always to solve problems, but often to predict problems." A constant stream of information from Unilever's companies all over the world comes to its own information, research, and press services at headquarters in London and Rotterdam.

Unilever's Common Market studies are among the most important of those which attempt to look to the future before making commitments for long run developments in the European area. From 1962 on, a series of Unilever Common Market Conferences[6] have been held for this purpose. In addition to short-term recommendations, these conferences have been used to prepare the groundwork for a long-term program for Unilever in the Common Market so that the company would be prepared for the eventual economic integration of the six nations of the European Economic Community. The Common Market Committee in Unilever's central services reports to the Board of Directors. The scope of reports of this kind has been extended to cover much wider geographic areas, such as those which include EFTA countries, and to cover trends toward common markets elsewhere.

Here we have some examples of the centralizing techniques available to a large multinational corporation as it expands the traditional corporate idea to cover global operations. Lord Heyworth, as chairman of Unilever Limited, London, declared, in an address to the annual general meeting of the company in 1959, that these techniques were not only valuable to the international concern but offered much as well to the national operating companies within the group: "First of all we make an investment, with all that that implies in the way of risk-bearing. Under the same agreements, where it is appropriate, we grant rights to use trademarks and patent processes . . . and we undertake to give our local companies help from Unilever's central fund of knowledge and experience."

This was the counterpart of the knowledge which locally recruited men bring in, a valuable asset arising from contact be-

6. M. Weisglas and R. A. Coope, "Planning in Unilever with Special Reference to the Common Market" in *Multinational Corporate Planning*, by George A. Steiner and Warren B. Cannon, editors (New York: Macmillan, 1966).

tween managers throughout the business. The resources of Unilever's Central Advisory Departments—running through the alphabet from Accounts, Audit and Buying, to Research, Taxation and Technical—provided an incomparable range and quality of experience and advice to local companies. While it had long been Unilever's principle "that operating companies know their own business, and should be left to get on with it in their own way," Lord Heyworth was clear that "we value the unity of the business and we do our best to foster a sense of loyalty to Unilever as a whole, as well as to one or another of its component parts."

Why was this principle of unity insisted upon? Because "the central resources of the concern would lose their value if they were neglected or disregarded by companies of too separatist turn of mind." In the linking of the center with the perimeter the Boards of the parent companies in Unilever play a vital role. Yet, Lord Heyworth said, if they were to become too dictatorial they might cramp the style of the enterprising. If they were to lean too far in the direction of becoming an advisory body of expert consultants, the business might fly apart by centrifugal force. Where outside partners had to be considered, he noted a clear limit to the authority of the Board to give direct orders—they could not, even if they wanted to, give orders to the Government of Pakistan or the Is-Bank in Turkey; and anyhow there was a disposition in Unilever to advise rather than command. At the center, however, "we must, and we do, keep and exercise the right of executive action, especially in the disposition of the resources of money and men. We keep our hand on major expenditure and on the placing of top management. If we didn't, Unilever would cease to be an operational company. It would become an investment trust, and most of the justification for its international activities would disappear."

The pattern of corporate unity in Unilever can be seen, with variations to suit the nature of the business, in other European countries: Nestlé, Imperial Chemical, Degussa, Philips, L. M. Ericsson, and Royal Dutch/Shell. Unilever's two identical boards are unique, but its strategies for unity from diversity are similar to all the others. The corporate idea, in late twentieth century practice, has proved to be of continuing value despite basic changes in cross-border business. The problem of cross-border industry in the nineteenth century, according to Kolde, was to maximize production, while that of today is marketing. Productive power has mounted to the point where it is necessary to organize transnationally to develop the uses, the users, and the markets to match that power.[7] Multinational corporations have met both these problems through various techniques of organization, using the corporate idea with imagination.

The Global Orientation

The modern state is the dominant political unit of the world today, just as the corporation is the dominant form of business enterprise; but the nation-state, with its claim to sovereignty, is a newcomer to the world stage. It is scarcely more than four centuries old. Corporate action, in many successive forms, is thousands of years old.[8] The modern state is in fact one form of the corporate idea. But there are numerous forms of expression for the central One-from-Many characteristic of the corporate idea.

The world is more than a mosaic of almost innumerable human associations; it is a complex of interwoven associations of many kinds. We nevertheless always come back to the international system as the basic pattern for global orientation of the multinational corporation because that is the pattern that governs men's minds today and will do so for decades to come. That this is so is evident in the nomenclature: the talk is mainly of multi*national*, inter*national* and trans*national* enterprises. Occasionally we hear of "world" corporations and global firms; but these terms are somewhat pretentious. Not even the United Nations can claim global coverage and the universality of a world government. No business enterprise today operates universally nor does any church or other corporate organization. The state successfully asserts sovereignty within its territorial jurisdiction; but the business corporation cannot do that within its "corporate domain."

The World Arena of Corporate Action

Corporations that stay at home within a single nation and live under the protection of the municipal law of that nation avoid

7. Endel J. Kolde, *International Business Enterprise* (Englewood Cliffs, N.J.: Prentice-Hall, 1968), p. 225.

8. See Dewing, *op. cit.*, Ch. I.

the special hazards of the world arena where no single supranational authority of global competence exists. Corporations which venture, with multiple managerial components, into that arena face a multiplicity of sovereign authorities claiming supreme competence to govern within their respective jurisdictions. The result is an incongruity of pluralistic entities, national and corporate.

The multicolored world map is divided up into mutually exclusive jurisdictional territories that are bounded by presumably precise political frontiers. These frontiers may or may not fix the real boundaries of political communities designated as nation-states; they rarely fix the geographic limits of other kinds of communities, associations, and functional entities such as corporate enterprises. Non-state entities and movements cross political frontiers in such complicated patterns that no world map has ever depicted comprehensively their territorial reach. There are innumerable non-state domains that are noncongruent with the standard patterns of power distribution in the world arena of the so-called international system. Noncongruence in the case of business domains produces tensions that concern us here.

Aristotle conceived of the city-state as the only natural society for the good life. It was a small community of perhaps no more than 120,000 inhabitants that a man could literally envisage. The dimensional requirements of the good life have changed radically. Even the vast dimensions of the modern superstate are not enough in our age of global interdependence.

Certainly the claustrophobic atmosphere of a totalitarian state of whatever geographic reach is too restrictive. But no state of the free world is expansive enough, either. For more than a century we have had free and open seas. But freedom of the seas is now in danger as jurisdictional claims of sovereign states reach hundreds of miles out beyond their shorelines. There is still another menace to the seeker after a global field for enterprise: even the freest of the free-world states tend toward restrictive nationalistic policies.

Nationalism is resurgent. Yet the counterforces of modern technology point to still more global interdependence. We must now speak also of space exploration far above and far below the conventionally defined surfaces of the globe: the outer space of the astronauts and the "inner" or ocean spaces of the oceanographers. Into these new realms of space, which must be regarded as part of the world arena of the future, the modern corporation will move along with other participants in the immensely varied activity of human life. For the future of the international system, the implications of vast new realms unclaimed, and perhaps unclaimable, by sovereign states, are unpredictable.

With characteristic social lag, our minds do not adjust readily to the social and political implications of technological change. Human aspiration for a more spacious environment on, above, and beneath the surface of man's earthly home is frustrated by out-of-date political institutions. Resistance to adaptive change bars the way to the better and more expansive life that technological revolution now makes possible. We stubbornly retain old and outworn pictures in our minds of supposedly permanent social arrangements that are not necessary, but only conventional. Among these sterotypes none is more pervasive than our "international system." That so-called system hampers the adaptation of political and economic institutions to the possibilities that now lie open to mankind to make a good home on this planet.

Barriers inherent in the international system test the ingenuity of multinational corporate managers. Their strategies are by no means merely copies of strategies used by political elites. Original business strategies appear. Among solutions to the problems of survival and prosperity for multinational enterprise in the world arena, one that beckons is the transformation of the multinational corporation into a basic building block in a reconstructed world order. So long as the dream of a world public order under law remains only a dream, enterprisers who venture forth into the world arena will do more than come to terms with national powers. They will also try to make their corporate entities a new kind of competing power with sovereign states.

Dynamism of the World Arena

The world arena of corporate action can best be described as a complex of interacting factors which includes national coercion and authoritative decision, as well as the wealth-producing and distributing processes that usually command attention when the multinational corporation is discussed.

The decision-makers in the world arena are usually regarded as officials in nation-states and public international organizations.

They are said to be the main movers in the process of authoritative decision. They use characteristic capabilities and strategies that are more or less fitted to the conditions that prevail in the political arena in order to achieve with more or less success certain common objectives.

These political objectives are variously described in the literature of international law and international relations at different levels of abstraction. In the most general terms, the authoritative (governmental) decision-makers seek "the *prevention* of alterations in the existing distribution of values among nation-states by processes of unilateral and unauthorized coercion, and the *promotion* of value changes and adjustments by processes of persuasion or by community-sanctioned coercion."[9] They also seek "the reduction to the minimum, when the procedures of persuasion break down and violence is in fact resorted to, of unnecessary destruction of values"—the term "values" being used here in a technical sense to cover both preferred outcomes and capabilities related to wealth, power, knowledge, skills, loyalties, well-being, respect, and rectitude.

In addition, there are significant decisions being made all the time by non-authoritative decision-makers in the private sector. Non-authoritative decisions at times determine the direction of world affairs more than official decisions.

This process of authoritative decision in the world arena is carried on in a pervasive atmosphere of potential or expected violence due to the fact that a process of coercion across the frontiers of nation-states is basic to the so-called international system. Coercion involves a high degree of constraint exercised by means of any or all of the various instruments of policy. In the case of nation-states these instruments are military, diplomatic, ideological and informational, and economic. With respect to the military instrument, coercion involves the use of force, that is to say, the infliction of severe deprivations by means of military weapons.

Nation-states are the primary authoritative users of force. But the process of coercion in general includes means other than

9. Myres S. McDougal and Florentino P. Feliciano, *Law and Minimum World Public Order: The Legal Regulation of International Coercion* (New Haven: Yale University Press, 1961), p. 41. Italics added.

force, and other participants than states. Private-sector and unofficial organizations and movements are also active in the coercive process. Non-state entities may, for example, with considerable effect, use economic and ideological instruments to achieve a high degree of constraint against each other, against other participants in the world arena, and even against nation-states.

Arenas of Power

The multinational corporation, when it leaves its home state, enters a situation in which an aggregate of interacting participants seek to optimize certain values, notably the value of power. Power refers specifically to participation in the making of important decisions: those which affect large numbers of people and involve relatively severe deprivations or substantial indulgences. [10] The role of corporations may be relegated to a secondary place because the relevant interacting aggregate of participants in international business is taken to be not an aggregate of *power-seekers* in an arena but rather an aggregate of *wealth-seekers in a world market*. But these are disparate types of aggregates. A market in economic parlance is an aggregate—defined functionally or geographically or both—within which the forces of demand and supply converge to establish a single price; functionally, it is an aggregate of individuals whose bids and offers disclose the supply and demand situation and thereby establish the price. A "perfect market," as hypothesized by Jevons, is one in which all traders have perfect knowledge of the conditions of supply and demand and the consequent ratio of exchange.

Multinational corporations are participants in both types of aggregates. Insofar as the theory of the perfect market fails to approximate the actual market situation, requiring one for the sake of realism to speak of "mixed" economic systems, then it is quite likely that the relevant arena is one in which other-than-economic values are used and sought along with economic values. In all mixed economies, one must look for strategies of the par-

10. See Harold D. Lasswell and Abraham Kaplan, *Power and Society: A Framework for Political Inquiry* (New Haven: Yale University Press, 1950), pp. 77*ff*; also H. D. Lasswell, "Introduction: The Study of Elites" and "The World Revolution of Our Time: A Framework for Basic Policy Research" in *World Revolutionary Elites: Studies in Coercive Ideological Movements*, by H. D. Lasswell and Daniel Lerner (editors) (Cambridge, Mass.: The M.I.T. Press, 1965).

ticipants in the market that go beyond bids and offers. When the state enters the picture as more than a preserver of peace in the marketplace, the stage is set for strategies of force.

Corporations and other participants, whose major aim is wealth-production and wealth-acquisition, are certain to have at least minor and auxiliary aims that must be described in terms of the power process. Strategies are used for power as a valued outcome. But power is also an instrumental as well as an end value. As an instrumental value, power includes not only coercive capabilities but also the right to use those capabilities. Multinational corporations, though business entities in a market aggregate, are also like nation-states, in that they cannot avoid the necessity of having specialists on their staffs who pay close attention to this power process in all of its phases. The nature of the world arena, lacking a supranational authority with enforcement capability, makes power indispensable to all participants in this arena. For complete analysis, one must consider the *many arenas of power*, and not merely the single world arena. The nation-states are subsystem arenas; and within each such subsystem there are public- and private-sector arenas.

Within each arena, degrees of centralization can be observed. In structure, the world arena appears to be anarchical; more accurately it is among the least centralized. Unitary states, as contrasted with those having federal governments, are relatively centralized. Private-sector organizations are similarly classifiable. A corporation may be a highly centralized or a relatively decentralized arena of power. Most multinational corporations appear to be relatively decentralized; but some are more nearly described as unitary arenas of power.

An important aspect of this structural account of corporate arenas of power is the identification of the decision-makers: the elites of the respective arenas. Those who seek power in the world arena tend to work within relatively centralized and highly organized arenas of power: nation-states and unitary corporations being among the prime examples. The interactions of an arena tend to become more stabilized in unitary systems, and in the more stabilized systems the decision process may yield greater rewards to the power-seeker. More fundamental may be the question of territorial bases of power. Entities other than nation-states, however well organized, lack the territorial base of power. Yet not all of the nonterritorial participants in the world arena suffer inferiority in all instances to all states. The elites of some nonterritorial entities—notably the elites of some of the largest multinational corporations—can at times deal on equal terms with sovereign states.

When one adds up all the factors that contribute to the relative power[11] of a state in the international system, it is at once obvious that many of these factors—such as wealth, the skills and the knowledge of a nation's people, and in particular the capabilities and outlook of a nation's leaders—also account for the power of non-state participants in the world arena, including such functional organizations as the multinational corporation.[12] A multinational corporation, lacking military power as well as territoriality, is a quasi-civic arena in which the expectation of violence is low.[13] It must, however, accept the possibility of involvement in interactions among other participants that do rely on military force. Business corporations have had, at times, to take protective measures that rely either upon their own paramilitary forces or directly and indirectly on the coercive capabilities of nation-states.

The Major Participants in the World Arena

A reconstruction of the international system might eventually lead to submergence of the nation-state to minor significance as transnational movements and institutions rise to prominence

11. See Hans J. Morgenthau, *Politics Among Nations: The Struggle for Power and Peace,* Fourth edition (New York: Alfred A. Knopf, 1967), Part II; and Raymond Aron, *Peace and War: A Theory of International Relations* (Garden City, N.Y.: Doubleday & Co., 1966), Ch. VI.

12. Ernst B. Haas, *Beyond the Nation State: Functionalism and International Organization* (Stanford: Stanford University Press, 1964), a study of functionalism with special reference to the International Labor Organization, discusses the general problem with extensive references to and commentary on the literature in the entire field. Cf. *Functionalism and World Politics: A Study Based on United Nations Programs Financing Economic Development* (Princeton: Princeton University Press, 1966); and Thorkil Kristensen (Secretary-General, OECD), "Economic Problems Confronting the Free World," in Herbert V. Prochnow (ed.), *World Economic Problems and Policies* (New York: Harper & Row, 1965), Ch. 2, on the possibilities of establishing a truly "ecumenical civilization" based on instruments of monetary, economic, and trade cooperation among nations.

13. Lasswell and Kaplan, *op. cit.*, pp. 252-4.

in response to the requirements of a global system of social inter-communication. Today, however, in the language of publicists, the major "actors" in the making of international law are undoubtedly sovereign states and public international organizations of which only sovereign states are members. Even the "international economy" is an interrelationship among sovereign states and not primarily among private-sector organizations. Even in the field of "international business," which mainly focuses on transnational business in the private sector, the student cannot exclude the impact of national policies. This has been so ever since the foundations of the modern state were laid at the end of the Middle Ages, and the contemporary state system emerged with the Peace of Westphalia in 1648.[14]

The dominant position of the sovereign nation-state in the world arena is often regretted, and its persistence in the age of space and the technological revolution that foreshadows a world community is often deplored. "Nationalistic economies with their nationalistic aims and procedures must be adapted and integrated into an international or world economy in the interest of all,"[15] declares one writer, with an emphasis characteristic of those who hope for a new era. Arnold Toynbee has said that the sovereignty of states looms as the great barrier to man's salvation in a non-suicidal global society. The transiency of the sovereign nation-state as a human institution that is destined for the scrap-heap of history, like many other institutions that have seen their day, has been underlined by many observers. "The modern nation-state will surely prove to be a passing phenomenon," writes Louis Halle in hazarding the judgment that "it will be identified primarily with the nineteenth century" and "historians of the future will . . . note how rapidly it was becoming obsolete in the twentieth."[16] He points out that typical nation-states of today such as those of Western Europe were unknown two centuries ago and may well have disappeared from the world of our grand-children.

14. Charles de Visscher, *Theory and Reality in Public International Law*. Translated from the French by P. E. Corbett (Princeton: Princeton University Press, 1957), Ch. I.

15. John Parke Young, *The International Economy*, Fourth edition (New York: The Ronald Press Co., 1963), p. 4.

16. Louis J. Halle, *The Society of Man* (New York: Harper & Row, 1965), p. 179.

Others have questioned whether the nation-state is "about ready to cash in its chips"[17] in favor of some new major actor in the world arena. It is, however, the peg to which erstwhile colonial peoples have fastened their rising expectations for the good life through the instrumentality of their new nations and the United Nations. In the case of many emerging nations, the peg of nationalism is more ego than reality, and can be removed as easily as it was put in place in the first instance.

Nationalism is, moreover, so strong a force today that it resists even the universalist doctrine emanating from new imperialist centers in Moscow and Peking where the vain theory of world-wide class warfare is still propagated. The Western state system has become a global international system with an open-ended number of sovereign states. The state system is the basis for the structure of the United Nations and other public international organizations. Nongovernmental organizations knock at the door but they are not admitted.

Membership in the state system can be precisely indicated. In addition to the 132 members of the United Nations (as of January, 1972), there are six non-member states which have maintained permanent observers' offices at UN headquarters in New York. These are the Federal Republic of Germany, the Holy See, The Republic of Korea, Monaco, Switzerland, and the Republic of Viet-Nam. To these must be added, for a complete list of all sovereign states in the international system, other non-members and newly-independent countries that have not yet become members of the UN.

The number of major participants in the world arena, using "major" to mean members and claimant members of the state system since Westphalia, now runs to not less than 137 and could perhaps be made—by suitable definition—to run to 150 or more. These "major" participants of the state system include mini-states as well as superpowers. The "minor" status of other participants in the world arena does not necessarily derive from lack of size or power; it derives, at least in part, from juridical concepts inherent in the system and from the massive fact of nationalism. The nationalistic element in the international system

17. Edward S. Mason, "The Corporation in the Post-Industrial State: At Home and Abroad," *California Management Review*, Vol. XII, No. 4, Summer 1970, p. 19.

strongly reinforces the juridical: sovereign states that are also *nation*-states, in fact as well as in theory, command the social process within their territorial jurisdictions by a rule of law that is grounded in imponderable but sinewy social ties. Functional organizations, national or transnational, cannot do that to the same degree. Transnational organizations, indeed, use nationalism or run up against its barriers in their effort to transcend political frontiers.

The Primacy of Nationalistic Politics

The future role of the multinational corporation depends heavily upon the future of nationalism. And the nationalism of the modern state system rests on three major principles: the concept of state sovereignty, the principles of international law (a law of nations, not an organized community of mankind), and the politics of the "balance of power". This balance was not necessarily one of equilibration in an exact analogy drawn from physics. Rather it was a balance that was supposed to sustain the sovereign independence of the states of the system, each of which jealously guarded its territorial integrity as best it could through self-defense, client status, or alliance. The state system never evolved into a mechanism for universal peace; rather it has become a multiplicity of more or less nationalistic communities.

The struggle for political community primarily at the national level has led to a hyphenated inter—*nationalism*, as contrasted with an idealized supranational global system. The nation-state persists against all universalist[18] movements, on the one hand, and against divisive particularistic movements, none of which has ever been transformed successfully into global systems of world order, on the other. It is the chief instrument for getting things done. Karl W. Deutsch observes that "nation-preserving, nation-building, and nationalism or the preference for the real or

18. Since the medieval claims of Church and Empire to universality there have been none to compare with the demands of the Communist world revolution centered at Moscow. Internationalism, with its pluri-polar (nationalistic) base has been defensive by comparison. Cf. M. M. Drachkovitch, *The Revolutionary Internationals, 1864-1963* (Stanford, California: Stanford University Press, 1966). The elites of other contemporary universalist forces have been less successful than the *Politburo* of Communism for reasons analyzed in detail in H. D. Lasswell and D. Lerner (eds.), *World Revolutionary Elites* (Cambridge, Mass.: The M.I.T. Press, 1965).

imagined interests of one's own nation and its members—these still remain a major and even a still growing force in politics, which statesmen of good will would ignore at their peril." [19] Managers of multinational corporations need to be fully aware of the dangers to transnational business operations inherent in the surge of nationalism.

Nationalism, however, is increasingly confronted by the forces of internationalism, supranationalism, and transnationalism, and not least, by the pressures for a world economy indicated—among other things—by the rise of the multinational corporation. The resultant tensions, latent or open, appear on every continent. [20] At the same time, there has been a notable expansion in the scope of tasks that national governments everywhere are undertaking. The stakes of politics have risen; more and more people in every nation have become the recipients of public or governmental services, and more people than ever before participate in politics. The implications reach into many areas of human activity. Higher levels of literacy, education for the many, and mass communications, all have significant effects on language and language rights; the right to have and use a language has become more important to more people than ever before, and they press their claims more urgently. Disputes over language, nationality, and the rights of ethnic, racial, and religious groups multiply. Minorities that used to be submerged have become vocal and truculent. Countries are harder to govern, even in self-governing nations. Intervention by outsiders becomes far more costly.

Resurgent nationalism has far-reaching consequences. The postwar, bipolarized world, for example, is being succeeded by multipolarity; alliances in West and East lose their cement. The nationalistic "protestants" on both sides of the line have begun

19. Karl W. Deutsch, *Nationalism and Social Communication: An Inquiry Into the Foundations of Nationality*, Second edition (Cambridge, Mass. and London, England: The M.I.T. Press, 1966), p. 4.

20. For the data and analyses on which this and the succeeding paragraphs on nationalism are based, see Deutsch, *op. cit.*, especially the introduction to the second edition, "Some Changes in Nationalism and Its Study, 1953-1965," with succinct observations on political developments after the first edition in 1953; also Chapter 9: "A Prospect for Nationalism." The bibliographical notes are comprehensive, indicating most of the significant work being done in the field today. See especially, K. H. Silvert (ed.), *Expectant Peoples: Nationalism and Development*, by the American Universities Field Staff (New York: Vintage Books, A Division of Random House, 1967).

to insist upon their own revisionist views of the once-prevailing doctrines, and this divisiveness occurs even within well-established nations. As all-out nuclear war between the United States and the Soviet Union becomes less and less credible, it is not the nuclear giants but rather the smaller powers with little or no nuclear capabilities that seem to endanger peace. Strength and moderation are the qualities that the giants have wanted to stress in their foreign policies; it is the smaller nations that could afford to act recklessly through threats of warfare by conventional means. In this age of resurgent nationalism, the chief nuclear powers have been deadlocked by mutual deterrence; and they have found themselves restricted in the use of limited warfare and the capacity to cope with revolution, civil wars, organized terror by guerrillas, and the provocative acts of other non-nuclear powers.

Some functionalists regard with optimism the strong trend in recent decades toward the extensive list of international organizations, a trend that seems to open up the possibility—in view of the great expanse of world trade—of building at least part of a better world order upon the foundations of a sound transnational and pluralistic structure for corporate business. Hope for progress in this direction is not to be discounted, and there is a strong presumption against the older and more orthodox views of international law and international relations which would bar even the recognition of private-sector organizations as actors on the world stage. The classicly recognized actors, the sovereign states of whatever size and power, present collectively a picture of highly unstable interdependencies that seems to indicate a period of turbulence at the level of public national and international organization. This turbulence is likely to endure for a protracted and indefinite period before there can be any prospect of a world order in which multinational corporate groups will be more than minor participants.

The Ambiguity of "Sovereignty"

One reason for this turbulence is the ambiguity about the "sovereignty" of actors. Sovereignty, in many of the new "mini-states" or "micro-states" of recent years, has questionable meaning. Some "sovereign" members of the United Nations, for example, are so small and their resources so limited that they cannot fulfill their obligations under the Charter, such as the obligation to participate fully in the Assembly's three-month (or more) sessions, in its seven, concurrently sitting committees of the whole (each made up of all members), and in such other committees to which the member-state may be named. Many have such small populations that they can send few diplomatic representatives abroad. The Maldive Islands, admitted in July, 1965, had a population of 97,000 (Staten Island's population is 295,500), and its area was 112 square miles (Queens' is 127 square miles). Theoretically, there were at that time sixty-five states, colonies, territories and dependencies which could have applied for membership in the United Nations, or could have done so on obtaining independence. They ranged from Mozambique (now a part of Portugal), with a population of 6-1/2 million, to Pitcairn Island, with eighty-six. Many multinational corporations, of course, outclass the mini-states in resources; but under present rules they could not join the state system nor be represented in the United Nations General Assembly.

Another basic cause of contemporary turbulence is the gulf between the rich and the poor nations. Deutsch's[21] arresting maps and tables, and especially the rank orders of human needs (population), potential power (income of nations), and human welfare (per capita incomes) for 141 countries, show that political power in the world arena is dependent on the highly uneven distribution of social communication facilities and of economic, cultural, and geographic interdependence. The world's poorest, more than one-half of mankind, will continue to exert whatever influence they can, acting mainly through nationalist institutions and blocs, to rid themselves of poverty. The rich nations will try through the same kinds of institutions to extend aid, to industrialize, and to lift agricultural production among the poor nations. To some extent the remedial job will be done by public international agencies; but the nation-states will be in control at the loci of actual operations.

21. Deutsch, *op. cit.*, especially Appendices VI and VII, the tables at pp. 64-71 ("Three Rank Orders of World Politics"), and the maps at pp. 54, 56, 58-59, and 62. Cf. Merritt and Rokkan (eds.), *Comparing Nations*, cited *supra*.

The divisiveness of this kind of institutional structure in the world arena is obvious. Yet nation-states are surely indispensable instruments for such an integrated effort at local levels. Nationalism at its best is a unifying force, channeling the efforts of diverse ethnic and other groupings within the sovereign's territory. With the help of other kinds of institutions, such as international organizations for reconstruction and development, nation-states may discover that new co-organic unities are more indispensable in tackling economic problems than the older unities. It is possibly one of the tasks of the multinational enterprise to become allied with such integrative efforts, not because the business corporation is an altruistic institution, but because it is only in the larger and better organized field of world affairs that the world company can survive and prosper.

The period of nation-building is hardly at an end. As Deutsch and Foltz have observed, "the formation and rise of nations were merely observed by scholars in the past. Today statesmen and voters increasingly want to *do* something about the process. They may want to establish or strengthen some national political entity of their own, or to merge it with or separate it from some other such entity. Or they may wish to strengthen, weaken, or otherwise change some other national political entity, so as to promote values and interests of their own. In any case, they will not leave peoples and nations as they find them. Old empires are to be broken up, new nations made, and new federations or communities established. . . . At this time, the world of developing countries is becoming more rather than less nationalistic. In country after country, modernization moves people out of their villages and their traditions into the modern world of mobility, insecurity, need for political and governmental services, and formal or informal political participation. . . . the larger powers [such as France and Germany] have not abandoned the substance of nationalism and national self-preoccupation" and even "the largest powers—the United States, the Soviet Union, and Communist China—have tended to represent to themselves and to others their national viewpoints and desires in the garb of international symbols and a world-wide mission." [22]

22. Karl W. Deutsch and William J. Foltz (eds.), *Nation-Building* (New York: Atherton Press, 1966), pp. v-x.

Nationalistic Modernization

Modernization and development are key words in the language of contemporary political economy. The "underdeveloped" or "developing" parts of the world capture our attention, however, mainly for political reasons. Modernization is a process that may—and often does—involve revolutions, however bloodless. The transformation of society required by modernization usually requires the transformation of the political order. Government becomes "the art of avoiding, delaying, or guiding such a revolution"[23] as the double transformation implies. The political system, in this view, is especially adapted to the necessary tasks: the rapid and decisive mustering of coercive power; organizing and giving effective institutional expression to the powerful salaried middle class; organizing mass participation in new types of roles for fashioning a nation and rebuilding the consciousness, organization, and material interdependence of society; developing and spreading new sets of ideas that can substitute for outworn faiths and set the path toward an emergent political culture.

Politics in its national garb tends to retain primacy because of the political system's superior and more immediate power to maintain or alter society's ability to generate and absorb persistent transformation. So nation-states proliferate in those vast areas of the world where they did not exist before, as well as in the older areas of long-established states, where dissatisfied regions rush toward modernization quite as zealously as do the "underdeveloped" nations. The nation-building we see going on apace in the Eastern Hemisphere today is, in a sense, an institutional tribute to the birthplace of the sovereign state, that old European cockpit of national power.

It was one thing to throw out the old colonial masters; it is quite another to reject their idea of the state. On the contrary, the masters in the newly-independent nations retain the old ideas of the sovereign state and nationalism. But the new elites of these

23. Manfred Halpern, "Toward Further Modernization of the Study of New Nations," *World Politics*, Vol. 17 (October 1964), pp. 157-181, at pp. 165-7. Cf. Lucian W. Pye, *Aspects of Political Development* (Boston: Little, Brown & Co., 1966); Gabriel A. Almond and James S. Coleman, eds., *The Politics of Developing Areas* (Princeton: Princeton University Press, 1960); Max F. Millikan and Donald L. M. Blackmer, *The Emerging Nations* (Boston: Little, Brown & Co., 1961); and Gunnar Myrdal, *The Challenge of World Poverty* (New York: Pantheon, 1970).

newer nations are bent on "development." Hence the debate about "developed," "less developed," and "developing" nations—a distinction that reflects both conceptual problems and dangerous conflict. The managers of multinational enterprise would do well to note this fact and not to be too preoccupied solely with the economic aspects of "development and modernization." Development has too often meant simply economic development, and mainly industrialization, but this is only one facet of a many-faceted revolution that is going on (not only in the "underdeveloped" parts of the world) toward modernization everywhere.

Economic development can be quite destabilizing in its radical alteration of values, demands, and power relations in a society, as, for example, in creating a class of the "*nouveaux pauvres*" [24] who turn into a political issue the poverty that they now see remediable. It can be destabilizing—perhaps with ultimate benefits to all—by forcing out old habits and institutions and making way for new ones so that investments can be secure and creative. It ought to be restabilizing, not merely by satisfying effective demands in the strictly economic sense, but also by satisfying aspirations, and in providing the means of overcoming social, political, and economic imbalances that arise from modernizing a society. The usual indices of "development," whether in terms of economics, education, skills, and so on, are not enough to assure a correct assessment of the "stability" of the new nations. Nor, indeed, is stability in itself any sound criterion for the degree of their modernization. The "revolution of modernization," which goes on whether one likes it or not, may in fact usher in tempestuous periods for these nations and for the world, since the goal of modernization is a well-nigh universal phenomenon. [25]

24. The term is used by Halpern in his article on "The Revolution of Modernization in National and International Society," in Carl J. Friedrich (ed.), *Nomos VIII: Revolution* (New York: Atherton Press, 1966), p. 211. Use of his analysis of the revolution of modernization is made at this point in order to call attention to an important new trend in the study of the international system and the world arena. Professor Halpern's contribution to *Nomos VIII* is a further extension of his ideas as set forth in the article from *World Politics*, cited above.

25. Halpern's comment on the "revolution of modernization" in Islam, in Japan, and in the United States, in *Nomos VIII*, pp. 202-3 and 211, makes the point. Further on modernization: William McCord, *The Springtime of Freedom: Evolution of Developing Societies* (New York: Oxford University Press, 1965); Claude E. Welch, *Political Modernization: A Reader in Comparative Political Change* (Belmont, Calif.: Wadsworth Publishing Co., 1966); C. E. Black, *The Dynamics of Modernization: A Study in Comparative History* (New York: Harper & Row, 1966); Bruce M. Russett, *Trends in World Politics* (New York: The Macmillan Co., 1965), Ch. 8, "Political Consequences of Economic and Social Change."

Problems of development and modernization are not to be solved by repeating old dogmas about dividing the world into two great camps, for example, East versus West, and the Communist World against the Free World. Nor is it very useful to speak of the "First World" of the United States and its Western allies and the "Second World" of the Soviet Union and its Eastern Bloc allies, a conception that makes no room for the so-called "Third World"[26] of nonaligned but variously committed nations of Latin America, Asia and Africa. Why three worlds and not four or five, depending upon one's conceptual purposes in spreading out the broad canvas on which to locate the multinational corporation? For the purposes of foreign policy, every knowledgeable chancery in the world has to distinguish the sub-camps within the major East-West confrontation; there are two superpowers, but there are also the up-and-coming lesser powers that challenge the leadership of the United States and the Soviet Union. The relevant world arenas of corporate action are similarly complex.

The goals of policy in all the world's powers shift with time and technological change. These shifts need to be observed in multinational board rooms and executive suites as well as in the chanceries of national governments. It is a dangerous fallacy to assume that the goals of nations, the desired outcomes of their strategies and tactics, can be neatly classified by dyads and triads, or any other way, that simplifies thought too quickly. The multinational corporate manager will find himself in a specific country, with unique characteristics, not in a nation cut from the template of a given ideology. He has to make a realistic assessment of the desired outcomes and goal values at the command of the decision-makers in power there. This is part of an indispensable strategy of corporate intelligence.

26. Irving L. Horowitz, *Three Worlds of Development: The Theory and Practice of International Stratification* (New York: Oxford University Press, 1966), p. 3. Horowitz argued that the United States was increasingly becoming isolated from the world political economy and, unlike the U.S.S.R. and mainland China, had already forfeited its opportunity to provide strategies and tactics with which nations in the Third World could identify. Thomas Patrick Melady, *Western Policy and the Third World* (New York: Hawthorn Books, Inc., 1967) and Cecil V. Crabb, Jr., *The Elephant and the Grass: A Study of Non-Alignment* (New York: Frederick A. Praeger, 1966) take different positions; speaking of the Afro-Arab-Asian countries, Crabb offers the African proverb: "When two elephants fight, it is the grass that suffers."

The goals pursued by those participants in the world arena that are designated as more or less developed or more or less modernized are often surprisingly paradoxical. Leaders in many of these countries reject liberal democracy, arguing that political freedoms will inhibit the necessary drive from economic stagnation to growth; they reject a wide and pluralistic diffusion of economic and political power as inconsistent with successful efforts to overcome poverty, disease, and a generally backward economy. Opponents of this position insist upon ending "the tyranny of the stomach without the tyranny of the slave camp." [27] The drift to authoritarianism is declared to be largely the result of a self-fulfilling prophecy of intellectuals who believe that the "underdeveloped masses" cannot rule themselves; the argument is that these masses must be "herded by benevolent dictators who will guide them to economic affluence" after which they will presumably relinquish power. [28]

It was long thought in Western countries influenced by the Enlightenment that faith in the inevitable triumph of reason would bring with it free social and political institutions. It was natural to classify governments into "democracies" and "dictatorships," and to relegate fascist and communist forms of government to the category of transient disorders and political pathologies. Recent developments on the world scene have put these conceptions in doubt. In the explosion of new states in the Middle East, in Africa, and in Asia, nations present such a bewildering variety of cultures, social institutions, and political characteristics that the old comfortable dichotomies have had to be abandoned. [29] The "advanced" nations of the Western political tradition no longer dominate the total scene; power and influence have been diffused into the former colonial and semicolonial areas. Communism has now emerged, not as a temporary aberration, but as a powerful competitor in the struggle to shape the structure of national politics and of the international system.

We can still speak of modern democratic and authoritarian

27. William McCord, *The Springtime of Freedom: The Evolution of Developing Societies* (New York: Oxford University Press, 1965), pp. 6-7.

28. *Ibid.*

29. Gabriel A. Almond and G. Bingham Powell, Jr., *Comparative Politics: A Developmental Approach* (Boston: Little, Brown & Co., 1966), p. 5.

forms of political systems but it is important to distinguish between primitive and traditional political systems and to classify these systems according to the degree of structural differentiation and cultural secularization. In modern political systems, there is a "specialized political infrastructure," consisting of associational interest groups, political parties, and the media of communication, [30] and in the "mobilized" modern systems one finds both a high degree of structural differentiation and a secularized political culture—both of some importance to the strategy of multinational corporations operating in the world arena.

Secularization is evident in societies in which traditional orientations and ties have begun to be broken down and large numbers of individuals have become available for new patterns of life and thought. Such societies may reach a much higher level of economic productivity and, consequently, of material resources. For this reason they are more likely to be readily available to the political system, [31] but with the expansion of capacity for more intensive extraction, regulation, and distribution, the political elites must respond to new pressures for more highly differentiated political infrastructures; there are increased demands for distribution or participation or both. The elite response is either

---

30. *Ibid.*, p. 255.

31. *Ibid.*, p. 258. In comparing modern systems, these authors note that the assessment of the level of political development involves three interrelated variables: role differentiation, subsystem autonomy, and secularization, and that there is a tendency for these processes of change to vary together (p. 306). In managerial thought, unattuned to the variety of foreign cultures, erratic judgment may result from attention solely to the second of these variables, with specific reference only to free enterprise.

Cf. Robert T. Holt and John E. Turner, *The Political Basis of Economic Development: An Exploration in Comparative Political Analysis* (Princeton, N.J.: D. Van Nostrand Co., Inc., 1966), Ch. 7; Richard T. Gill, *Economic Development: Past and Present* (Englewood Cliffs, N.J.: Prentice-Hall, Inc., 1963), Chs. 5 and 6; Richard N. Farmer and Barry M. Richman, *Comparative Management and Economic Progress* (Homewood, Ill.: Richard D. Irwin, Inc., 1965), Ch. 2, pp. 55-62, and Ch. 7; Hadley Cantril, "A Study of Aspirations" in John J. Coyle and Edward J. Mock (eds.), *Readings in International Business* (Scranton, Pa.: International Textbook Co., 1965), pp. 238-250; on the differences and the nuances in capitalist ideology, Paul A. Samuelson, "Personal Freedoms and Economic Freedoms in the Mixed Economy" in Earl F. Cheit (ed.), *The Business Establishment* (New York: John Wiley & Sons, Inc., 1964), pp. 193-227; T. R. Brennan and F. X. Hodgson, *Overseas Management* (New York: McGraw-Hill Book Co., 1963), Ch. 6: "Inducing Purposive Cultural Change"; Roy Blough, *International Business: Environment and Adaptation* (New York: McGraw-Hill Book Co., 1966), pp. 45-52 on "Values, Attitudes, and Motivations"; Howe Martyn, *International Business: Principles and Problems* (The Free Press of Glencoe/ Macmillan Co., 1964), Ch. 7: "International Enterprise and Economic Growth."

to develop support for various activities or to manipulate and control them. In the latter case, there is an attempt to preserve system stability; in the former, the system is directed toward new goals. For the managers of transnational business, it is always necessary, in order to operate in such environments, to be currently informed on the nature of these goals.

There are other ways to classify types of political systems.[32] Democratic systems have ranging degrees of subsystem autonomy, e.g., in the private sector, and of participant culture, ranging from the high subsystem autonomy to be found in Great Britain, through the limited subsystem autonomy to be found in France, and to the low subsystem autonomy characteristic of Mexico.

Authoritarian systems (i.e., those with subsystem control and only subject-participant culture) may be subclassified into four kinds: radical totalitarian (Soviet Union), conservative totalitarian (Nazi Germany), conservative authoritarian (Spain), and modernizing authoritarian (Brazil). Among the "premobilized modern systems" (i.e., with limited differentiation and secularization) are to be found the authoritarian (Ghana) and the democratic (Nigeria prior to January, 1966) systems. This typology is not necessarily definitive, but it is empirically based and not derived from abstract conceptions of national goals.

International Entities: Organized and Otherwise

Among the organized groups in the world arena there are nation-states, transnational intergovernmental organizations, political parties with certain claims to universality, and other transnational private associations, both nonprofit and for profit, including multinational corporations. The unorganized and partially organized participants include religions, civilizations, languages, markets, races, and other aggregates. These aggregates are all of immense importance to the decision process and to corporate policy, and will command more and more attention in the intelligence function of multinational corporations of the future, a matter to be discussed in a later chapter. As of September 30, 1968, one list[33] of 38 public international organizations showed

32. E.g., by Almond and Powell, *op. cit.*, Chs. IX and X.

33. "International Organization," *Britannica Book of the Year: 1969*, pp. 431-2.

varied memberships by 137 states. Of these, the United Nations and its specialized agencies (some of which, such as the International Labor Organization and the Universal Postal Union, antedated World War II) aimed at universality, while others had more restricted membership; regional political groupings such as the Organization of American States (OAS) and the Organization for African Unity (OAU), military alliances such as the North Atlantic Treaty Organization (NATO) and the Warsaw Pact, and organizations with a primarily economic orientation such as the European Economic Community (EEC), the Council for Mutual Economic Assistance (COMECON), and the Organization for Economic Cooperation and Development (OECD), were all less than universal yet public, governmental, and international in the full sense of that term.

Nongovernmental, nonprofit organizations that are called international are decidedly minor actors in the international system, if admitted at all—they are not among the makers of international law, but they are among the more influential initiators of law, practice, and convention. Like some private-sector corporations-for-profit on the world scene, they may in fact intervene significantly at several stages of the decision process in international public affairs. These nonprofit organizations have been divided[34] into the following categories: business and finance; communications, transport and travel; labor; agriculture; arts and science; press; education; religion; social welfare; sports; international law and the legal settlement of disputes; and the pursuit of peace. These NGOs, while nonprofit, are in some cases nonetheless organized and controlled primarily by profit-making institutions, some of the latter including influential multinational corporations.

The Corporate "Actor" in the International System

Private corporations have begun to occupy a more important place in international law than was formerly conceded them by

---

34. Lyman C. White, *International Non-Governmental Organizations: Their Purposes, Methods, and Accomplishments* (New Brunswick, N.J.: Rutgers University Press, 1951). Cf. J. J. Lador-Lederer, *International Non-Governmental Organizations and Economic Entities: A Study of Autonomous Organization and Ius Gentium* (Leyden: A. W. Sythoff, 1963).

the jurists. The consequences for multinational enterprises are considerable. Wolfgang Friedmann[35] has called attention to four different perspectives that have to be used in an understanding of the new dimensions of international law. In the first place, this field of the law has been extended "horizontally" from its original nucleus of European nations several centuries ago to the non-Western group of states that have more recently become members of the family of nations. The international law of this "expanded world"—to use Röling's terms—is undergoing basic changes as different cultures, religions, and political and economic systems the world over now introduce legal principles that were unknown to Gentile, Grotius, Wattel, and other founders of the modern law of nations.

In the second place, there is the dimension of social control exercised through the organization of the modern state. With a wide spectrum of degrees of control over the economic activities of nations, over their natural resources, over the political and social activities of individuals and groups, and over human welfare measures that lead to new types of international conventions, the law of nations today bears little resemblance to the older personal agreements among sovereign princes; it bristles with subjects such as international labor conventions, multilateral trade agreements, conventions on the conservation of resources, on the control of propaganda, and on the uses of atomic energy.

Thirdly, there is a new dimension due to the inclusion of new participants in, and "subjects" of, international law, especially public international organizations, as well as the older sovereign states, and private corporations, as well as individuals. Finally, there is the new dimension of subject matter formerly regarded as outside the sphere of the law of nations; here there are matters of direct interest to multinational enterprises.

The doctrine that private corporations are properly regarded as participant-actors in international law is by no means universal. It contravenes the principles of analytical positivists who insist that only states can be the "subjects" of international law.

---

35. Wolfgang G. Friedmann, *The Changing Structure of International Law* (New York: Columbia University Press, 1964); also his article, "The Changing Dimensions of International Law," *Columbia Law Review*, Vol. 62 (Nov. 1962), pp. 1147-1165, reprinted in Coyle and Mock, *Readings in International Business* (1965), pp. 47-66.

For the positivists, law is nothing but the command of a superior will to an inferior, and only the sovereign state can utter supreme commands. The objections to the positivist view are partly moral; Brierly declared that "the result of positivism has been to secularize the whole idea of law and thus to weaken the moral foundation which is essential to the vitality of all legal obligation,"[36] and he pointed to the "curious metamorphosis which transformed the doctrine of sovereignty from a principle of internal order, as Bodin and even Hobbes had conceived it, into one of international anarchy"—the modern state having thus so far departed from classical teachings of law as the embodiment of justice.

International law, in Brierly's opinion, has suffered from this "incubus of the doctrine of sovereignty" in the prevalent view that "international law is the sum of the rules by which states have *consented* to be bound, and that nothing can be law to which they have not consented." Against this positivist position, Brierly urged that the source of obligation to obey international law had to be sought outside the law itself and beyond any merely juridical explanation; the explanation was rather in institutional terms: "states . . . are merely *institutions*, that is to say, organizations which men establish among themselves for securing certain objects, of which the most fundamental is a system of order within which the activities of their common life may be carried on."[37]

This suggests a further objection to the positivist view which would exclude all but sovereign states from the participants and subjects of international law. The modern state is not the only institution established by men to reach their objectives, and in the world arena it becomes more and more obvious that the sovereign state sometimes stands dangerously in the way of new and needed institutions. We cling to the idea of the state and of national independence because it is an anchor to windward in a tumultuous age of rapid social change and stupendous confrontations of power. The nation-state does serve purposes that cannot be served in any other way, not least in carving out parts of

36. J. W. Brierly, *The Law of Nations*, Sixth edition edited by Sir Humphrey Waldock (New York and Oxford: Oxford University Press, 1963), p. 44.

37. *Ibid.*, pp. 45-55.

the earth's surface where reliable jurisdiction makes the framework for a life of meaning and human dignity.

When all this has been conceded, however, we face the fact that there are and must be new dimensions of international law to make room for intermediate institutions: instruments for getting things done in the world arena that must be done and cannot be done by states or public international organizations alone. Here enters the case for recognition of private international organizations, private corporations, and individuals as participants and subjects of international law.

The trend in this direction is indicated in Jenks's[38] monograph on a global common law. There the author insists that international law "represents the common law of mankind in an early stage of development, of which the law governing the relations between States is one, but only one, major division," and goes on to elaborate among the substantive elements of international law such topics as property rights of an international character, including copyright and patent; common rules established by international agreement which apply to public services, corporations, and individuals rather than states; human rights protected by international guarantees, including civil liberties and political, economic, and social rights; activities in space; employment policy; colonial policy; the integration of Europe; atoms for peace; and many others that would never have been found, except as footnotes at best, in the traditional texts.

Modern transnational business practice,[39] as business interlaces with diplomacy and interstate agreements, points in the direction of a broad transnational law. Corporations do play a significant part in international transactions to which states are parties. Private corporations do undertake at least quasi-public functions in many parts of the globe. An outstanding example of

38. Wilfred Jenks, *The Common Law of Mankind* (New York: Frederick A. Praeger, 1958); see also Philip Jessup, *Transnational Law* (New Haven: Yale University Press, 1956); Bernard V. A. Röling, *International Law in an Expanded World* (Amsterdam: Djambatan, 1960); Georg Schwarzenberger, *The Frontiers of International Law* (London: Stevens and Sons, Ltd., 1962); Alfred Verdross, *Völkerrecht*. Fifth edition (Wien: Springer, 1964); Wilfred Jenks, *Law in the World Community* (New York: D. McKay & Co., 1967).

39. Stephen J. Brams, "Transactional Flows in the International System," *American Political Science Review*, Vol. 60, No. 4, December 1966, pp. 880-898.

the role of private corporations in contemporary international transactions of a public character is the Iranian Oil Agreement of 1954. In that agreement, the government of Iran concluded what some have called a "quasi-treaty" with a consortium of eight foreign oil companies for the nationalization of Anglo-Iranian properties. Active participants in the negotiations that led to the agreement were the diplomatic representatives of the countries of which the companies were nationals alongside the representatives of the companies themselves. Some of these countries had controlling interests in the companies. The arbitration provisions of the agreement have served as models for similar international transactions.

The Quasi-Public Status of Corporations

While it is true that many economic matters in the world arena are dealt with by public international organizations reared simply on the basis of inter-state treaties and conventions, there are also—and in growing numbers—remarkable, mixed, public-private entities that arise through combinations of state and private-corporation action. The strictly public international organizations, such as the World Bank and the International Monetary Fund, do not exhaust the need for institutional growth in world affairs. Important examples of a new trend are companies constituted by joint action of governments and private enterprises, such as Eurofirma (1955), Eurochemic (1957), and the International Mosel Company (1956). Eurochemic has shareholders ranging all the way from governments through public atomic energy authorities, public and mixed public-private corporations, to private companies engaged in the production and distribution of energy. The establishment of joint ventures of this kind requires, in the absence of a single constituting authority, a network of public and private actions and agreements.

The necessity for such a mixed network of agreements arises, again, from the pluralism of authorities in the world arena. In areas reaching toward the goal of a common market, this pluralistic problem has to be met eventually by a supranational corporation-creating authority, or at least certain constitutional arrangements that facilitate "freedom of establishment" within the entire common-market area. In the United States, the pluralistic structure of federal government presented a similar problem that has been at least partly solved through the supremacy clauses of the United States Constitution and the linkage of this clause by the Supreme Court with the commerce clause and key provisions of the Fourteenth Amendment. The extension of corporate business throughout the country by means of "foreign corporations" (created in one state of the union and doing business in others) has proceeded under the protection of federal law. Little use has been made by businessmen of the corporation-creating capacity of Congress as the national legislature. Our common market has been opened up through a century and a half of constitutional development. A comparable development for opening a continental market to the companies of Western Europe will take time and ingenuity.[40]

The status of private corporations in the international law of pluralistic Europe—with its failure to date to achieve political unity—may be expected to become a kind of municipal-law status if unity ever occurs. In the meantime, there will be networks

40. The most comprehensive study ever made of the problem of a European company law can be found in *Project d'un Statut des Sociétés anonymes européennes* (Brussels: Commission of the European Communities, Competition Series No. 6, 1966), a report made by a group of experts from the six countries under the chairmanship of Professor Pieter Sanders, dean of the Faculty of Law of the University of Rotterdam, proposing a draft statute for European limited-liability companies; see comment by Guido Colonna di Paliano, "Why Europe Needs Continental-Scale Firms," *European Community*, No. 116, September 1968, and Alan Parker, "The European Company" in the same number. For more recent developments see "European Company Law: Common Market Commission Sends Final Draft to the Council," *European Community*, No. 137, August 1970, and the proposal to the Council by the Commission of the European Communities in *Bulletin of the European Communities*, Supplement to Issue No. 8, 1970, published in French and English. Cf. Dennis Thompson, *The Proposal for a European Company* (London: PEP, European Series No. 3, December 1969). Charles P. Kindleberger, "European Integration and the International Corporation," *Columbia Journal of World Business*, Vol. I, No. 1, Winter 1966, pp. 65-73, discusses the need for a European corporation with a European—not a national—charter for operation freely throughout the Common Market. See also J. J. Servan-Schreiber, *The American Challenge* (New York: Atheneum, 1968), Ch. XI, "State of the Union"; Jean Maynaud and Dusan Sidjanski, *L'Europe des Affaires: rôle et structure des groupes* (Paris: Payot, 1967) on the structure of business concentration since the inauguration of the Common Market and the consequences for industry of the lack of coordination between the political and the economic integration of Europe; "Industrial Property Laws Impede Economic Union," *European Community*, June 1968, No. 113, pp. 17-18; "Regulation for the Block Exemption of Bilateral Exclusive Distributorship Agreements Takes Effect," *European Community*, April-May 1967, No. 102, p. 22; "Legal Disparities Obstruct Intra-Community Mergers," *European Community*, June 1966, No. 93, pp. 6-7; Pieter Verloren Vom Themaat, "Does Europe Need Larger Firms?", *European Community*, April 1966, No. 91, p. 12.

of public-private arrangements, involving both the governments of the several nation-states and the private corporations that operate transnationally. The increasingly important role of private corporations in international transactions of a public character, especially at Brussels and in Luxembourg—the seats of the new communities—is due to the mixed economies. Nations operate industries, exploit natural resources, build highways and canals, conduct foreign trade, and do many other things that may be put in the hands of private, semi-private, and government-owned corporations.

Often there is a close working relationship between private companies and governments that have delegated power to get things done through other than bureaucratic channels of the governments themselves. For the lawyers and the students of public policy, the precise status of corporations of this kind raises difficult problems. On the one hand, they cannot be regarded as strictly private entities, unrecognized in public law; on the other hand, to make no distinction between such entities and public corporate bodies seems unacceptable, and especially in international law.

Friedmann comments that "the elimination of differences in status between states and public international organizations, representing public interests and constitutionally responsible to the public, and private corporations, representing private interests and pursuing private objectives, would be subversive of the basic objectives of public international order. It would be no more tenable than the elimination, in municipal law, of the distinction between governmental and other public authorities on the one part and the private legal subject on the other part."[41] He comments further that "it would be as dangerous to uncritically accord subjectivity to the private corporation in international law as it would be to deny its factual participation in the evolution of public international law," referring here to Sigmund Timberg's warning against powers exercised by unregulated and powerful private corporations in international cartels in steel, oil, chemicals and certain metals.

These cartels are alleged to have exercised powers of a quasi-sovereign character, often contrary to the professed public policies

41. Friedmann, *The Changing Structure of International Law*, cited, pp. 223-224.

of the sovereigns to whom they were supposed to owe allegiance, according to Friedmann. His position is that any strengthening of the role of the private corporation in public or "quasi-public" international legal processes must be accompanied by a corresponding measure of public regulation.[42] The corporation in international affairs, he observes, is not the "person" of jurisprudence but a collectivity with organizational and economic power that in some instances surpasses that of many of the smaller states in the family of nations.

There is a whole new branch of international law of which the structures, organizations, and functions of the public international agencies, the multinational companies, and, to an as yet more loosely defined extent, private international corporations, are a part. Like the relatively new fields of international labor law, international tax law, and the law of international investment, there seems to be an emergent field of international commercial and company law in which the multinational enterprise plays a major role.

---

42. Friedmann, "The Changing Dimensions of International Law" in Coyle and Mock, *op. cit.*, p. 59.

Chapter IV

THE GOALS OF MULTINATIONAL CORPORATE POLICY

The goals of those who govern a firm are humanly various,[1] and personal goals apparently tend to shape the goals of the firm itself. Goals so derived are not describable in simplistic terms of economic orthodoxy. Most corporate enterprises are small and entrepreneurial, and the giant corporations have to be studied separately for the sake of accuracy. Size introduces differences of kind in corporate structure, processes and functions.

It is also important to distinguish between the role of business in "society"[2] in some abstract sense and business in specifically named social environments at specific points in time. The large multinational corporation operating in a score or more of national societies may face radically diverse situations unknown to the firm that operates exclusively in the market of a single nation. The role of the multinational corporation in any given environment may be substantially different today than it was before World War II, or will be in another decade. It has been said that "the primary habitat of the multiple-goal firm is the protected market"[3] but it could hardly be concluded that when an enterprise moves out into an unprotected market in the world arena, its goals are perforce reduced to one.

It is one thing to postulate entrepreneurial objectives, at an analytically theoretical level, of directors and executive managers of the multinational corporation as an ideal type, operating in a

1. *E.g.*, Harold L. Johnson, *Graphic Analysis of Multiple-Goal Firms: Development, Current Status, and Technique*. Occasional Paper No. 5, Center for Research of the College of Business Administration, Pennsylvania State University, 1966.

2. "Business and the Realm of Values," in Clarence Walton and Richard Eells, editors, *The Business System: Readings in Ideas and Concepts* (New York: Macmillan, 1967), Vol. III, pp. 1905-2352, presents the views of many contemporary writers on this subject.

3. Johnson, *op. cit.*, p. 32.

conceptualized international economy. It is quite another thing to observe what real people in these positions actually do. A further distinction has to be made between *preferred* goals as stated by responsible directors and executive managers and the *operative* goals, as shown by objective study of managerial direction. This distinction implies no judgment in advance on the worth of stated preferences. The operative goals may rate higher on some scale of values than those devised and declared for public relations output.

Profit-Maximizing and Social Responsibility

There is no generally acceptable answer to the elementary question: What is the business of a business firm? Return of a reasonable profit to the owners would seem to be an elementary answer, but who owns the modern large corporation and what principles operate to determine who gets what, when, and how as gross receipts are divided up? The problem is complicated enough without introducing the cross-border aspects of business in the multinational corporation.

A distinguished conservative economist declares that a corporate executive's sole responsibility as a businessman is that of "an agent serving the interests of his principal." These interests— presumably of stockholders as the corporation's "owners"—are interpreted in the plain language of profit.[4]

There are many difficulties with this formulation, not the least of which is the notion of agency—a legal concept that hardly explains the scope of directors' authority. But there is an even greater difficulty. The shareowners own only paper claims on the directors of a corporation who, collectively, are the true holders of corporate property. The shareholders are only one class of many contributor-claimants.[5] There are also creditors (including bondholders) to consider, as well as employees and customers. In addition, there are home and host governments, whose contributions may be considerable and whose claims may be substantial. How are the returns of a corporate enterprise to

4. Milton Friedman, "A Friedman Doctrine: The Social Responsibility of Business Is To Increase Its Profits," *The New York Times Magazine*, September 13, 1970.

5. See Richard Eells and Clarence Walton, *Conceptual Foundations of Business*, revised edition (Homewood, Ill.: Richard D. Irwin, Inc., 1969), pp. 215-300, esp. Ch. 8.

be allocated among all these claimants, who have in their various ways contributed to a profitable outcome?

In practice, we know that in the large modern corporation the answer to this question is not left in the hands of share-holders. They have little or no power to decide, except in the vague sense of their indirect and diluted power to vote their shares. That power rests in the hands of professional managers, according to the original Berle-Means[6] principle that ownership and control are separate in the modern corporation, or according to the Galbraithian theory, in the hands of influential members of committees of the "technostructure," none of whom may hold any shares at all. The technostructure is that part of the modern corporate organization which supplies "specialized talent and organization." Management, in Galbraith's account, is a rela-tively small group that embraces the chairman, president, vice-presidents with important staff or departmental responsibilities, and some division and department heads. The technostructure is much larger, embracing "all who bring specialized knowledge, talent, or experience to group decision-making," and this, not management, is said to be "the guiding intelligence, the brain—of the enterprise."[7]

The locus of control in the modern corporation is a matter of debate. But in large corporate groups, the allocation of receipts among all the contributor-claimants involves an exercise of power at decisive points within the corporate organization that are not easily discoverable.

In the larger content of the allocation of scarce resources to alternative uses in society at large, the classic doctrine is that the determination of this allocation has to be left and ought to be left to market mechanisms, and emphatically not to political decision-makers. "The market governs." That this is a useful nor-mative principle for a theoretical construct of the distribution of

6. Adolph A. Berle and Gardiner C. Means, *The Modern Corporation and Private Property*, Revised edition (New York: Harcourt, Brace & World, 1968).

7. John Kenneth Galbraith, *The New Industrial State* (Boston: Houghton Mifflin, 1967), Ch. VI. This "technostructure" is distinguishable from "technocrats" regarded as the scientific and technological community, both as it exists and as it forms the basis of contemporary industry and government; see W.H.G. Armytage, *The Rise of the Technocrats: A Social History* (Toronto: University of Toronto Press, 1965). Ante-cedent usages were those of Veblen's, in *The Engineers and the Price System* and Howard Scott, in his abortive notion of "technocracy" as a political movement.

power over resource-allocation among public- and private-sector power-holders in society might be conceded for the sake of argument. That it describes what actually happens is clearly incorrect. As to the internal distribution of decision power in a corporation, when decisions must be made as to allocations among contributor-claimants, it takes more than a vivid imagination to conceive of this allocative function in terms of market mechanisms.

A more realistic view is that the internal governance of corporations runs on principles that refer only partly to market forces and heavily to pressures of a very different kind. As to corporate subordination to market forces in national and world arenas, it is evident that under both older and current mercantilist policies of nation-states, the corporation has not had to play so passive a role. The current debate about the social responsibility of business, as applied to the corporate goals of multinational corporations, is a new phase of a very old problem: What do business enterprisers owe to national governments and vice versa? Yet, throughout modern history, business corporations often have had to serve nationalistic social purposes in one way or another, while pursuing the goal of profit.

Old and New Mercantilist Goals

The multinational corporate executive is literally fenced in today by political considerations that arise from the modern state system. He cannot move out into the world as though it were a great free marketplace. It is not a situation in which he can carry on his company's business under the "obvious and simple system of national liberty," postulated by Adam Smith as productive of the greatest possible prosperity and harmony so long as natural economic laws are not interfered with. Instead, at nearly every turn he faces massive interference by protectionist national governments in host countries. At home, the autonomy of a self-regulating market economy of national dimensions is equally out of the question.

Everywhere, the multinational corporation executive faces pressing problems of *political* economy. He may prefer to believe in the doctrines of classical economics, whether unreconstructed by Keynesian thought or otherwise. He may assume that complete freedom of economic exchange within nations and across frontiers would produce a natural harmony of interests, which only needs to be let alone in order to produce optimum economic advantage to everyone. In practice, the multinational corporate executive runs up against the nationalistic as well as the corporate facts of life.

The "invisible hand" of natural economic laws must move aside from time to time, not only for the nation-state but also for the quite visible and immediate hand of corporate policy-makers themselves. In the Ricardian version of classical economics, the pursuit of individual advantage was thought to be admirably connected with the universal good of the whole, but the Ricardian individual was a natural person, not a fictitious person in the form of a powerful enterprise. And of what "universal good," of what "whole," did Ricardo speak: For the whole of mankind an ecologically defined good life, or only the "wealth of nations"?

The contemplative multinational corporate executive looks in vain for a twentieth-century philosophy that updates the classics of economic theory while conserving their strong points and fitting the theory to international realities. The equivalent of Adam Smith's inquiry into "the nature and causes of the wealth of nations," done by a genius of equal intellectual strength and moral certitude in our time, might be entitled "An Inquiry into the Nature and Causes of the Wealth of Man in His Global Biosphere."

The sweep of Smith's work cannot be minimized, nor its relevance both to the mercantilism of his day and the neo-mercantilism of our own. He was a professor of moral philosophy before he became collector of customs at Edinburgh. "Moral Philosophy" in his day meant the sum total of the sciences that we now call social, as distinguished from "Natural Philosophy" that denoted the physical sciences plus mathematics. In the *Wealth of Nations* (1776), he did more than analyze coolly and objectively what trade and laissez-faire stood for; he was a leading force in their victory through his writing.[8] Nearly a quarter of the book was given over to a scathing criticism—as well as an exposition—of mercantilism as a protectionist and monetary system.

8. Joseph A. Schumpeter, *A History of Economic Analysis* (New York: Oxford University Press, 1954), p. 181, called Smith "the most famous of all economists" and the *Wealth of Nations* "the most successful not only of all books on economics but, with the possible exception of Darwin's *Origin of Species*, of all scientific books that have appeared to this day."

As a conception of society, mercantilism was a unifying system that marked progress away from the disintegrative particularism of feudalism and away from the sterile universalisms of medieval Europe. The essence of mercantilist policy, in Schmoller's words, was "the total reconstruction of society and its organization, as well as of the state and its institutions, by substituting for the local and provincial economic policy that of the state and the nation."[9] Considered as a phase in the history of economic policy (and not as a phase of economic development per se) in Europe between the Middle Ages and the age of laissez-faire, mercantilism was connected with certain political conditions, notably the rise and consolidation of the nation-states, which grew up on the ruins of the Holy Roman Empire. These states were limited in territory and influence, but they were sovereign within their own borders; and as soon as they were sovereign the state stood at the center of mercantilist policy.

The emergence of the sovereign nation-state as the predominant social institution was due in part to mercantilist policy, which was directed—in the interest of the state—inward against parochial forces as well as outward against that feeble heritage of medieval universalism, the Holy Roman Empire. It was the internal threat to state power that most concerned the proponents of state supremacy. This threat was institutionalized in more narrowly confined social institutions than the nation-state, namely in cities, provinces, and corporations. The adversary of mercantilism, in the early modern period, was the medieval combination of universalism and particularism.

Instructive parallels might be drawn, for our contemporary age, to the multinational corporation, which seeks a more comprehensive unifying agent than the nation-state of mercantilism. The prime goal of mercantilist policy was to make the state's purposes decisive in a uniform, national, economic sphere. It sought further to make all economic activity subservient to considerations corresponding to the requirements of the nation-state.

9. Gustav Schmoller, in his *Jahrbuch 1884*, as quoted by Eli F. Heckscher, *Mercantilism*, in the revised edition edited by E. F. Söderlund, from the authorized translation by Mendel Shapiro (New York: Macmillan, 1935), Vol. I, p. 28. My account of mercantilism is drawn in part from Heckscher's study and Schumpeter, cited. In describing mercantilism as a "unifying system," Heckscher wrote that it "opposed everything that bound down economic life to a particular place and obstructed trade within the boundaries of the state." *Op. cit.*, Vol. I, p. 273.

The domain of the state required national uniformity. In our day, the goal of a comparable policy of *global* dimensions would be statable almost in the same terms, except that one would have to substitute "a world legal order" for "the state."

The difficulty of solving the global problem is, however, much greater than the difficulty faced by the king's ministers in England, France, and other European states of the early modern period. Their problem proved not unsolvable, for they could surmount disintegrative toll systems and medieval municipal policies, and, on the positive side, build state bureaucracies that were national in scope. But the king's minister's ambitions might far outrun the administrative means at his disposal. It is notable that a major source of power in the most successful, early, empire-building companies was administrative capability, evident in their relatively advanced bureaucratic structures, as compared with the pretentions of the nation-state of the time.

The nation-state of today has developed powerful bureaucracies. It also has at its disposal advanced techniques for turning the economic forces of individuals and firms to national advantage. But in some places and for some purposes, even major nations must and do fall back on the superior administrative expertise and organizational structures of industrial firms.

One object of the early mercantilists, in using economic forces in the interest of the state, was to strengthen the state authority and thus to augment the state's external power in relation to other states. They did not seek to advance the interests of the king's subjects, a point noted by the early classical school of economic analysis and of interest to us today when multinational corporations do seek through corporate policy to serve humane purposes.

Part of the critique of early laissez-faire liberals was that in pursuing the mercantilist policy objective of national power through national unification, the early modern nation-state and the corporations of that day were indifferent to humane considerations. The individualism of Adam Smith and David Ricardo was not indifferent to the problem of unification as against ancient particularism, but both men were relatively indifferent to the nationalism of mercantilist doctrine. Their care for human life persists today against neo-mercantilism. It is still a relevant question whether unification of *national* power is a necessary step toward a global order of economic welfare for all, and whether the multinational corporation can and should shape its policy to that end. It can be argued that mercantilism, in seeking to bolster the power of the state, did in fact contribute to human welfare because a strengthened state was the only road to a form of nationalism which, in turn, stood for the rights of men as citizens.

Central to mercantilist doctrine was a theoretical danger from which economic policy was chiefly to protect a country, namely, the danger of having *too much* goods. A protectionist system grounded on this theory is as great a threat to individual liberty today as it was under mercantilist policy; it can hardly be regarded as centered on the rights of man and human welfare. The closely related balance-of-trade theory in neo-mercantilism raises a similar issue for multinational corporate policy: where does the multinational corporation stand in priorities of human values relative to national, transnational, international, and supranational goals of home and host countries? Both the modern state and the modern corporation have been charged with policy aims that fly in the face of these values.

The liberalism of Adam Smith, in opposing monopolies and business combinations generally, was rooted in an ethics that precluded artificial disturbances of the system of "natural liberty." The corporate form of industry and large-scale enterprise were such disturbances, although he would allow exceptions for canals and a few other cases. He was thinking mainly of commercial and financial big business, of colonial enterprise particularly. Governments of national states in the sixteenth and seventeenth centuries were variously motivated in creating or favoring the great chartered companies. Most of these companies enjoyed a monopolistic position in that their policies and practices kept both foreigners and co-nationals out of protected markets and restricted the output of the favored group itself, regulating distribution of the output between markets.

The policy is explainable. At a time when these countries were far from having fully developed capitalist economies, powered by a great onward rush of competitive enterprise, governments used defensive tactics. To foster industrial development, it was a rational policy to grant monopolistic privilege, especially

93

since enterprise would not have been possible at all without the grant; in some instances, governments had to permit monopolistic practices on the part of the businessmen concerned whether they wanted to or not.

Given the fact that capitalism had not at the time burst forth full-grown but was developing slowly from the guild system, new production methods and new forms of enterprise were bound to meet with resistance. The craft guilds and other established pressure groups were quite successful in resisting the newer "free" enterprise; they resorted to legislation and state administration. The new capitalists—merchant traders and masters—responded in kind. Being themselves the product of an age when organization and corporate action were quite acceptable, they organized to resist. Nor were they at all ashamed to make use of their own powerful organizations for this purpose of resisting the old in favor of the new. The individualism later advocated by Adam Smith would not have appealed to them. In unity they saw strength, and that meant much aping of the older corporate methods. In ironic tones, Schumpeter has described the "Worshipful Company" as accepting the going "ethical" and religious codes and enjoining standardized behavior, complete with prayer meetings but also with more direct strategies.[10] These new companies were political powers in overseas trade. They had to be, in order to provide for physical protection and aggression. Aggression? Yes, because there were joint stock companies formed for no other business than piracy, and even the more respectable (by today's standards) of overseas businesses had to use force to keep peace in the marketplace.

The use of force and exclusionary policy by companies that resisted the old in favor of the new was not necessarily a progressive step. It looked backward in some respects. The chartered companies, organizational shells for the trade of their members, often allied themselves, for example, with the old medieval staple system. That system required foreign trade to pass only through certain staple cities or even staple countries, as in the old colonial systems of Spain and England. Staple policy was related to the discriminatory treatment of "merchant-strangers," the principal means of preserving trade in the hands of a city's burghers. The

10. Schumpeter, *op. cit.*, pp. 152-3.

laws against intermediary trade were not directed against production as such.

The alliance of the chartered company with such a policy was—from our twentieth-century vantage point—a reactionary policy, but it was an alliance explainable in early modern circumstances. Evidently Queen Elizabeth "participated personally in the gains (and losses) of 'monopolistic' ventures, even in the proceeds of downright robbery," granted letters patent of monopoly to her favorites, and squeezed the monopolist organizations like sponges. It was easier to squeeze them than it would have been to squeeze a large number of independent enterprisers. That may seem to us a corrupt use of business organizations by the state; but the monarch's tax collectors were not so efficient as the Internal Revenue Service. The connection between government and business, moreover, had long been one of dependence of the former on the latter in medieval Europe.

Medieval Italian city-states, for example, in order to replenish empty treasuries, had to grant their bondholding creditors guarantees for interest in the form of claims on definite state revenues. At length they found themselves confronted with a corporate organization of creditors carrying out economic functions with special privileges. Colonizing enterprises, such as the Giustiniani, and the *compere*—notably the Casa di San Giorgio of Genoa—developed from these circumstances. These associations of state creditors in Italy were the first real corporate associations of capital, with a guarantee for the perpetuation of an enterprise irrespective of the personal fate of the individual shareholder, as contrasted with partnerships. These Italian creditors' associations used the state to launch enterprises. In both England and Italy the line between what we call the public and private sectors would have been difficult to draw at the time.

The line was especially difficult to draw when the new Age of Discovery brought sixteenth- and seventeenth-century companies directly into the business of government. Companies trading on the African coasts, in India, and in the Americas, had to provide capital not only for long-term investments in ships and facilities in newly discovered lands, but also for defense works, for military forces, and for all the machinery of administration including diplomatic representation. The legal branch of the *Casa de contratación* in Seville, Spain, for example—an office that regulated trade with "the Indies" (the Americas)—was controlled by a corporation of merchants who were able to extract special privileges from a Spanish state that was continually in financial straits; these extracted privileges permitted smuggling, undercutting, and other violations of law. The Portuguese picture had been no less dark. It is worth noting that the Spanish-American trade was carried on far more by other Europeans than by Spanish companies, insofar as non-state trading was allowed. Dealings in slaves were among the advantages extracted from the Spanish state by the capitalists of other countries.

Neo-Mercantilism

All this may sound like irrelevant ancient history. Far from it. We live in an age of neo-mercantilism. The situation is especially clear in contemporary statism versus transnational business. The multinational corporation of today may strive, ideally, to surmount the barriers of the political frontiers erected by nation-states or by combinations of nation-states (as in the European Economic Community) in order to reach a world market as a natural domain. In practice, the multinational corporations of today are confronted with high walls around the old national domains. Within these domains, under the powerful control of national political bureaucracies, the old exclusionary policies of mercantilism take new form in the use of business corporations for national—not transnational—purposes.

The best examples[11] of this trend have been in Japan and Europe during the recent postwar years—"postwar" despite the fact that World War II ended a quarter of a century ago; the economies of both Europe and Japan have grown spectacularly

11. See Simon Kuznets, *Postwar Economic Growth* (Cambridge: Harvard University Press, 1964); Endel J. Kolde, *International Business Enterprise* (Prentice-Hall, 1968), Ch. 3: "The Legal Environment of International Business"; Raymond Vernon, "Multinational Enterprise and National Sovereignty," *Harvard Business Review*, March-April 1967; also "Economic Sovereignty at Bay," *Foreign Affairs*, October 1968, and *Manager in the International Economy* (Prentice-Hall, 1968), Ch. 5: "National Control of International Trade"; George Thomson, "The New World of Asia," *Foreign Affairs*, October 1969; Richard N. Cooper, *The Economics of Interdependence* (New York: McGraw-Hill, 1968), Ch. 6: "National Economic Policy in an Interdependent World Economy"; George W. Ball, *The Discipline of Power* (Boston: Little-Brown, 1968), Ch. IV: "The Failure of the European System"; Howe Martyn, *International Business* (Free Press of Glencoe, 1964), Chs. 3, 14, and 15, on national policies; Richard D. Robinson, *International Business Policy* (New York: Holt, Rinehart & Winston, Inc., 1964), Ch. 1: "The Historical Dimension."

partly as a result of postwar recovery programs. In Europe, in order to do battle with giant American corporate invaders, scores of companies were merging in the late sixties and early seventies. The result was to form corporate goliaths that were the direct outgrowth of national neo-mercantilist policy. Instead of looking toward the wider natural domain of a World Market—to say nothing of a European market—this remarkably anachronistic policy harked back to the old idea of sufficient national, natural domains.

It remains to be seen whether this has been a transient reactionary phase of corporate development, or a major step backward in a general neo-mercantilist trend. If it is such a step, the relationship of this trend to the general breakdown of internationalism in the world arena raises fundamental questions about the future of the multinational corporation, especially in Europe. The Europeans' pained reaction to "the American challenge"—as described by Jean-Jacques Servan-Schreiber—has been twofold. On the one hand, there has been the growth of the European communities in an attempt to overcome the old particularism. On the other hand, there is this move in the opposite direction to strengthen the nation against foreigners by mobilizing corporate power into vast concentrates.[12]

In England, the national government created in 1966 the Industrial Reorganization Corporation (I.R.C.) to carry out this task. A Labor government had already nationalized (more accurately, re-nationalized) the steel industry; this I.R.C. program went much further without nationalization, but with strong governmental pressure behind it. Under the direction of Charles Villiers, a former merchant banker, the I.R.C. moved from industry to industry reorganizing industries through mergers that were sometimes forced.

The I.R.C., for example, used its persuasive powers to get one company to sell a part of its operations to another; it supported the new ventures with infusions of debt and equity capital (it could draw up to $360 million in government funds); it was able to put its own watchdog on the new company's board. The I.R.C. helped to block attempts by foreign firms (General Foods and SKF, the Swedish ball-bearing company, have been named) to acquire British firms. Insisting that it was not opposed to

12. See Philip Siekman, "Europe's Love Affair with Bigness" in *Fortune*, March 1970.

foreign investment in Britain, I.R.C. nevertheless urged that a prime mission was to create British companies large enough to resist the battering onslaught of United States subsidiaries. In the field of automobiles and computers, industries in which the British-owned units were up against stiff United States competition, I.R.C. planned to counter with two British corporations: British Leyland Motor Corp. and International Computers Ltd.

In half a decade the I.R.C. had been involved in more than twenty industries. Although some British businessmen were fed up with it, hoping for its early demise, spokesmen for I.R.C. declared that work remained to be done in many medium-size industries such as machine tools, specialty steel, and footwear. Its director thought that the time had come to look across the English Channel, to search for ways to correct what he called the "surprising failure" of European companies to join forces across national boundaries. On the Continent, he and his associates were trying to foster interest in a version of the I.R.C. that would be funded by a number of governments and would guide and encourage inter-European mergers.

In France, the Institut de Développement Industriel is a new organization, founded in the seventies, mainly concerned with medium-size companies. The French government used the state planning agency to encourage concentration of most of France's largest industries. Two companies, Usinor and Wendel-Sidelor, accounted in 1970 for two-thirds of France's crude steel production. Renault and Peugeot, the only surviving all-French carmakers, were as much partners as competitors. Three nationalized companies, Sud-Aviation, Nord-Aviation, and SEREB (missiles and rockets) were merged, and a government-inspired reorganization of the electrical-equipment and chemical industries was on the way in early 1970.

Companies accounting for 60 per cent of the sales in the electrical and electronics industries were absorbed into two large enterprises: Cie Générale d'Electricité and Thomson Houston-Hotchkiss Brandt. Even these two seemed headed for some sort of merger. They already owned jointly a number of companies, including Compagnie Internationale pour l'Informatique (C.I.I.) the flag-bearing computer company created as part of the government's Plan Calcul, which is designed to strengthen the French-owned computer industry. A regrouping of the chemical industry culminated in the summer of 1969 in the creation of a combine that included Rhone-Poulenc, the industry leader, plus Progil, Naphtachimie, and Pechiney-Saint-Gobain. It had consolidated sales of $2.1 billion in 1969 and accounted for about a third of French-controlled chemical production.

In Germany, the government of the Federal Republic aided in the creation of Ruhrkohle A.G., an amalgamation of twenty-five coal companies that together account for 75 per cent of the national output. In Italy, the state-owned holding company, I.R.I., together with E.N.I., the state-owned petroleum company, gained control in 1968 over Montecatini Edison, a chemical giant resulting from a merger four years earlier; I.R.I. controls companies accounting for 15 per cent or more of Italy's total industrial output, and is now reaching out for more. In Austria, the nation's second largest industrial enterprise arose from the merging of two state-owned petroleum and chemical companies, OeMV and OeSW.

These and other examples indicate a strong trend toward *national* policies of industrial strength, using corporate mergers as a major weapon. This policy is not, of course, uniquely European. "Buy American" is a watchword that is enforced by law; but there is a difference in European policy that favors single suppliers and feeds selected companies to foster growth. This is done in many ways: giving the new giants a monopoly on research-and-development contracts, on procurement orders from national and local authorities, including the school systems and state-owned corporations, buying only locally made computers, supplying police departments with cars made in the country, acquiring generating and transmission equipment for public power companies from national suppliers, and above all by protection from outside competition so far as possible.

Monopolistic positons of these companies are to some extent threatened by the more nearly free cross-border movement of industrial products among Common Market countries. For Europe, economic—to say nothing of political—integration was a long way off in the early seventies. There was no uniform European corporation law, and even if there had been—it was being discussed—United States multinational corporations might have gained thereby a distinct advantage in buying up companies. Cross-border mergers of European companies did occur, but not on a massive scale; nor could that soon be expected because of the persistence of nationalism and the nation-state system.

"The real obstruction to integration of Europe's industries is national egoism," a French government official had declared with no great prescience, for it was plain that the nation-state was by no means on its last legs. And as long as the nation-state dominated the world arena, there was likely to be a very long road to transnational—rather than multinational—corporations that owed nothing to, and asked nothing of, national powers. The main barrier to trans-European mergers was more than "a lingering notion of national prestige."[13] It was rather the durability of a nationalism expressed contemporaneously in many ways. All nations, large and small, seem to seek the location of prestige industries within their frontiers. Cross-border mergers are difficult to carry out when a big company, dominant in its industry, becomes the source of national pride. A French company that represents nearly its entire electric-appliance and electronics industry might find national pride a bar to merger with Siemens or with G.E.C.-English Electric. Italian pride could bar the merger of Montecatini Edison chemical complex with Imperial Chemical. A British Leyland merger with Volkswagen would be equally difficult. The merging of two legally nationalized companies would present well-nigh insuperable obstacles.

Political or diplomatic considerations arise. Britain, for example, could not merge its flag-bearing International Computers Ltd. with Siemens' computer division without taking into consideration the extremely damaging effect this might have on France's C.I.I. and thus, indirectly, on the attitudes of the French Government toward cooperation with the British on other matters.[14] If C.I.I. were brought into the deal, what would happen to the other weak European computer makers? Politicians might prefer to put them all together. An enlarged market for the surviving company, a new supergiant with few worries about European competitors, might be inefficient. Even with a continent-wide market a European producer of high-technology equipment, such

13. *Ibid.*
14. *Ibid.*

as computers of aircraft, would still find it hard to compete effectively with United States corporations like I.B.M.

Will Europe have to choose between an industry divided into separate national monopolies or a single European monopoly achieved as a result of the concentration of large national units? A move toward international mergers of companies that do not represent the whole of a given national industry would be one possibility. In this way, three nuclear power equipment groups could be set up, each containing what were formerly independent British, German, and other national companies. In prestige industries these mergers would be difficult to arrange. Avoidance of domination, in the new combine of managers and owners, by one of the predecessor national companies—or at least avoidance of the appearance of such domination—might open the way.

If most of the major industries have been or soon will be boiled down to what is, in effect, one company per country, as an English observer has indicated, this alone would present practical barriers to the plan just mentioned. Perfectly balanced mergers in which no partner would dominate would be hard to arrange. Any automobile company in Europe (except Volkswagen or British Leyland), to take a clear case, would be overwhelmed if it joined with Fiat. Any one of the three German chemical makers might be overshadowed by Imperial Chemical Industries. Paired deals in which, say, France accepted a minority position in one venture in return for a major role in some other industry might be more practical; and such deals would result in an industrial structure closer to the one that would result in a free market. "But such continental wheeling and dealing," he concludes, "is about as unlikely as is a concerted agreement by the governments to let the industrialists work it out for themselves." [15]

Such restructuring need not be arbitrarily limited to the European continent, he goes on to say, suggesting that transnational mergers that include United States corporations would make a great deal of economic sense. If half of the European computer industry, for instance, combined with Control Data and the other half joined with Honeywell or Univac, both the Americans and the Europeans would be in a far better position to

15. *Ibid.*

compete with I.B.M. But here again, there is the problem of balance, of creating a company that the Americans would not dominate.

Transnational Goals in Europe

It would be hyperbole to declare that all multinational corporations are headed toward neo-mercantilist status with a strongly nationalistic bias to their corporate objectives. But the evidence of that trend is indeed strong and disquieting to those who see the multinational corporation as the harbinger of a world order, leading to peace in the world's marketplace. There is evidence for another view of the situation that indicates at least the possibility that the business of multinational corporations is business and not politics. Agfa-Gevaert is a merger of Belgium's Gevaert Photo-Producten with Agfa, a subsidiary of Germany's Bayer. Zentralgesellschaft VFW-Fokker mbH is the result of merger between Royal Netherlands Aircraft Factories Fokker and Vereinigte Flugtechnische Werke in West Germany. There are many cross-border acquisitions of subsidiaries by well-known companies such as Philips, Unilever, Siemens, and Nestlé. Some mergers are extra- as well as intra-European, with consequences for trans-Atlantic corporate action. Thus the Dutch Algemene Kunstzijde Unie (AKU) merged with KZO, a Dutch chemical and pharmaceutical company, to form a new group that holds a controlling interest in International Salt and American Enka.

It is also true that among the technocrats in the European communities one finds hope, even enthusiasm, for transnational industry that will lead away from the old nationalism to a new and expansive conception of business enterprise. Four of the seven in EFTA (European Free Trade Area) are waiting hopefully at the door to the presently six-nation EEC (European Economic Community). The Dutch, the West Germans, and the British have agreed on joint construction of uranium-enrichment plants. The Six have agreed to form a consortium of companies to develop a gas-cooled breeder reactor. There are other straws in the wind.

Are they blowing in the direction of a united Europe? Would a united Europe simply lift neo-mercantilism to a continental scale, doing nothing for transnational business freed from political goals? Jean Rey, president of the Commission in EEC, has predicted that by 1980 Britain will be a member of a Community with a single currency and its own parliament directly elected by universal suffrage. That would require much harmonization of legislation and a reversal of the neo-mercantilist trends discussed above.

The "European Idea" has been badly battered, as a European correspondent for *The Economist* has observed; the victory of integration over the nation-state, if that victory ever occurs, would be a qualified one, and the status as well as the resources of European institutions will be crucial. "The presence of ten or more states (hopefully a democratic Spain and Greece among them) will make it more necessary than ever for the European Community's Council of Ministers to move beyond the power of national veto into the era of decision by majority"; and "that will not count for a great deal unless the Commission gets much larger resources, and a directly elected Parliament with much larger powers."[16]

Present proposals on the table for realizing the European Idea in the Community appear to be modest. Commission resources for this purpose, carried up to 1974, are proposed at a level not to exceed 1 per cent of the Community's gross national product, although most national governments take 30-35 per cent of their national GNP. "Unless an astonishing surge of federal feeling materializes, national governments will still be the main initiators and decision-makers in the Europe of 1980; and intergovernmental cooperation, albeit in a spirit of good will rather than the suspicion of the last few years, will still play a major part in framing common policies. If so, neither direct election nor the hoped-for legislative powers of the European Parliament will count for much."[17]

That the nation-state stands firmly across the path to a world economy in which multinational corporations could be single-

16. Stephen Hugh-Jones, "Europe in the Seventies," *European Community*, January 1970, p. 9.

17. *Id.* See "The Scorecard" in the January 1970 issue of *European Community*, pp. 20-21, comparing goals and performance of EEC. The goal of establishing "common rules preventing practices which distort or restrain competition, whether by private business or member governments" had reached this stage of performance: "Definition of unfair business practices has been clarified in a body of case law, and the Commission has imposed heavy fines on firms operating cartels, competition still distorted by state aids and monopolies and by national public-procurement policies."

minded, profit-seeking business enterprises is all too obvious, even in Europe where the Common Market was once so optimistically welcomed by the integrationists. John Pinder, director of PEP (Political and Economic Planning) in London, has put the matter bluntly: the Rome Treaty focused on the bars to integration rather than the positive tasks of reconstruction, on the removal of discrimination and distortions, and on the common market chiefly as a consequence. His view is that in an age when all governments of modern states use economic policies for many purposes beyond the minimal, neo-liberal one of removing distortions from the economic system, it is quite inconsistent for the Community to confine itself largely to this negative task. Indeed, he writes that it will probably be found that the free trade system cannot be indefinitely maintained unless the Community undertakes many of the positive tasks that modern citizens demand, and that national governments may not be able to perform when they belong to a common market. A "second Rome Treaty" might be required, embodying a firm commitment to move forward to economic union: providing for the formation of a whole range of positive economic policies according to a definite timetable and for the stronger and more democratic—and thus federal—institutions that will be required to accomplish these policies.[18] Perhaps a unified European system must be conceptualized in order to find the goals of the multinational corporation in the system.

Europe as a System

The eventual shape of a European system and the place of the multinational corporation in it are provocative issues for several reasons. In the first place, there are conflicting views about Europe as a "system." Secondly, the possibility of a federal structure developing into a single European nation has to be considered, with all that this implies for the policies of multinational corporations that enter this putative political unit in the international system. Finally, there are questions of corporate efficiency, simply in terms of entrepreneurial operations, to say

18. John Pinder, "Is the Rome Treaty Biased Against Common Policies?", *European Community*, January 1970, p. 23.

nothing of the political dimensions of a multinational corporate business.

To take the last point first, multinational corporations have been called "a substitute for the market, as a method of organizing international exchange" and "islands of conscious power in an ocean of unconscious cooperation."[19] As large firms operating typically in imperfect markets, there is a question of their efficiency in oligopolistic decision-making. This is an area where welfare economics seems to falter. If competition allocates resources efficiently, and if there is a harmony between private profit maximization and the general interest—a basic proposition in economic theory—how does this square with what one sees in the actual operation of the multinational corporation in the international economy? To one economist, multinational corporations "bring into high definition such social and political problems as want creation, alienation, domination, and the relationship or interface between corporations and national states (including the question of imperialism) which cannot be analyzed therefore in purely 'economic' terms."[20]

The European case is instructive for other areas of the globe in which problems of federation, political unification, and corporate role, also arise. Federalism and, more broadly, a systems approach to the political and social environment of the multinational corporation are the key issues.

Europe, within the Common Market, may be seen as an emergent nation, or as a federal state, or as a federation of states, or perhaps no more than a commercial unity that falls far short of being a political system. How one sees it will affect one's ideas about multinational corporate goals for firms that enter this arena. Some form of effective organized cooperation between groups on the continent of Europe (including the United Kingdom and Ireland)—nations and also groups of a less clearly political cast—is certainly emerging; multinational corporate policy makers must take careful notice of this development and prepare for it with adequate company goals.

19. Stephen Hymer, "The Efficiency (Contradictions) of Multinational Corporations," *American Economic Review*, May 1970, p. 441, quoting D. H. Robertson in R. H. Coase, "The Nature of the Firm," *Economica*, New Series, 1937, pp. 386-405.

20. Hymer, *op. cit.*

European businessmen had at the start given qualified support to the idea of a common market, their qualifications having been dictated to a considerable extent by distinctive national situations and interests—or what was believed to be such interests and situations. The affirmative attitude was generally dominant, and the courage to take the road to the Treaty of Rome was at length rewarded by a notably forward industrial movement.

At the same time, corporate managers restructured their enterprises for a new era: *L'Europe des Affaires*—The Europe of Business. This was evident both as to the structure of corporate objectives and as to cooperative association with other firms. The new scope of corporate objectives can be seen in the multiplication of entrepreneurial undertakings which, in turn, called for more complex forecasting and planning in production and marketing, more attention to modernization and to the rationalization as well as the augmentation of production. Joint ventures in other countries of the Common Market became the goal of some firms. The most significant change came in political and business mentality in these expansive enterprises, a change that is observable not only on the continent of Europe but also in goals of American multinational corporations that moved into Europe.

Although American multinational corporations have been more active in pushing over frontiers into and about the Common Market than European firms, among the latter there appears to be the beginning of broader geographic—and even social— scoping of goals. This comment must not be taken to mean a new emphasis on "social responsibilities." The social dimensions of corporate goals, however, are clear enough in the recognition by corporate boards and executive managers that technological advance demands large new programs, joint financing of major research projects, coordination and division of labor between the member states of the Common Market in their national research, and promotion of cooperation by industry with the aid of tax and economic policy.

Another field in which business goals in the Common Market have undergone change is corporate governance. Worker participation in management through elected representatives, long established in Germany, is now a problem for managements elsewhere. On the management level, the problem of new specializations, with organizational and procedural implications for the entire corporate structure, has arisen because of the pace of technological change and the expanding market area. A "Europeanized"—rather than a strictly local or national—cadre of personnel attuned to the larger market effects a change in political outlook in corporate governance. The legal structure of corporate governments, too, is headed for change; model laws for a European corporation have been drafted. The growth of corporate giants has given new impetus to antitrust measures in the Common Market countries and to concern within corporate governments about appropriate reactions to such measures.

Systemic Goals of the Multinational Corporation

Parsons and Smelser conclude that economic theory is a special case of the general theory of social systems and hence of the general theory of action; that the economy is a special type of social system; that the economy, like any social system, exchanges inputs and outputs over its boundaries with other cognate, functional subsystems of the same society, with its institutionalized value system; that interchange between the economy and these functional subsystems is not randomly distributed, but that particular input-output categories are concentrated vis-à-vis other specific cognate societal subsystems; that concrete economic processes are always conditioned by noneconomic factors, most clearly apparent in the parametric characteristics of the noneconomic subsystems of the society; that a theoretical scheme other than economic theory is the only possible way to analyze these noneconomic factors in such a way as to articulate successfully with economic theory; that the problem of institutional change in an economy is a particularly striking case of the foregoing proposition because the primary factors involved cannot be economic; and that economic theory need not remain an "island" of theoretical specificity totally alone in an uncharted "sea" of theoretical indeterminacy.[21]

The relevance of this formidably abstract account of systems theory to the immediate problem of multinational corporate

21. Talcott Parsons and Neil J. Smelser, *Economy and Society: A Study in the Integration of Social and Economic Theory* (Glencoe, Ill.: The Free Press, 1956), pp. 306-308.

goals is this: the goals of corporate policy need to be seen against a background of social policy in a given society, and this is possible only with a sound theory in hand to describe that social policy. When we are considering the relationship of corporate policy to the *national* policies of a given nation-state, it is obviously necessary to comprehend the content and sweep of the national aims. When we turn to a consideration of multinational corporate policies in relation to the larger society of nations—or any group of nations—it is likewise required of us that we comprehend the aims of that society. An economic theory of these aims is not enough; what is required is a general theory of social systems that includes polities as well. And, as we see from the Parsons-Smelser exposition, the economy is but one of four "functional subsystems" of a society.

Similarly, the other functional subsystems—the polity, the "pattern-maintenance" subsystem, and the "integrative" subsystem—are analytically conceived. The multinational corporation, as a concrete collectivity, is not a sub-subsystem of the economy. Like all concrete collectivities, it is multifunctional, and its goals are accordingly assignable to each of the four functional subsystems of the society.[22]

The economy, in the Parsons-Smelser exposition, is the primary "adaptive" subsystem. Insofar as a multinational corporation acts as a unit of the economy, it is governed (in the cybernetic sense) by the value-principle of utility. Production, as a process of value-implementation, is the use of combinations of the factors of production to increase the utility of goods and services available in the economy as a subsystem and, through its outputs, for consumption. A measure of utility is money, in one of its classical roles. Money, thus used, "coordinate[s] producing units with each other and with interchanging units outside the econ-

22. See Talcott Parsons, *Politics and Social Structure* (New York: The Free Press, 1969); also his *System of Modern Societies* (1969); *Sociological Theory and Modern Society* (1967); *Societies: Evolutionary and Comparative Perspectives* (1966); "The Ideas of Systems, Causal Explanation and Cybernetic Control in Social Science" in Daniel Lerner (ed.), *Cause and Effect* (1964); "Sociological Theory" in *Encyclopedia Britannica* (1965); "The Political Aspect of Social Structure and Process" in David Easton (ed.), *Varieties of Political Theory* (1966); "Components and Types of Formal Organization" in P. B. LeBreton (ed.), *Comparative Administrative Theory* (1968); "Systems Analysis: Social Systems" and "Interaction: Social Interaction" in *International Encyclopedia of the Social Sciences* (1968).

omy [as a functional subsystem] through the standard of solvency," a standard which, fully applied, means "the expectation that, over requisite time periods, the money costs of economic operations can be met by the money proceeds of these operations,"[23] that is to say, the sale of products as the typical case.

This exposition of the function of "the economy," it should be observed, is the exposition of a function that applies not alone to concrete business collectivities but to non-business collectivities as well, such as universities, churches, associations of all kinds, with appropriate variation of terms. The other subfunctional systems—the polity, the "pattern-maintenance," and the "integrative"—similarly apply to all concrete collectivities, the multinational corporation included, although Parsons and Smelser do not elaborate their exposition with specific reference to the multinational corporation.

Because the goals of the multinational corporation have to be sought not only in action assignable to the economy—as an analytical subfunctional system of society—but also in action assignable to the other subfunctional systems, these must be distinguished from each other. They must also be distinguished from the concrete collectivities that we see and deal with every day.

The polity, for example, is not "government" in the concrete sense of legislative, executive, and judicial organs, or of persons as public officials. Parts of the subsystem designated as polity are organizationally independent of government, as for example in central banking and businesses "affected with a public interest" but deliberately—or historically—separated from the official governmental structure. The polity, analytically conceived, is the "goal-attainment" subsystem of any social system. (Note that the polity is not the goal-*defining* system.)

The primary political system of a society becomes its "governmental" system in a sense parallel to that in which the primary economic system is its market system. As money has held a carefully codified place in economics, there is a close equivalent for power in political science. Polity is conceived analytically as "the aspect of all action concerned with the function of the collective pursuit of goals," and since "the collectivity in question may be any system involving the coordinated action of a

23. Parsons, *Politics and Social Structure*, p. 443.

plurality of individuals oriented to the attainment of a collective goal or a system of collective goals," [24] we are entitled to conclude that the multinational corporation reveals the functions of a polity. The collective goals of polity are of all kinds, but the central significance of a "goal" is that it "exists only if the desired state differs from the actual or expected state at the inception of action," [25] and that commitment to the goal implies the use of appropriate measures to effect the desired goal-state.

The multinational corporation may be regarded as carrying out the functions of polity in two ways: internally, through goal-attainment measures aimed at a goal-state defined in terms of self-interest; and externally, through goal-attainment measures aimed at a goal-state defined in terms of others' interests, for example, a particular economic order or the economies of home and host nations. In the latter case, the multinational corporation is the agency for goal-attainment by larger collectivities than the firm.

Another aspect of polity is the value-standard in terms of which this type of functional action must be regulated. Parsons adopts C. I. Barnard's standard of "effectiveness" for this purpose, as parallel to utility in the economy. Barnard had declared that "when the purpose of a system is attained, we say that the cooperation was effective; if not attained, ineffective," and that the "effectiveness" of the effort of an individual in cooperation is judged from the cooperative point of view with reference to its bearing on the attainment of cooperative purpose, and not from the point of view of the individual cooperating as a means of satisfying his own personal motives. [26]

Effectiveness, in this sense, contributes to the functioning of corporations in that the values institutionalized in the subsystem of polity are implemented; and whereas the coordinative standard for measuring the parallel contribution in the economy was solvency, here it is success. Here Parsons makes the interesting observation that concrete collectivities with primary functions other than political have to be " 'subsidized' by an extra infusion

24. *Id.*, p. 318.

25. *Loc. cit.*

26. Chester I. Barnard, *The Functions of the Executive* (Cambridge: Harvard University Press, 1938), p. 43.

of the factors of effectiveness, parallel to the financial subsidization of collectivities other than firms."[27] The implication, for multinational corporations, is that their effectiveness in goal-attainment may depend upon externally derived resources of power for action to implement goal-values.

Power is the measure of effectiveness in the polity as a functional subsystem, just as money was the measure of utility in the economy, where the standard was utility. Power, for Parsons, is "generalized capacity to activate obligations of member units in the interest in the implementation of goal-oriented decisions binding on [a] collectivity,"[28] in our case the multinational corporation. Power, as a differential evaluation of success, serves as a standard for the allocation of resources; operatively it accomplishes this by serving as a "generalized medium of interchange" from one subsystem to another. Accepting the proposition that "concrete economic processes are always conditioned by non-economic factors which are most clearly apparent in the parametric characteristics of the noneconomic subsystems of society,"[29] it follows that multinational corporations are not only conditioned by politics but carry out, themselves, characteristic "polity" functions.

Power, in the multinational corporation as in nation-states, is a medium of interchange across functional subsystem boundaries. Power in the multinational corporation is a capacity to activate corporate goal-oriented decisions. In the case of the multinational corporation, the relevant goals are clearly social and not strictly entrepreneurial in the classical and neoclassical senses of enterprise (including Schumpeter's "innovative" purpose). The multinational corporation functions as a polity by seeking directly through its own organizational means—as well as indirectly through governments of states—to achieve a standard of success in implementing these goals.

As to the substantive goals of the multinational corporation, one need not assume that they are in any sense borrowed from

27. Parsons, *Politics and Social Structure*, p. 443.

28. *Loc. cit.*

29. Parsons and Smelser, *op. cit.*, p. 307. The scope of their book is indicated on p. 295: "Our central proposition is that economic theory is a special case of the general theory of social systems, which is in turn one of the main branches of the developing theory of social action."

the state, delegated to corporations by the state, or otherwise devolved upon a firm. The polity subfunctions are universally derivative from concrete collectivities by reason of their collective characteristics. That economic goals may be primary in the multinational corporation can be taken for granted. That non-economic goals are merely ancillary to economic purpose does not follow at all; for all collectivities are multifunctional.

A major goal of *corporateness* is unity of action for entrepreneurial and other purposes. The multinational corporation must indeed draw upon extra-corporate sources for success in attaining unity. Insofar as the sovereign state is the source of corporateness—under the concession theory—then the multinational corporation will seek from many states the "right" to act corporately. On the other hand, if concession theory is a delusion and a snare, the real voluntary effort of associated men and capital resources constitute the foundation of unity in corporateness, and the "subsidy" in that case is from some functional subsystem other than polity. The practical answer to this dilemma is that both sources of unified action in the multinational corporation are required for success in goal-attainment.

The governing value-principle in integration is "solidarity" in Durkheim's meaning: a state of cohesion achieved through the complementarity of units that make their contributions to the society as a system in quantitatively differentiated functional action. The integrative function resists the centrifugal forces of factionalism and particularism, and reinforces the centripetal and coordinative forces of a society, and of its concrete collectivities. Influence, as a measure of contributions to solidarity, refers to a combination of factors, including commitments to valued associational ties and to legitimate policy decision.

The "integrative" system may be seen not only in consensus but concretely in federative and unitary forms of organization. The integrative system of a society will be paralleled in a concrete collectivity, such as the multinational corporation, by forms of cross-border corporate organization. New consensus, new associational ties, and new forms of organization are needed from time to time to meet changing situations. Influence is a "medium of interchange" in the multinational corporation, especially as a means of securing commitments to association with

112

units across borders, to supportive political units in the international system, and to the capitalistic or at least non-Communist system of the "free world." There are also commitments to other units in the economic system resulting from corporate decisions that bind the multinational corporation and its members to certain collective obligations.

The primary function of "pattern-maintenance and tension-management" is cybernetic control and integrity of the value-pattern itself. In the three other subsystems there were values specified to less generalized levels, while the pattern-maintenance subsystem presents the problem of *integrity* of the value-pattern. Here, commitment-maintenance is "the central normative *condition* of the process of implementation," that is to say, the "maintenance of integrity of commitment to the pattern over a wide range of different actual and potential decisions, in differing situations, with differing consequences and levels of predictability of such consequences."[30] At the same time, the door must be left open for exploiting diverse opportunities to implement values relevant to the situation and to reject false possibilities.

Parsons' theory of social action is not suggested as the only possible approach, but it illustrates a degree of contemporary sophistication that the student of the multinational corporation cannot afford to neglect. He need not accept it; but he will need to take it into account and then go on.

Systems theory is not a sufficient approach. This is evident when one begins to break the problem of goals down by geographic focus. As one looks at contemporary Europe, for example, it would seem that if there is a new system on that continent—including the United Kingdom and Ireland as well—based on the Treaty of Rome, then the essence of that system is statable in organic terms, and not in the mechanistic input-output conceptions of much systems theory. The goals of multinational corporations operative in the Common Market area, and eventually within a European political unity of some kind, are to be discovered empirically as well as analytically. One must study—company by company—what managers must do to survive and prosper in this emergent system; and insofar as it is a system, the approach to governing values in the system and in corporations

30. Parsons, *Politics and Social Structure*, pp. 444-5.

that operate there must be historical, comparative, and descriptive in the more traditional ways of analysis.

The same thing can be said of corporate action and corporate goals in the larger international system. While systems theory is indispensable, it is not sufficient. We live in a revolutionary age comparable with that which ushered in the international system of nation-states at the end of the Middle Ages. Historical perspective is prerequisite to a full understanding of present tensions as compared with those of earlier epochal changes. In political science and sociology, there are provocative and useful new approaches that will throw light on the nature and scope of corporate goals in the midst of our revolutionary period. These approaches, however, do not alone suffice.

Finally, it is necessary to add a caveat concerning the scope of values involved in policy-making for multinational corporations. A revolutionary age brings to the surface conflicts over man's purpose on earth, deep division over ends as well as means, sharp conflict over allowable aspirations in the young, and, as an inevitable consequence, profound debate over the meaning of business. This debate reaches into the top echelons of corporations. It forces the student of business institutions to reexamine the anatomy of values,[31] the problems of personal and social choice, and notably these problems as they arise in the rapidly expanding field of transnational business.

This reexamination has already led executive managers of multinational corporations to recognize, in their planning work, the macroeconomic significance of big concerns in world markets.[32] But beyond that is their political significance as potential contributors to—or resistors against—the coming reconstruction of polity in the world arena.

---

31. See Charles Fried, *The Anatomy of Values: Problems of Personal and Social Choice* (Cambridge: Harvard University Press, 1970); and Kurt Baier and Nicholas Vascher (eds.), *Values and the Future: The Impact of Technological Change on American Values* (New York: The Free Press, 1969), especially Kenneth Boulding on "The Emerging Superculture" and Part IV: "Controls."

32. His Royal Highness, Bernhard, Prince of the Netherlands, "The Promotion of International Business," in George A. Steiner and W. M. Cannon (eds.), *Multinational Corporate Planning* (New York: Macmillan, 1966), p. 151.

Chapter V

EXTERNAL CONDITIONS OF MULTINATIONAL CORPORATE ACTION

The preemptive strike, it has been said, will be the characteristic strategy of the future, at the climax of confrontation between the superpowers. This terrifying possibility overshadows all other considerations in any comprehensive survey of the external conditions that affect multinational corporate planning and policy in the world arena. It is often a marked or hidden consideration that corporate planners and policy makers would rather banish even from the unconscious labyrinths of their minds and hearts.

But there it is. One reason it is there, remarkably enough, is that superpower and multinational corporate policy makers depend, and know that they must depend, upon those strategic calculators[1] that provide instant information. The more astute policy makers, moreover, know that instant information can create instant crisis. Whether a crisis "exists" depends largely on whether it is perceived. The incredible accumulation of information by memory banks, coupled with the speed with which such information can be transmitted to those in command of war, may be a liability. We can learn of a crisis too quickly. Knowing of it tends to make us act quickly in response to it, perhaps at suicidal speed. In the age of electric circuitry, the *first knower* is likely to be a computer that can foresee the strategic moves of a potential enemy more clearly and more speedily than mere human policy makers.

Tuning in on world politics as well as world economics is an elementary requirement of good corporate planning when a firm has affiliates and subsidiaries in a score or more countries. Beyond this elementary requirement, however, is the necessity for

1. Harvey Wheeler, "The Strategic Calculator," in Nigel Calder (ed.), *Unless Peace Comes: A Scientific Forecast of New Weapons* (New York: Viking, 1968).

an adequate perception of conditions external to the corporation so that in policy decisions there will be no dangerous gaps in staff work on the whole range of relevant facts and forces.

Current works on the multinational corporation tend to focus on the problem of the barriers of economic nationalism to the flows of the factors of production in direct investment. Some writers even equate the multinational corporation with direct investment, as though this form of doing business would disappear if factor movements across political frontiers were to cease for some reason and the flow of transnational trade were to revert mainly to commodities. It seems more than doubtful that the proliferation of the multiple-management form in scores of multinational corporate groups now scattered over the surface of the earth would pass into history if all cross-border barriers were to be abolished tomorrow.

This hypothetical situation will not be put to the test of experience very soon. The international system, however anachronistic and obsolescent it may seem to be, is far from dead. The sovereign power of states, reaching everywhere more and more into economic processes and showing few signs of delegation of this power upward to supranational authority or downward to the private governments of corporate enterprise, will find new ways to control transnational business, with the consequence that transnational enterprises will serve still undisclosed functions in their pluralistic pattern of multinational management centers. But although one cannot test the hypothesis, it seems fairly clear that expansion of the territorial basis for corporate governance—as in the "universal church" and other noneconomic institutions with a global perspective—resulting from the revolution in communications, will necessarily lead to numerous outposts of the corporate empire. And, the outposts of empire, whether political or not, have a way of becoming nuclei of independent entities. We shall arrive at a sound theory of institutional proliferation of this kind when the theory of federalism—now best understood in its political context—is accepted for nonpolitical entities such as the multinational corporation, where it must be understood in the broadest possible manner so that no influential force in the total environment will be overlooked.

Eventually, we shall see a corporate science that takes the corporate form of economic production—whether local or global, capitalist or Communist—as its point of departure and then draws into the necessary model-building usable contributions from all disciplines. An alternative approach is suggested in John P. Davis's historical account of the corporation in its many forms: the ecclesiastical and municipal corporations, the guilds, educational and eleemosynary institutions, regulated companies, regulated exclusive companies, colonial companies, joint-stock companies, and, finally, the modern corporation. A perusal of his and other historical works on this broad subject leads one to the conclusion that history is one of the disciplines usable in contemporary model-building, but not the decisive discipline required by corporate policy makers. The inquiry has to be multidisciplinary from the start.

In all the social sciences, there is the danger of confusion arising from uncontrolled factors, using "control" in the sense in which it is used in the process of scientific verification. The control of factors demands experimentation, but experimentation in which the variable factors in a situation are controlled so as to make it possible to observe the varying factors one at a time—in most cases this is impossible in the social sciences. That kind of scientific investigation is hard enough in the physical sciences.

Sovereignty is an increasingly debatable concept, even an anachronistic one, as man-on-earth moves irrevocably toward a unified (although not a unitary) global system of government. A global system that reduces the chance of total self-annihilation requires that no state is or can be sovereign in the absolute sense. The nineteenth-century international system was based mainly on a balanced Western-states system centered in Europe. Colonial ministries in European capitals controlled the nerves of government that ran to most of Asia and Africa. In the Americas, many new states were born south of the Rio Grande before the middle of the nineteenth century; but the Monroe Doctrine brought these under the "protection" of the United States while their commercial credit was underwritten by the great trading companies located in the leading industrial nations—mainly in New York.

Of the 132 sovereign states in the United Nations today, how many are *major* protagonists on the world stage? Certainly many of them are weak. Assimilated into the United Nations on the basis of a "carefully maintained fiction of sovereignty," "given

117

'purchasing power' in the world markets by grants and loans," and "propped up against rivals and near neighbors by imported armaments,"[2] these weak entities[3] nevertheless claim a status in the General Assembly equal to that of the strongest states, while in political fact a few of the major sovereign protagonists have not joined the United Nations at all. In the meantime, a good many non-state protagonists, such as the top ten or twenty multinational corporations, have become weighty factors in the world arena.

The multiplication of new states, especially in the light of their unrealized expectations, reflects strongly destabilizing tendencies in the global environment. That we are in the midst of a succession of revolutionary systems and not on the verge of a stable one[4] is a more realistic view than the hope often entertained that we live in an international system that is only temporarily disturbed. The study of acute international crises,[5] based on the nature and meaning of social conflict and drawing upon several disciplines of the social sciences, gives no comfort to the hopeful, even though the most ominous forecasts are not necessarily supported. The global political environment is a hazardous one; it is closer to anarchy and chaos than to unity and world order, and there is sparse evidence that it is moving toward the latter goal.

The "systemic perspective"[6] proposed by Riggs, envisages as an ideal goal, an integrated world order in which the organs of a world government would require a direct relationship to individuals as actors in the same way that a national government

2. Wayne Wilcox in "The Protagonist Powers and the Third World," *Annals* of the American Academy of Political and Social Science, November 1969, p. 4. This number of the *Annals*, entitled: *Protagonists, Power, and the Third World: Essays on the Changing International System* is hereinafter referred to as *Annals*, November 1969.

3. See Leo E. Rose and Roger Dial, "Can a Ministate Find True Happiness in a World Dominated by Protagonist Powers? The Nepal Case," in *Annals*, November 1969, pp. 89-101.

4. Stanley Hoffmann, "International Systems and International Law," in Klaus Knorr and Sidney Verba (eds.), *The International System* (Princeton, N.J.: Princeton University Press, 1961), p. 237.

5. Charles A. McClelland, "The Acute International Crisis," in Knorr and Verba, *op. cit.*, pp. 182-204.

6. The "systemic perspective" is expounded by Fred W. Riggs, "International Relations as a Prismatic System," in Knorr and Verba, *op. cit.*, p. 145.

deals with its citizens. In the systemic perspective, the failure of mankind to achieve such a world government reflects a patho- logical condition that should be overcome.

Riggs has called attention to earlier work[7] that distinguishes economizing and traditional systems. The "economizing" or "nationalizing" concepts and institutions that are employed in modern economic structures (whether based on the market, as in free enterprise societies, or on state planning in the Soviet model), differ fundamentally from traditional systems which subordinate economic to religious, political, and social considerations. Riggs proposes the "bazaar-canteen" as the intermediate, or "pris- matic," model.[8] While this terminology may seem somewhat esoteric, the implications are clear.

The characteristics of this analysis are illustrated by reference to the "canteen," whose prices are typically higher (in the "tribu- tary" canteen of captive customers) or lower (in the "subsidized canteen" open only to an elite) than those to be found outside the canteen.

The canteen-concept is applicable to contemporary "macro- polity"—i.e., to contemporary international economic relations where one sees exchange controls, import quotas, tariffs, and so on, in "stable" as well as transitional societies; where the infra- structure of schools, roads, welfare programs, transport, power,

7. Gabriel A. Almond and James S. Coleman (eds.), *The Politics of the Developing Areas* (Princeton, N.J.: Princeton University Press, 1960), and Gabriel A. Almond and G. Bingham Powell, Jr., *Comparative Politics: A Developmental Approach* (Boston: Little, Brown & Co., 1966) indicate this methodological trend as to the developing countries. See also Lucian W. Pye and Sidney Verba (eds.), *Political Culture and Political Development* (Princeton, N.J.: Princeton University Press, 1965). Also, Karl Polanyi, Conrad Arensberg and Harry Pearson, *Trade and Market in Early Empires* (Glencoe, Ill.: The Free Press, 1957).

8. Riggs, *op. cit.* and his "Prismatic Society and Financial Administration," *Adminis- trative Science Quarterly*, June 1960, pp. 1-46. Cf. Marion Levy, Jr., *The Structure of Society* (Princeton, N.J.: Princeton University Press, 1952). Riggs' "prismatic model" is drawn by analogy from the physics of light: the prism through which fused light passes causes the light to become refracted. Thus, he terms a system for which a single structure performs all the necessary functions of a society as a "fused" model. In a "refracted" society there is for every function a corresponding structure. The "refracted" and "fused" models are polar extremes for a scale on which Riggs places the "prismatic" model in an intermediate point. Traditional agricultural and folk societies—as in Modelski's Agraria—approximate the fused model which is "function- ally diffuse"; modern industrial societies—as in Modelski's Industria—are "functionally specific." See George Modelski, "Agraria and Industria: Two Models of the Inter- national System," in Knorr and Verba, *op. cit.*, pp. 118-143.

etc., reduces the costs necessary for profitable investment; and where further—although not generally conceded until quite recently—prerequisites of economical production also include political and administrative structures and processes. The current market model for the global macro-polity is inadequate because it fails to take into account these prerequisites.

In the "world super-canteen," on the one hand, there are some countries in which the potential customer for capital enjoys a heavily-subsidized super-canteen; there enough capital is available even at relatively low rates of interest (prices). On the other hand, there are countries where the market for capital is a highly tributary super-canteen; there, capital is scarce and interest rates high. Capital, in the case of the latter countries, is found only for industries in which anticipated profit rates are very high.

The Transnational Network

It has been said that the heart of the problem with multinational corporations is that "business has gone international" while "the countries of the world have not"—referring, among other things, to "the fractured character of present-day national regulation" that impairs efficient business operations.[9] The truth is, rather, that business has tried to go *transnational* in the face of an anachronistic international world of fixedly sovereign states. The countries of the world do not have to "go international"; they are the protagonists *par excellence* of a pluralistic international system in which multinational corporations labor against nationalistic barriers that would disappear in a world order under law.

It can hardly be maintained, of course, that all multinational corporations would thrive under a unified world order; some of them are bound in goals and strategies to the national purposes of their home countries, and few indeed pretend to act as supranational entities that have cut all bonds of dependence on national governments' legal systems and infrastructures. The managers of multinational corporations, when they consider this problem, do not demand or hope for a unitary world order; rather some form of federal structure seems indicated as the

9. Richard J. Barber, *The American Corporation: Its Power, Its Money, Its Politics* (New York: E. P. Dutton & Co., Inc., 1970), pp. 284 and 280. Cf. the discussion of "integrated areas" in Richard N. Cooper, *The Economics of Interdependence* (New York: McGraw-Hill, 1968).

practical requirement. What we have at the present is a nation-building stage in the development of the hoped-for world order, and, at that stage of development, the new states seize and cling zealously to the old trappings of sovereignty.

The superpowers, least of all, would surrender national sovereignty to a truly federal world order. All national powers resist transnational forces that threaten—or are suspected of threatening—sovereign authority over their territorial jurisdictions. The "public interest," at the present stage of development in world politics, means, as a rule, a *national* interest rather than a putative transnational interest in the welfare of mankind as a global goal. It is true that in the less publicized functional activities of the UN—such as WHO, ECOSOC, UNICEF, and UNESCO— remarkable strides have been made in the direction of developing the concept of a global public interest. But their activities are not ordinarily stressed by multinational corporate managers as indicators of the road to secure "international business," because "international business," as a form of mixed transnational and international activity, looks both ways and makes abundant use of the institutions and strategies peculiar to the international system as well as the emerging transnational system.

Functions of Organizations in the Network

In general, transnational organizations derive from strong transnational movements which seek to transcend national frontiers in some way. They are either indifferent or hostile to these state-made jurisdictional lines on the global map, which impede the transnational movement of ideas as well as the factors of production. In these cases, Parsons speaks of a strong "communicative complex" that is without primary territorial reference. Communication, in this sense, covers a good deal more than simply the transmission of messages; it includes all the media for the transfer of persons and things as well as signs and signals. This reference to things and persons sent uses "message," which derives from *mittere*, to send—in a semiotic sense.[10] In social theory, "communication always implies a *common culture*," with the communicative process starting "in a matrix of *given*

10. As defined by Charles W. Morris in *Foundations of the Theory of Signs* (University of Chicago Press, 1938).

'understanding,' and ending in a modified system." [11] This is all of direct relevance to multinational corporate action.

The communicational ties of transnational movements and organizations often transcend political frontiers with no difficulty, although sometimes with great difficulty, if at all. Religious movements, for example, run into trouble when their organizations pursue objectives that national governments regard as subversive. Ethnic movements may become explosively irredentist. Even scientists and educators—presumably imbued only with universal ideals of truth-seeking and the development of mind, skill and character—whose community transcends political frontiers, can be stopped at those frontiers, also for anti-subversive reasons. Sport, the arts, and a hundred other pursuits of man, give rise to communities—and at length to transnational organizations—which have their own value systems and their own private governments that are distinct from the public governments of nation-states and public international organizations, and all are subject to blockage by these governments.

The "organizational revolution" described by Boulding [12] —a world-wide increase since about 1870 in the number, size, and power of non-state organizations, and especially those whose activity has been directed toward the economic betterment of their members—seems to have arisen from several causal factors. In the first place, there are the needs that only organizations satisfy. Organization formalizes the human desire for status, and not only the status of a "job." Nonmaterial benefits can be obtained by organizational status, if it helps to assuage the frustrating sense of anomie in mass societies that produces feelings of disorientation, anxiety and isolation. Further causal factors appear in improvement of organization skills in the techniques of private government, and in the ability of organizations to grow horizontally in a societal ecosystem that transcends artificial frontiers. The parochial bonds of other centuries have been rent asunder by modern media of communication—using the latter term in the widest sense, as indicated by Parsons' analysis.

11. Talcott Parsons, *Structure and Process in Modern Societies* (The Free Press of Glencoe, Illinois, 1960), p. 269.

12. Kenneth E. Boulding, *The Organizational Revolution: A Study in the Ethics of Economic Organization* (New York: Harper & Bros., 1953).

Other causes of the organizational revolution have been suggested by Boulding: technical changes extending environmental limitations on growth; new types of structure in the organizations themselves, better adapted to the larger environment; the dynamic effect of an ethos of growth, especially the idea in Western culture that growth is good in itself and that a static organization may be a dying one; the attempt to correct disproportionalities, as in the move to a bigger house to shelter more children; and the search for new sources of social energy through organization.

The "birth of the liberal creed," and especially the policy of laissez-faire, early in the nineteenth century—as described by Polanyi [13]—was undoubtedly a major stimulus to the organizational revolution. In terms of economic liberalism, the new creed stood for three classical tenets: that labor should find its price on the market; that the creation of money should be subject to an automatic mechanism; and that goods should be free to flow from country to country without hindrance or preference. Institutionally, this liberal creed took the form of a labor market, the gold standard, and free trade.

The principle of economic liberalism, however, was but one of two organizing principles in society, according to Polanyi. A counter trend of interventionism finally brought the liberal era to an end in the 1930's. Polanyi refers to the principle of "social protection"—protection of family life against the destructive force of the factory system; protection of neighborhoods from devastation, of forests from denudation, and of rivers from pollution; protection of craft standards from deterioration; protection of the martial character of a nation; protection of "infant industries"—as evidence of demands that led to protective national legislation, restrictive lobbying associations and pressure groups, and other instruments of interventionism.

The self-regulating market—more nearly, the laissez-faire market, the core of economic liberalism, since intervention by the state to establish and maintain the self-regulating market is often justified by economic liberals—was conceived by "old liberals" as a transnational institution that public governments

13. Karl Polanyi, *The Great Transformation: The Political and Economic Origins of Our Time* (New York: Rinehart & Co., 1944).

ought to protect by appropriate legislative and administrative measures. Yet, the argument can be, and is, made that the market economy was a "threat to the human and natural components of the social fabric" and that counteraction by a great variety of people had to be expected in pressing for organized protection against this threat. [14] Polanyi denied that there was any left wing "collectivist conspiracy" in this protective reaction; on the contrary, he held it to be a spontaneous reaction. But the evidence also shows some powerful transnational movements and organizations on the protective side, and these do include proletarian parties; more important, they include numerous nonpolitical transnational associations, some of a business character. Neonationalism and neo-mercantilism in the early 1970's has obscured the more general trend toward the hated "globaloney"—as neo-nationalists termed it—of the fifties.

The diverse transnational movements of the postwar decades —now perhaps better designated as pre-21st century decades— portend a vast *transnational system* that could well take shape before 2000 A.D. The quarter-century of social change that lies ahead, however, is likely to be at least as rapid and revolutionary (although not necessarily in the political sense) as the first six decades of the twentieth century. The world has already moved much farther toward supranational organization in non-state entities than most people realize. There is now evolving a vast matrix of non-state governments whose writs run in many directions, in many fields of human interest and at all levels of social action. [15] This evolution is hidden from public view by verbal devices such as the myth that the state has exclusive power and authority to govern. Nonsovereign governance goes on meanwhile in many places, including transnational organizations.

On radically empirical grounds it will be maintained by some that we know nothing about the transnational network unless we know it all. But a caveat has to be entered against the claim of ignorance of some facts as a bar to any useful science of transnational organization and of the multinational corporation in

14. *Id.*, p. 150 (in the Beacon Press Paperback edition of 1957).

15. See Bertram Gross, *The Managing of Organizations* (The Free Press of Glencoe, 1964), Vol. I, p. 289, and generally, Ch. 12.

particular. Weber's methodology was the correct one on this point: empirical knowledge is, in the nature of the case, abstract and never includes "all the facts," even those that can be easily ascertained, but only those which are relevant to certain interests of the investigator.[16] Subjective categories, as in Weber's "specific concepts" (*Idealtypus*), will not be squeezed out of social analysis in a rigorous empirical method that excludes all but "the facts." But the real task of the social scientist, centered for Weber on the process of systematic conceptualization, notably in his classification of four types of action; and this task has been carried toward completion in Parsons' structure of social systems of action.

Parsons' critique of Weber's work, together with his own work on social action, are prerequisites to a fully systematic knowledge of the multinational corporation as a part of the transnational network.[17]

Aspects of the Economic Environment

The economist as well as the corporate executive is apt to turn first—and too often first and last—to the world economy in the more limited sense of "international business" or "international economies." As we have seen, the first of these is not so much international as more and more transnational, while international economics, though truly inter-*national*, is not primarily business but an aspect of action in the international system.

Factor Mobility and Direct Investment

From the economist's point of view, the multinational corporation is interesting because of its movement of factors across political borders but within the firm. The theory of factor flows has been a subsidiary topic of economic theory, mainly in the subfield of location theory, and of economic history. Recently, it

16. See Max Weber, *The Theory of Social and Economic Organization*, translated from Part I of *Wirtschaft und Gesellschaft* (1921) by A. M. Henderson and Talcott Parsons and edited with an introduction by Talcott Parsons (The Free Press of Glencoe, Illinois, 1947), Part III, p. 9.

17. See also from *Max Weber: Essays in Sociology*, translated, edited, and with an introduction, by H. H. Gerth and C. Wright Mills (New York: Oxford University Press, 1964; also as a Galaxy Book paperback in 1958), especially Part II: "Power," and "The Discipline of Large-Scale Economic Organizations," p. 261.

has become a topic in development theory. Baldwin,[18] noting the contributions of Bertil Ohlin[19] and Paul Samuelson,[20] nevertheless stresses the importance of a model showing the interrelationships between output and input flows in connection with the study of the operations of multinational corporations.

This relatively new approach to the economics of the multinational corporation, and particularly to the subject of efficient economic allocation, is now becoming an established subfield of economic theory in its own right. The writers on this subject are beginning to produce a body of literature that will throw much more light on the external conditions of multinational corporate action in the world arena, with special reference to cross-border factor flows.

The subject would not attract the attention of economic theorists if it were not for the pluralistic structure of the international system of sovereign states. It is true that *within* federal systems of sovereign states, where cross-border factor flows are also significant for the economic theorists, the basic situation has long existed. It is the current concern about direct investment, in the political headquarters and the capital-market centers of the world, that brings the whole subject to a new and urgent focus.

In Kindleberger's theory of perfect competition, "domestic firms would have an advantage over foreign firms in the proximity of their operations to their decision-making centers, so that no firm could survive in foreign operation . . . for direct investment to thrive there must be some imperfection in markets for goods or factors, including among the latter technology, or some interference in competition or by firms, which separates markets."[21]

---

18. Robert E. Baldwin, "International Trade in Inputs and Outputs," *American Economic Review*, May 1970 (Papers and Proceedings of the 82nd Annual Meeting of the American Economic Association, December 1969), p. 430, citing as an example G. Haberler, *The Theory of International Trade* (London: William Hodge, 1936), pp. 4-5.

19. Bertil Ohlin, *Interregional and International Trade* (Cambridge, Mass.: Harvard University Press, 1952).

20. Paul A. Samuelson, "International Trade and Equalization of Factor Prices," *Economics Journal*, June 1948.

21. Charles P. Kindleberger, *American Business Abroad* (New Haven: Yale University Press, 1969), p. 13.

From this point of view, it is clearly a world of *political* economy that constitutes the conditions for transnational corporate action, since interference by *governments* as well as by firms is posited; but the emphasis in his theory is on the market— an economic construct. Kindleberger rejects the popular doctrine of some businessmen that direct investment across frontiers is stimulated by markets rather than profits, observing that explanations which businessmen give of their thought processes must not be taken with literal seriousness. Businessmen maximize profits in transnational business rather than merely follow promising markets.

Other explanations are frequently given for the development of corporate organization and transnational business. One is that direct investment involves the reinvestment of corporate funds, earned abroad, that firms are reluctant to distribute to shareholders; retained earnings form cheaper capital than borrowings or the sale of new equities, and besides, extra dividends only lead stockholders to expect more and more. But Kindleberger rightly insists that cross-border direct investment involves much more; direct investment means entering into commitments, taking risks, and the establishment of control centers abroad. The latter point was underlined by Stephen H. Hymer in his argument that direct investment belongs more to the theory of industrial organization than to the theory of international capital movements.[22] It is an important point because it links in significant ways the internal and external conditions of corporate action in the world arena.

Transfer Logistics in the Multinational Corporation

The ultimate theoretical constructs of multinational corporate action in the world arena will derive from a competition of ideas in the academic marketplace. In the meantime, the student of the multinational corporation must continue to observe the way in which this competition is influenced by studies of factor flows. A good example of this is Baranson's study of technology

22. Stephen H. Hymer, "The International Operations of National Firms: A Study of Direct Investment," a doctoral dissertation (1960) at the Massachusetts Institute of Technology, cited in Kindleberger, *op. cit.*, p. 11, note 9.

transfer through the international firm.[23] This study discusses the transfer environments in donor and recipient countries, recipient and donor firms' characteristics, and conflicting interests over licensing as against investment choices. He notes that the multinational corporation has emerged as an important instrumentality of resource allocation in the world economy; that its role goes well beyond the classical concept of market mechanisms and is more in the mainstream of Schumpeter's contribution on the entrepreneurial role; that major factors influencing pricing and allocation efficiencies are the way in which the contracting parties view the costs and benefits of technology transfer, as well as the competitiveness in donor and recipient markets.

He adds that it does not necessarily follow that "an intensification of technological dissemination will lead to more effective utilization of world resources," and that "transfer induced by protection of national markets increases overall resource costs of world production and nurtures technological stagnation." Flexibility on the part of multinational corporations, on the other hand, in their choice of alternative modes of transfer "can lead to a wider dissemination of technology and better resource utilization throughout the world."[24]

The environment of multinational corporate action from this point of view—which is generally that of economists who have no nationalistic or parochial axe to grind—is not a narrowly drawn economic model but a model of world political economy based on certain universal value premises. In this regard, Baranson points to issues of public policy that lie beyond the scope of his paper, namely, how to induce practices that will contribute to technological progress through open-licensing and cross-licensing procedures between industrially-advanced partners. Also, under the heading of public policy, would be measures to assure competitive pricing of technology, a matter related to "larger issues of competition in supplier markets and the relative bargaining

23. Jack Baranson, "Technology Transfer Through the International Firm," *American Economic Review*, May 1970, pp. 435-440. This paper was based in part upon correspondence and interviews with some 30 corporate executives of multinational corporations with overseas manufacturing affiliates. Mr. Baranson was with the International Bank for Reconstruction and Development.

24. *Id.*, p. 440.

position of purchasers." Larger questions of market structure and bargaining positions include the matters of excessive rent to technology donors, and of returns to indivisible packages of production and marketing services.

Baranson's study of industrial technologies for developing countries yielded concrete examples of the fact that certain multinational corporations are more willing than others to adjust industrial transfer to the specialized needs of developing economies. DuPont of Mexico, for example, had been active in adapting acquired technology to the scale of demand of the Mexican market without incurring an excessive cost premium. Cummin's Engine Company had designed and built a diesel series to meet market demands both in developing countries and in certain specialized markets in industrialized areas. Massey-Ferguson in Mexico and Fiat in Yugoslavia have both structured their investments to minimize diseconomies of small-scale production and built-in technological obsolescence. [25]

In the light of studies of the kind just described, some general conclusions can be drawn concerning the big shift, after World War II, from the *commodity-trade* pattern of transnational business to a pattern of *transnational production* characterized by a factor mobility of increasing volume and significance for world politics as well as for world economics. For world politics, it means that more attention has to be given to the policies and strategies of the multinational corporation as a major emergent entity in the world arena along with sovereign protagonists. For world economics, it means that new theory is required to explain the economic role of the multinational corporation and to furnish the premises for both corporate and national policies that are realistic in relation to given business and government goals. The big shift also has organizational implications for both multinational corporations and governments.

Before the big shift, transnational business was carried on mainly by uninational firms that reached out to the world beyond national frontiers through trade in commodities; now they do so increasingly through transnational intrafirm production. The concomitant factor mobility challenges earlier economic

25. Jack Baranson, *Industrial Technologies for Developing Economies* (New York: Praeger, 1969), pp. 45-53.

doctrine of comparative advantage or comparative cost; it assumed that while commodities moved transnationally, productive resources did not, and that the resultant factor specialization tended to maximize world output if there were minimal restrictions on the transnational flow of trade. With liberal national trading policies, the world as a whole could thus approach an optimal global allocation of resources. The result would be an optimal level of human well-being.

The rapidly increased movement across frontiers, bringing in its train new kinds of national restrictive policies, indicates the need for revised doctrines of comparative cost and comparative advantage to deal with these policies. Some of them reflect national autarkical goals, others regional and global goals. Competing doctrines are designed to meet or counter these respective goals. As to corporate policy, some firms have goals that parallel or complement national goals, others are either indifferent or hostile to these goals. A few multinational corporations may reflect commitment to the doctrine of comparative advantage—revised to account for the transnational movement of factors.

New forms of business organization are required for this new form of transnational business in which capital (as man-made things useful in further production, including technology) and labor (including managerial effort) move on an unprecedented scale across political frontiers, but *within* a firm or a corporate group.

Shifts in Centers of Power

Among other external conditions that influence corporate policy, as multinational corporations move into the world arena, are major shifts in the centers of power *within* nations, as well as within the international system as a whole. These shifts seem to be characteristic of the present transitional epoch. In the international system, the big shift of centers of power since World War I has been from Europe to non-European political capitals: in the first instance, to the capitals of the superpowers in Washington and Moscow, but, with nuclear proliferation and modernization in the Third World, to an increasing number of capitals. The effect of all this has been to create radically new external conditions of political economy for all multinational corporations.

Within nations, especially those industrialized countries that constitute the major protagonists of the international system, the shift from financial and industrial centers of power to national governments has modified basically the pluralistic structure of power in these countries, with consequences for conditions in the entire world arena.

The shift of power to national governments is best illustrated for Americans by examining what has happened in federal legislation since 1933. The national government's authority over many aspects of United States economy was vastly extended to cover the securities markets and holding companies; to increase the output of the nation's productive plant; to maintain that output more evenly through business cycles, which legislation has also tried to reduce; to distribute the national income more widely both for human satisfaction and for creating a larger mass market, to be served, in turn, by more productive enterprise; and to provide for reasonably full employment and to counter depression, control inflation, and reduce poverty. Centers of private government (including corporate centers) remain strong; but there has been a redistribution of the power to govern the economy, with labor unions as well as federal and state governments placed in a new—and changing—pluralistic pattern of governance.

All national governments today tend to maximize the social welfare function; one consequence for the multinational corporation is that as it moves into such nation-states, the governments of these countries may try to use it for these and other national purposes.[26] For the world political economy as a whole, there may be, as there is in each country, a considerable shift in the centers of power over the next few decades—a shift that has less to do with transformations of the international system of states than with the relations between states and multinational corporations.

Multinational corporate managers have become concerned about a world of "discrete governments with positive purposes."[27]

---

26. In this paragraph, I have drawn from my comments in *The Company: Law, Structure and Reform in Eleven Countries*, edited by Charles de Hoghton for PEP (New York: Macmillan, 1970), pp. 93*ff.* For European trends see the bibliographies at pp. 383-387.

27. Kindleberger, *op. cit.*, at pp. 192*ff.*, comments on this trend as it affects factor-price equalization and the problem of monopolies.

It is a world that stands in contrast to a hypothetical world of laissez-faire—without tariffs, with fixed exchange rates, and with "minimal taxation because of minimal government," thus yielding a hypothetical situation in which multinational corporations of truly global perspective could scan the world horizon "to improve the efficiency of goods and factor markets that function less than optimally because of distance, ignorance, and local monopoly."[28]

With the waxing of the welfare state and economic nationalism everywhere, however, the multinational corporation cannot become a strong instrument of allocative efficiency in a global economy. Aligned with the economic nationalists, moreover, are business interests that stress the infant-industry argument, the external diseconomies, and other formulae that work against international harmonization.

We are probably in for a long and stormy period of hostilities in the relations between corporate enterprises and nation-states; any hoped-for transition from nationalistic jurisdictional conflict and overlap to international coordination and harmonization will be eyed with reserve. As Raymond Vernon has said, American businessmen are likely to view the absence of an international coordinating mechanism—in the form of treaties, for example—as generating more benefits than pain. A few years ago, he wrote that the decision to fashion and support a system of international harmonization of national policies affecting multinational corporations would probably be imposed in the end "by circumstances rather than by thoughtful forward planning of those who stand to gain most from it."[29] And more recently he has observed that with varying degrees of intensity, nation-states had a sense that the locus of their power is challenged by an open international system in general and by multinational enterprises in particular; what some nation-states were searching for was the means of "checking their sense of ebbing control and of retaining a tolerable amount of power."[30]

28. Kindleberger, *op. cit.*, p. 189.

29. Raymond Vernon, "Multinational Enterprise and National Sovereignty," *Harvard Business Review*, March-April 1969, p. 172.

30. Raymond Vernon, "Economic Sovereignty at Bay," *Foreign Affairs*, October 1968, p. 122.

Modernizing Trends

Modernization[31] is the name of another major trend in the external conditions of multinational corporate policy. Multinational corporate managers have to be familiar with competing ideologies of modernization as well as its practice. Multinational corporations do most of their business in the world of developed industrial nations; but these nations are deeply involved in the Third World of the less developed countries (LDC's). Quite aside, then, from direct involvement with these LDC's in factor and commodity movements, multinational corporations are indirectly affected by their home-country policies vis-à-vis the Third World.

The United States, for example, is involved with Vietnam, a Third World country. The United States position concerning Vietnam—not only as to the war, its aims and the way the war ought to be ended, but more importantly how the outcome will affect the status of the United States as a Pacific power—is closely related to and may in the long run determine the government's position on all Third World countries. The results for all United States-based multinational corporations could be pervasive and profound.

Even if the Vietnam experience does not become generalized in American minds to embrace all Third World countries—or generalized also in the minds of men in the home bases of other multinational corporations in Europe, Africa, and Asia—official actions could undergo a drastic alteration that would be critically harmful to all of these countries. In a world of rising expectations, development may lead eventually to stability; but along the way the world is learning that there may be violent instability

31. Cyril E. Black, *The Dynamics of Modernization* (New York: Harper & Row, 1966); Richard Butwell (ed.), *Foreign Policy and the Developing Nation* (Lexington: University of Kentucky Press, 1969); Lester D. Pearson, *The Crisis of Development* (New York: Praeger, 1970); Gunnar Myrdal, *The Challenge of World Poverty: A World Anti-Poverty Program in Outline* (New York: Pantheon Books, 1970); David Hapgood (ed.), *The Role of Popular Participation in Development* (Cambridge: M.I.T. Press, 1969); Clive S. Gray, *Resource Flows to Less-Developed Countries: Financial Terms and Their Constraints* (New York: Praeger, 1969); Alfred Maizels with others, *Exports and Economic Growth of Developing Countries* (New York: Cambridge University Press, 1969); Jack Baranson, *Industrial Technologies for Developing Countries* (New York: Praeger, 1969); John H. Adler (ed.), *International Development, 1968: Accomplishments and Apprehensions* (Dobbs Ferry, N.Y.: Oceana Publications, 1969); Hiram S. Phillips, *Guide for Development: Institution Building and Reform* (New York: Praeger, 1969); and Raymond W. Goldsmith, *Financial Structure and Development* (New Haven: Yale University Press, 1969) are among the leading titles.

engendered by change. It is a still-unanswered question whether the response of the more developed countries will be world-weariness and recoil, or a more sophisticated approach based upon full review and analysis of experience—military (as in Southeast Asia) and economic (as in foreign aid)—and involving new foreign policies that may be radically different from the old and current ones.

Development and the Multinational Corporation

The general approach of the more developed countries toward modernization in the LDC's—or perhaps a long period of inaction due to a sadder-but-wiser attitude—will be a basic element in foreign policies. The Third World may be regarded as less than vital to the national interest [32] of one or more of the major protagonist powers, with far-reaching results for multinational corporate affiliates in Third World countries. The tendency in nations to turn inward [33] and to avoid new commitments while reducing the old could leave many a firm holding the bag without much protection from home and host governments. But either way—the abandonment of LDC's or their buildup through external aid—involvement with the Third World is full of enigmas.

In the struggle between foreign investors in raw materials and host governments in the LDC's, for example, these governments may press investors for an increased share of the profits and an increased measure of control over the exploitation of these natural resources. [34] It is debatable whether the aggregate profits will thereby shrink under an illusory control acquired by these

32. Thomas Perry Thornton, "A View from Washington," *Annals*, November 1969, cited above, pp. 19-30. Dr. Thornton was Chief of Research on South Asia in the Department of State when this article was written. I have relied on its substance in the next few paragraphs.

33. For the debate in the United States on national interest in this respect, see Kermit Gordon (ed.), *Agenda for the Nation* (Washington, D.C.: The Brookings Institution, 1968), especially the papers by Edwin O. Reischauer (on "Transpacific Relations"), John C. Campbell (on "The Middle East"), and Max F. Millikan (on "The U.S. and Low-Income Countries"); James A. Johnson, "The New Generation of Isolationists," *Foreign Affairs*, October 1970; Robert E. Osgood and others, *America and the World* (Baltimore: Johns Hopkins Press, 1970); Willard L. Thorp, "Foreign Aid: A Report on the Reports," *Foreign Affairs*, April 1970.

34. Raymond Vernon, "Foreign Enterprises and Developing Nations in the Raw Materials Industries," *American Economic Review*, May 1970, pp. 122-126.

LDC's.[35] Governments on all sides would be involved. To what extent the United States and other governments in the more advanced countries would be prepared in the future to pursue a policy of supporting the cause of multinational corporations as against modernizing countries is not predictable. If a minimum level of economic growth in the LDC's is a necessary, if not a sufficient, precondition for political growth—which growth governments in the more advanced countries may or may not favor in varying situations and at various times—the corporate cause will get varying responses to pleas for government support.

Another aspect of the general issue is the corporate role in resource transfers to the LDC's. Trade and investment have not met the need, nor can it do so in the foreseeable future: From 1955 to 1967, the LDC's total share of world trade dropped from 28 to 21 per cent. At the same time, these nations have been finding it more expensive to buy what they need. During this period, their terms of trade dropped 9 per cent. The United Nations Conference on Trade and Development (UNCTAD) underlined the gap between the Third World and advanced countries (including the Communists) but brought forth no general solutions. The regressive movement in the United States and Europe toward protectionism worsens the picture. If trade and investment are the only alternatives to aid, a policy of trade-liberalization is indicated in the more developed countries, which, moreover, can gain at length through exports to these potential markets.

Investment, the other half of the trade-and-investment alternative to aid, commands attention to a sober problem. But multinational corporations hesitate to invest too heavily outside the more developed nations. They fear expropriation, limited domestic markets, paucity of skills, unfamiliarity with the milieu, and a general economic weakness in the LDC's. President Nixon, in his 1969 aid message, proposed the formation of a semipublic entity to encourage investment and to assume the investment-guarantee functions of the Agency for International Development. Other measures would help: a further relaxation of United States balance of payments controls on investment in LDC's, and tax

35. See the comments by Marshall Hall and Chandler Morse on Vernon's paper, cited above, *American Economic Review*, May 1970, pp. 128-131.

incentives for such investments. On the side of the LDC's, the abandonment of doctrinaire prejudices against the entrance of foreign capital for development on equitable terms would help. There are mutual opportunities in this area, such as devising a form of investment that will combine the advantages of equity investment (not adding to an already overwhelming debt burden in an LDC) with those of fixed-term investment and turn-key projects that become the property of the recipient country as soon as they are completed.[36]

These alternatives will not replace the urgent need for resource-transfer in the form of aid from the more developed countries at the rate of from $15 to $20 billion annually. In 1968, the non-Communist Development Assistance Committee (DAC) countries provided some $12.8 billion of aid, while the Communist states provided about $0.7 billion. United States aid and commitments have decreased since then, although the Perkins Committee (the President's General Advisory Committee on Foreign Assistance Programs) advised that United States commitments for aid ought to rise five per cent annually from the 1967 level, i.e., from $3.2 billion in 1967 to about $5 billion in 1973. (The assumption was that there would be constant growth in United States GNP, of which United States aid would constitute a constant proportion).

In July, 1970, the Committee for Economic Development (in the United States), the Japan Committee for Economic Development (Keizai Doyukai), and the Committee for Economic Development in Australia, after two years of study, jointly issued a report[37] urging that the world's industrial nations increase their development aid to nine Southeast Asian nations: Burma, Thailand, Laos, Cambodia, South Vietnam, Malaysia, Singapore, Indonesia, and the Philippines to an annual flow of one per cent of national income within the shortest possible time, and in the longer run to one per cent of GNP. The report urged further that

---

36. Thornton, *op. cit.*, p. 28.

37. Committee for Economic Development, *Development Assistance to Southeast Asia* (New York, July 1970). See also CED's *Assisting Development in Low-Income Countries: Priorities for U.S. Government Policy* (New York, September 1969) and *Trade Policy Toward Low-Income Countries*, A Statement on National Policy by the Research and Policy Committee of CED (New York, June 1967). These reports usually have reservations by dissident members of the panels.

an increasing share of official assistance should be channeled to the nine nations through multilateral international organizations.

The CED report was critical of past emphasis on the promotion of the narrow economic and political self-interest of the assisting countries, with humanitarian concern for the people of the recipient country tending to recede into the background. The proposed aid formula was premised on the belief that rapid economic development in Southeast Asia can best be achieved through a judicious mixture of private initiative and public planning in the developing countries themselves.

The CED report declared that official bilateral aid should be "substantially liberalized," and that "an increasing proportion of such assistance should be provided in the form of grants and concessionary loans with longer maturities and grace periods as well as lower interest rates." It also recommended that "united official aid should be expanded at a faster rate than the total volume of development assistance." To control rapid population growth, a serious problem in the area, the report called on developed countries and international organizations to assist in studies, make their own specialists available, and promote training of population and family planning specialists.

Jan Tinbergen, chairman of the United Nations Development Planning Committee, declared in January, 1970 that better statistics were needed on production costs, industrial investments and production processes, in order to determine which industries should be shifted to developing countries. "If we are interested in a stable world order, we will have to change our aid and trade policies," he declared; "otherwise, there will be increasing mass unemployment, increasing internal conflicts, disaster." [38] Developed countries should raise their aid to one per cent of GNP, he said, and then get rid of the protective barriers against products from the poor countries by multilateral action: "The only way out of the antiquated international structure is a shock therapy consisting of the simultaneous acceptance of commitments."

The revolutionary implications of Tinbergen's proposal appear in his prescriptions for the developing countries: they must improve their governments, provide better education, turn

38. From an interview with Clyde H. Farnsworth at The Hague published in *The New York Times*, January 16, 1970.

out more blue-collar workers, and then "cut away at the power of the feudal landlords" whose land holdings are held as a hedge against inflation and not specifically for food production. A Nobel prizewinner in economics, he proposed to spend the $36,500 grant (shared by Ragnar Frisch) on a major study of the progressive land tax that would force better utilization of the land. In addition to reducing the gulf between the two classes in developing countries, the very rich and the very poor, the result would be greater tax revenues and more agricultural production to earn more foreign exchange.

The Global Political Economy

No ideal order has ever been designed for all multinational enterprises; they have no common goals that would form the basis for blueprinting such a generally favorable environment. Yet, in the literature, there are highly suggestive normative studies that provide points of departure for such blueprinting. At a time when, as now, the world stands at a turning point in world trade policy—when there is a possibility that a relatively free trade era may give way to a highly restrictive period—the perspective of some earlier studies can be useful.

Such a study, called "Shaping the World Economy," was prepared a decade ago by a team organized under the auspices of the Netherlands Economic Institute Division of Balanced Economic Growth and headed by Jan Tinbergen, then professor of development planning at the Netherlands School of Economics. [39] The study was undertaken in order to deal mainly with "the economic problems of a world faced with the threat of nuclear war, misery in the developing countries, and the challenge of the Communist economic and political system."

The team asserted several premises. Emphasizing the need for an "undoctrinaire approach," it took exception to two "Western doctrinaire approaches," first, as to economic systems, to a purely free-enterprise economy; secondly, as to political matters, to an insistence upon autonomous national policy making. The report took the position that mixed systems are better than either a pure free enterprise economy or a completely regimented

39. See Jan Tinbergen, *Shaping the World Economy: Suggestions for an International Economic Policy* (New York: The Twentieth Century Fund, 1962).

one. The right mixture would depend upon circumstances; it had to be the subject of "careful engineering."

Autonomous national policy having been rejected as the way to guide the affairs of the international economic community, the report asked for more centralized use of certain instruments of global economic policy. The use of these instruments might be coordinated at the international level; better still, they could be handled by supranational agencies. In any event, they could not be used with maximum efficiency if decisions were to be taken at the national level. These major "optimum instruments of economic policy" were designated in the following terms: a world treasury, a world bank, and a world budget; investment criteria on a world scale together with something like a "Mutual Investment Insurance Corporation" as an affiliate of the World Bank; a World Economic Survey under the auspices of ECOSOC; and an "international economic order," at least in non-Communist areas.

For optimum use of these instruments, and for the required solidarity in solving any given problem, the degree of centralization would vary from case to case. But clearly some functions of national governments would have to be transferred to a "higher level" because of certain conspicuous lacunae in the international economic machinery. These were in "financial policy, in the realm of stabilizing the revenues of countries producing primary commodities, and in the field of insurance against noneconomic investment risks."[40] Centralized expenditure for development purposes was a primary need, national and international institutions being unable to correct two basic faults: a low level of expenditure and an unsatisfactory geographic distribution. Just as any central government makes a considerable portion of its development expenditure on a current basis, a strong international financial institution was needed to make current expenditures, as well as to provide loans and to finance its expenditures through current contributions from member countries. Such an authority could exert its influence on the business cycle and create incentives for intergovernmental cooperation. The report mentioned two other needs: agencies for dealing with the problem of stabilizing the revenues of countries producing primary commodities, and the provision of an international insur-

40. *Id.*, p. 183.

ance scheme against noneconomic risks in order to further private foreign investment in developing countries.

Then, the report charged that certain existing institutions were being used against the best interests of the world community because of inadequate centralization of authority. The trade policies of some nations failed to conform to the rules set by GATT. There were unjustified quantitative restrictions on Asian industrial products. There was excessive protection of European agriculture. There was unduly restricted trade with Communist countries. There were inefficient item-by-item methods of reducing impediments on trade.

Regional approaches to the General Agreement on Tariffs and Trade (GATT) idea for Asia and Africa were proposed. Reduction in the level of the Common Market's agricultural protection was urged, and its discrimination against non-associated areas was condemned.

The necessary financial central authority, according to this report, might be organized within IDA or possibly OECD if the latter could extend membership to developing countries. There was an urgent need for more commodity agreements, at least among the non-Communist countries, especially on cocoa, some non-ferrous metals, bananas, and cotton. Insurance against export declines was suggested. "Lower level" forms of bilateral cooperation and ad hoc organizations such as the Colombo Plan were held to be good so far as they went, "provided that the organs at the highest levels are sufficiently endowed with supplementary means to carry through a program of optimal intensity and optimal geographic distribution." [41]

The report did not stop with recommendations for the better economic organization of the non-Communist world. A "truly international order" was envisaged through the use of the United Nations, and especially of ECOSOC and regional commissions of the United Nations. Here the report turned to the larger problems of political security on a global basis, suggesting a three- or four-power system to replace the current bipolarity, the hypothesized "fourth power being a neutralist force, organized by the 'South,' the uncommitted countries." [42]

41. *Id.*, p. 185.
42. *Id.*, p. 190.

The recurrence, during the decade succeeding this report, of many of these themes in debate about public policy on a world economy indicates how far we are from solutions of the problems that the report underlined. The nations of the world continued to flounder in a sea of uncertainty about the way out of their global troubles, and there were important changes in world politics, as well as in world economics, that brought new issues to focus.

Crisis in International Development

A crisis in international development[43] arose in the late sixties, reflecting many of these changes and bringing to the fore new conditions affecting multinational corporate policy. In the days of the Cold War, development assistance had been recommended in the West as an aid to the bulwark against Communism in the LDC's. On a more positive note, it had been recommended as a means of strengthening democratic institutions in those countries, but as neutralism spread in the Third World, and as it became obvious that democratic institutions could scarcely flourish where deep poverty prevailed and social tensions rose, support for development assistance began to wane in the more developed countries.

Then, too, the LDC's themselves changed. On the one hand, the Green Revolution—due to the increased use of fertilizers and the technological breakthrough in high-yield varieties of wheat and rice—created optimism; on the other hand, population growth threatened to cancel out much of this technological advance, while the LDC's failed to convince the more developed countries that measures would be taken to increase exports fast enough to meet development needs. Other measures, especially the development of human resources through educational reform and the broadening of skills, were only slowly taken, if at all. The balance of payments problem was worsened in some LDC's by the policy of increasing domestic production of manufactured goods to substitute for goods that had been imported, with the result that the foreign exchange saving proved to be less than

43. See Irving S. Friedman, "The Crisis of International Development," *Britannia Book of the Year: 1970*, pp. 284-286.

expected as imports for equipment and intermediate goods mounted.

High-cost production behind high-tariff walls, the bane of many LDC economies and, by the opening of the seventies, a general threat to the world economy, had begun to show dramatically how dynamic growth resulting from internationally competitive export sectors could be suppressed by restrictive nationalistic economic policies. International development, which had been regarded as an essential step toward a healthy world economy, faltered as a result of all these causes, and for other reasons as well, not the least a fading from the public conscience everywhere of the long-term objectives of development and the failure to coordinate the long-term objectives with short-run tactics.

As the industrialized nations have begun to face their own balance of payments problems and have reduced their national budgets, they have rationalized the drop in aid in various ways. Aid, it was said, had been wasted in the LDC's. Too much had been used for local political purposes, and for uneconomic projects. No more aid would be forthcoming unless reforms proved competence to use native resources more effectively. Neutralism was an added ground. In the meantime, the gap between rich and poor nations widened. In many poor countries, per capita income of $100 per annum contrasted with that of $2000-$3000 or more in the rich ones. The revolution in communications has made the gap obvious to all. Political leaders have taken advantage of this. The ideological gap has widened. Ideological tensions between countries have now become more complex than they were in the earlier postwar period of East-West bipolarity.

Crisis in Foreign Trade Policy

The net result, by 1971, had been a crisis in foreign trade policy[44] in all the more developed countries, and especially in the United States, the home base of the largest and the greatest number of multinational corporations. In the United States, the lure of the quota captured majorities in Congress. The most restrictive trade bill (HR18970) since the Smoot-Hawley Tariff Act of 1930, moved perilously near adoption. It would have man-

44. Discussed in the *Monthly Economic Letter*, October 1970, of the First National City Bank of New York.

dated quotas rather than tariffs whenever the President decided to limit imports for national security reasons, as in the case of petroleum. The bill could have led to trade barriers on a large range of products by making it much easier for all industries to qualify for escape clause relief. In a provision of major significance, the bill established a presumption of added trade barriers, if import growth and market penetration were to exceed certain limits.

Advocates of protection pointed to the rapid growth of competing imports, arguing that this growth, both in volume and market shares, had caused or threatened to cause serious injury through lost production, closed plants, idled workers, and impaired profits. It was argued, too, that foreign producers in many cases enjoyed wage-cost advantages beyond the ability of American domestic firms to offset with advanced technology and efficient operations. Foreign producers, it was charged, sometimes benefitted from hidden government aids, direct subsidies or tax rebates. Shielding of markets abroad in textiles was held to be only one of a more general range of cases.

The receptivity of Congress to these arguments was due in part to growing resentment concerning the restrictive action of other traders, notably Japan and the Common Market. Japan had to some extent relaxed its quantitative restrictions on a wide range of agricultural and industrial imports after pressure from her trading partners. The Common Market's many preferential association agreements had discriminated against United States exports and the exports of non-EEC nations in violation of the General Agreement on Tariffs and Trade (GATT), and more were under negotiation. Common Market barriers against the import of farm products had harmed United States exporters; at the same time, Common Market agricultural policies had generated a large volume of heavily subsidized exports to markets in which the United States had to compete. All of this helped protectionists in the United States.

The return to protectionism in the United States and elsewhere threatened international specialization of production, a basic principle for a world economy and fundamental to multinational corporate strategy. While trade expansion on this basis promotes noninflationary economic growth, improves resource allocation, and fosters a rise in real income, protectionism leads in the opposite direction. Quotas, in particular, set precise limits on imports and can damage trading relationships more than tariffs. Quotas are outlawed in the GATT. When quotas are imposed, the danger is a sequence of retaliatory trade restrictions that could eventuate in a bitter trade war among the major protagonists in the international system.

One of the gravest aspects of the trade bill (HR18970) was its threat to the bargaining power of the United States in countering restrictive actions by other protagonists. The President's bargaining power was important for diplomatic strategy in countering trends that might isolate the United States. In Europe, for example, the Common Market was on the way toward monetary unity and a degree of political solidarity and Britain was on the way toward entry into that new political and economic entity—soon perhaps to be a great power in its own right. Tensions, too, were being relaxed between the U.S.S.R. and West Germany, with unforeseeable results. In the Middle East, the Soviet presence was another factor; and in general, the United States stood at bay before a hostile foreign attitude concerning the war in Southeast Asia. The developing countries in Asia, whose growth the United States had fostered with billions of dollars in aid, would be especially hard hit by United States quotas. The imposition of quotas would undercut the efforts of many years to strike a better balance between aid and trade, to shift the impetus for promoting growth abroad from subsidies to free enterprise and the market system.

Opponents of quotas argued further that they would tend to undermine the efficiency of the market economy by insulating domestic industry against the forces of change in the world economy and to freeze existing patterns of operation; that they would shift decisions from the impersonal marketplace to government bureaus; and that officials—through complex procedures that cannot be easily insulated from politics—would have to decide who would be allowed to import, how the overall quota was to be divided among importers that would get the nod, which countries would qualify as suppliers, and how much of the quota was to be assigned to each country. The arbitrariness of such a system, its inefficiency, and its vulnerability to improper influence were stressed.

The most damaging of all the feared results of the quota system was described as extensive government involvement in business. The government of the United States in setting quotas would acquire a powerful lever over corporate policies. What the government would give it could also take away. A consumer protection clause in the bill before Congress would, for example, permit the President to enlarge quotas on footwear and textiles if inadequate supplies were available at reasonable prices. Once an industry had made itself dependent on quotas, it would be vulnerable to the actual or threatened exercise of this option by a President anxious to compel certain business actions, or simply by a new President with a different view of what constitutes adequacy of supply or reasonableness of price.

The multinational corporate manager, assessing the external conditions of corporate action in the world arena, might have mixed feelings about the arguments just cited. Some multinational corporations—and some enterprises within a given corporate group of enterprises engaged in transnational business—would profit, others would suffer losses, in a general return to protectionism. All, however, would be required to make the most careful forecasts of which their intelligence services were capable concerning the general direction of the world economy and the effect of such measures as quantitative barriers on their own ideal global system.

Expansion of national production in their home and host countries, and expansion of world trade generally would hardly suffice for this ideal. There could be serious "imbalances" that would threaten their intra- and extra-firm relationships. Strong price-cost pressures within these nations, and severe disturbances in the balances of payments among them, together with recurrent crises in the foreign exchange markets, would all have to be considered. An upsurge of economic activity in the world, with considerable growth of real output in the nations concerned, would not alone point in ideal directions. It would depend on the causes of the growth of industrial production, the rate of public consumption and for what purposes (e.g., the arms race, better infrastructures in home and host countries, tax policies), shrinkage in the value of money and pro- or anti-inflationary measures of governments, the shortage or plethora of capital, and so on.

The world economy during the sixties grew beyond the most optimistic expectations. In many countries, standards of living rose spectacularly, but the demands for goods and services everywhere exceeded supply. The revolution of rising expectations was general. Military insecurity aggravated the shortage of resources. Nor would the end of warfare in Southeast Asia promise respite in demand. The two superpowers were not on the way toward substantial enough arms limitations to reduce demand for the goods and services of security-minded nations, large and small. The demand for productive capital, on the other hand, was growing at an unprecedented rate. On two scores this demand would exert enormous pressures for years to come: first, for the exploitation of discoveries at the frontiers of science, and secondly, for the application of technology throughout the world economy. The demand could not be met within the structure of the political economy of the world of the sixties. Would there be any better chance in the seventies and the eighties?

These were among the problems of external conditions for multinational corporate action as the world faced 1970 and thereafter. But multinational corporations were among the institutional channels that some observers hoped to find improving trade opportunities and transnational investment in the years ahead; and some thought that multinational corporations could be more powerful forces in promoting economic development than government aid as it had developed since the fifties.

The Ecology of Multinational Corporate Action

Bridgman's *Logic of Modern Physics* in effect announces the end of an idea of causality that he identified with the Renaissance: "We do not have a simple event A causally connected with a simple event B"; rather "the whole background of the *system* in which the events occur is *included in the concept*, and is a vital part of it." Parts of this passage are here italicized to make several points. First, systems analysis now irreversibly changes the whole field of social theory and its application to governmental and corporate policy, current and surely temporary relegation of some systems analysts to the doghouse notwithstanding. Next, there is a special implication of this method as applied to information systems. Today, "at the end of the Neolithic age," ac-

146

cording to McLuhan, electronic circuitry has brought a new tool into existence, the first in a thousand years, to create a total environment.

McLuhan says that the interdependence of all events and of all people becomes a direct experience under the conditions of the instant information movement provided by electronics. The popular conclusion that is often drawn from the communicational revolution—that it unifies mankind—is not supported by McLuhan's analysis. He asserts that the paradox of the electronic age is that while it creates an environment that is total, it is also decentralist.[45] Now, the multinational corporation is presumably a transnational force opposed to the decentralizing tendency of the international system of nation-states; but the multinational corporation could hardly be the unifying force that it is in the absence of our instant electronic culture. If electronic circuitry makes the world one for transnational business, it may have other effects that run counter to transnational unity. Its effects in propaganda may, for example, far outrun its production of communicational efficiency.

The resurgence of nationalism, often in virulent form, is vastly stimulated by electronic circuitry as used by propagandists. Propaganda "reprocesses any existing psyche or society" and can become the master and not the servant of man. Electronic technology takes as its nutrient "the most common feelings, the most widespread ideas, the crudest patterns," and this places it "on a very low level with regard to what it wants man to do and to what end"—here McLuhan quotes Ellul, who goes on to say that "hate, hunger, and pride make better levers of propaganda than love or impartiality."[46] And, one might add, better levers than rational modes of resource allocation by transnational corporate business. Merely by seeking the broadest and least articulate substratum of social feelings, and by raising these to new intensity, the myth-making of propaganda can arouse the most ancient and forgotten impulses. The machine, with its frag-

---

45. See Marshall McLuhan's criticism of Jacques Ellul as being "quite blind to the centralist aspects of the instant electronic culture," in a review of Ellul's *Propaganda: The Formation of Men's Attitudes* (1965) in *Book Week*, November 28, 1965. But he was in general laudatory.

46. *Book Week*, cited, p. 27.

menting and specialist patterns, had tended to suppress all the old folk and tribal awareness in favor of private and individual outlook. Not so electronic circuitry. Electronics are at home in the subconscious, private or collective. Merely by pushing dimly felt and scarcely apprehended assumptions of our social existence into higher intensity and definition, the electronic media create potent new stereotypes and myths.

This is one aspect of the new age of technics, an age much derided by its critics for having produced a deplorable environment for man, yet one that the multinational corporation does not always find so uncongenial. Nor could the multinational corporation have come into existence without technics and the indispensable scientific foundation. In Lewis Mumford's *The Myth of the Machine* (1967), a major recapitulation and extension of the themes in his earlier work, especially *Technics and Civilization* (1934) and *The Condition of Man* (1944), he questions and hopes to demolish "both the assumptions and the predictions upon which our commitment to the present form of technical and scientific progress, treated as if ends in themselves, have been based." The "tool technics" of our time are but a fragment of "biotechnics: man's total equipment for life" with his own "mind-activated body" nourished by ritual, art, poesy, drama, music, dance, philosophy, science, myth, religion—all as essential to man as his daily bread. The work activities that directly sustain him are his barest minimal activities; his true life consists in far more than this. It is the symbolic activities that lend significance both to the processes of work and their ultimate products and consummations. The humanist's critique of the contemporary, basely cramped, little dreams of man's possibilities on earth follow, in general, this line of attack; and it leads, for our discussion, to the question: Is the multinational corporation no more than a new, but unexciting, instrument for the maintenance of the minimal level of human life? The contribution of this new instrument toward the production of our daily bread—with all the variations on a theme of "better living"—can be interpreted as no contribution at all to our significant symbolic activities. On the other hand, the contribution may be a necessary, if not a sufficient, one for the production and distribution that supports the significant symbolic activities of men everywhere.

At any rate, the technics of our new age, and the science that underlies technology, are an indispensable condition of multinational corporate action. The interplay between corporations and this technological and scientific environment will undoubtedly consume more attention in board rooms and managerial suites as time goes on. We all draw on the heritage of science and technology; hence, we must defend and strengthen these sources of innovation. There are negative as well as positive sides of this obligation, both of which are relevant to multinational corporate policy. Take first the negative side of preventing deterioration at the source. Here we refer not mainly to the persistent enemies of science and technology in superstition and recurrent waves of anti-intellectualism, important as these are, but rather to the protection of Nature. From St. Francis of Assisi to Rachel Carson, the awareness of ecological ethics has grown to the point where it must now be taken into account among the external conditions of multinational corporate policy making. It is not simply that corporations must avoid befouling the environment. The issue is deeper: What are the necessary and sufficient ecological conditions for *corporate* survival in the world arena?

One must expect the future development of a new science of corporate ecology that will research the whole range of relationships between multinational corporations and their environment. In some respects, this knowledge will be basic to new technology, as in the exploitation of the resources in the oceans and the ocean beds. In the social sciences, corporate ecology will deal, among other things, with changes in man's understanding and use of the physical environment.

Another part of the coming corporate approach to technology will deal with corporate involvement in the phasing of technological advance with science. A committee of the American Association for the Advancement of Science in 1965 declared that we live in an era in which scientific ideas are given large-scale technological application before the relevant basic scientific knowledge has been sufficiently developed to provide an adequate understanding of the effects of the new technology on nature. Fuel additives are a case in point. Society is greedy for short-run payoffs, often enormous, on its investments in science; the corporation is but the instrument, and not the source, of this greed. But, as Nobel prize winner Joshua Lederberg has said, greed, if it continues to foster a scientifically ignorant and imperceptive technology, responsive only to narrowly drawn goals and blind to larger human needs, can have no other consequence than "a terminal cosmic bellyache."[47]

Charles A. Lindbergh, after declaring that the very survival of man depends on our ability to foresee and control the fantastic forces of the various technologies our scientific knowledge has released, has demanded government control. "Much as I believe in the utmost practical freedom for man," he wrote to Representative Emilio Q. Daddario of Connecticut from a village in the mountains of Mindanao, "I do not see how his essential environment can be maintained in this technological era through commercial organizations acting independently." He asked for quick and firm governmental action against "contemporary pressure lobbies" bent on "ruthless exploitation and spoliation of our country." He went even further than that. "We need a policy and plan that covers our entire planet and extends to the utmost of human capability into space and time."[48] The role of the multinational corporation in such a policy and plan is still an unwritten chapter.

---

47. Joshua Lederberg, "Greed to Cash in on Science Can Cause Cosmic Bellyache," *The Washington Post*, May 24, 1969.

48. AP dispatch in *The New York Times*, July 7, 1970. For other comment on ecology that will affect multinational corporate policy see F. Fraser Darling and John P. Milton (eds.), *Future Environments of North America* (Natural History Press/ Doubleday, 1967); "Fighting to Save the Earth From Man," *Time*, February 2, 1970; Paul Shepard and Daniel McKinley (eds.), *The Subversive Science: Essays Toward an Ecology of Man* (Boston: Houghton Mifflin Co., 1969); Robert Rienow and Leona Train Rienow, *Moment in the Sun* (New York: Dial, 1967); William R. Ewald, Jr. (ed.), *Environment for Man: The Next 50 Years* (Bloomington: Indiana University Press, 1967); Lawrence B. Slobodkin, "Aspects of the Future of Ecology," *General Systems Yearbook*, Vol. XIII, 1969, pp. 115ff.; LaMont C. Cole, "Can the World Be Saved?" *The New York Times Magazine*, March 31, 1968, pp. 35ff.; Philip H. Abelson, "Global Weather," *Science*, January 13, 1967; R. Buckminster Fuller, *Operating Manual for Spaceship Earth* (Southern Illinois University Press, 1970) and *Utopia and Oblivion* (Bantam Books, 1970); L. Dudley Stamp, *The Geography of Life and Death* (Cornell University Press, 1965); Roger Revelle, "Human Ecology and Ethics are Inseparable," *The New York Times*, January 12, 1970; Harrison Brown, "The Combustibility of Humans," *Saturday Review*, June 24, 1967; and Abel Wolman, "Pollution as an International Issue", *Foreign Affairs*, October 1968.

Chapter VI

INTERNAL CONDITIONS OF
MULTINATIONAL CORPORATE ACTION

The literature on corporate structure and strategy in the sense of enterprise activity is growing at an enormous pace. The best of this literature is both analytical and descriptive; it depends not only upon case histories and comparative studies of corporate practice, but also upon provocative theoretical constructs that guide the inquiring mind on some urgent issues of public as well as corporate policy. These issues concern the role of the multinational corporation both as a survivor in, and as a contributor to, a global political economy. The latter role should surprise no one who takes seriously the problem of man's surviving the multiplex dangers of the coming decades. The modern corporation will be expected to make a positive contribution toward solving many world problems without abandoning its enterprise function.

The Corporation: Master Magician or Sorcerer's Apprentice?

So lofty a role for the multinational corporation, as a contributor to a global political economy, may be dismissed by some as too pretentious. The multinational corporation, as a business enterprise, it may be argued, simply seeks a profit for its owners and thereby contributes indirectly to the general welfare. This was the classical rationale. But a new development in our Age of Technology has altered this argument. Those who manage the modern corporation, like those who manage the modern state, now stand at the controls of potentially life-destroying, as well as life-giving, machines.

151

The "technetronic"[1] machine age has put in the hands of multinational corporate managers fabulous tools that were undreamt of a few decades ago. To cite only one example, General Electric (U.S.) has announced that it will eventually set up an international computer network, using satellites, that will permit subsidiaries throughout the world to gain immediate access to any information the company will have deposited in a central computer. A time-sharing system such as this—which allows users at many different locations to use the same computer at the same time, utilizing a teletypewriter connected to the computer by telephone line—would open the way for simultaneous use by many different organizations. The marvels of the technetronic age are not limited to multiple independently targeted reentry vehicles.

Lewis Mumford, commenting on the social meaning of automation, has alluded to Goethe's fable of the sorcerer's apprentice. In the fable, the apprentice, having overheard his master speak magic words that moved inanimate objects at will, tried out these words in the master's absence. The boy was delighted to find that if he pronounced the words, a broom and a pail would fetch water from the well and do his work; soon, however, the tubs were full and overflowing and he was ignorant of the magic words that could stop the process. He seized an axe and chopped the broom in two. Each piece went right on, and at greater speed. More chopping only produced more brooms and a flood that would have drowned the apprentice had his master not returned to pronounce the right words.

With the marvelous technics of our civilization, we have found the magic formula for setting scientific, technological, and industrial brooms and pails to work by themselves, in ever increasing quantities and at ever increasing speeds. But Mumford asks whether we have the Master Magician's formula for altering

1. Z. Brzezinsky, *Between Two Ages: America's Role in the Technetronic Era* (New York: Viking, 1970). Cf. H. I. Ansoff, "The Firm of the Future," *Harvard Business Review*, Vol. 43, No. 5, September-October 1965, pp. 162-78; Harold J. Leavitt and Thos. L. Whisler, "Management in the 1980s," *Harvard Business Review*, November-December, 1960, p. 85; Herbert A. Simon, "The Corporation: Will It Be Managed by Machines?" in M. Anshen and G. L. Bach (eds.), *Management and Corporations 1985* (New York: McGraw-Hill, 1960); and J. C. R. Lickliker, "The Man-Computer Partnership," *International Science and Technology*, May 1965.

the tempo of the process and for halting it, when it no longer serves human functions and purposes. The magician's saving spell is compared with the foresight and feedback that is plainly written on every organic process; yet we benightedly pursue the mindless apprentice's role as though a narrowly conceived use of technology were enough.

The logic of technology carried to an extreme indicates a system of control over many natural processes and organic functions. The processes of technology and automation, stubbornly pursued, could create a whole race of acquiescent and obedient human automatons, although Mumford suggests that it has already reached a terminal point, confronted by natural reactive forces. The forces of life then begin, sometimes with stealth, sometimes with ostentation, to reassert themselves; and when they do, there is "an explosive affirmation of the primeval energies of the organism." Reactions to the technics of modern civilization can be epochally desperate; they may take the form of withdrawal to the most primitive and to the primal underlayer of the human personality. Automation, of bright promise, also has its twin, a dark shadow-self: "defiant, not docile; disorderly, not organized or controlled; above all, aggressively destructive, even homicidal, reasserting the dammed-up forces of life in crazy or criminal acts." This "subversive superego" may seek to destroy the higher attributes of man. It is these higher attributes, the "gifts of love, mutuality, imagination and constructive aptitude" that have enlarged all the possibilities of life. Man must now reappraise the dreadful subjugation of nature that replaces his own functions with collectively fabricated, automatically programmed and operated, mechanical and electronic equivalents.[2]

The reappraisal of technics that is called for in this indictment—an indictment that now reverberates widely, but with which I, along with many others, heartily disagree—is at some point bound to involve the multinational corporation. The modern corporation in its most advanced form, reaching out into the world arena, is a prime bearer of technics. Without the corporation, it is difficult to imagine how the great onrush of technology

2. Lewis Mumford, *The Pentagon of Power. Volume Two of the Myth of the Machine* (New York: Harcourt Brace Jovanovich, 1970).

could have occurred in the first place and could then have been applied to the development of a world economy. The corporation has not been the sole cause, but certainly a necessary one.

If the corporation is not *the* master magician, with power and responsibility to steer man through the hazards of our technetronic age, it must be more than a sorcerer's apprentice. While the power over and the responsibility for the use of technics reside mainly in the modern state because of its claim to primacy, this power and responsibility is shared with many other important decision centers; clearly the multinational corporations of our time are among these decision centers.

Managerial intentions at corporate centers cannot be divorced from the goals of environing societies and suspended in the mid-air of an amoral world market. The goals of the home and host countries, and at length the goals of the macro-society that multinational corporations serve directly or indirectly, are interlinked with corporate goals. This is an uncomfortable, but inescapable, fact. Corporate centers, like other centers of power and responsibility—the churches, the academies, the labor unions—take cues from and give cues to governments. The modern corporation is more than a powerful instrument, available for whatever uses its managers may wish to make of it. As an instrument of profitable enterprise, it has successfully advanced economic growth through the multiplication of its ventures; but are production, profitability, and economic growth enough as the ends and motivating forces of corporate action in the world arena? Necessary, but not sufficient, must be the answer.

Extra-Corporate Ends of Corporate Policy

The spur of profit seeking has to be distinguished from managerial intent that serves extra-corporate purpose. The point here is not the one usually made in distinguishing profit that is passed on to shareowners from profit that serves other intra-corporate demands such as managerial rewards, corporate growth, reserves for security, and so on. The point is rather that there are ends to be served in the extra-corporate environment.

The extra-corporate ends of corporate policy are of two kinds: those that are traceable to enlightened self-interest and are essentially defensive—such as the support of governments that preserve order where a company operates—and those which enhance the total environment.

These two kinds of corporate policy objectives respond to two distinguishable kinds of demands that are made on multinational corporate management: the demands of investors as risk-takers for a return on their investment, and the demands of others in the corporate environment. Demands in the first category arise from internal contributor-claimants; demands of the latter kind arise from outside the corporation considered as a financial and organizational entity. One of the best examples of the latter kind of extra-corporate demands is found in the Canadian Task Force report on foreign ownership and the structure of Canadian industry.[3]

The Task Force distinguished between "national," "multinational," and "global" corporations—all of which, by our definition, would be objectively definable as multinational corporations, but not by the normative standards set by the Task Force.[4] A "national" corporation, according to the Canadian report, operating internationally "insists on the primacy of the methods it uses at home, and even on the laws of the home country." Its structure will be designed with cool indifference to host country norms. The "multinational" corporation, on the contrary, is "sensitive to local traditions" and respects local jurisdictions and policies. The "global" corporation, however, has "such pervasive operations that it is beyond the effective reach of the national policies of any country" and is "free to some extent to make decisions in the interest of corporate efficiency alone."

These three types of multinational corporations are defined in terms of extra-corporate norms that influence both structure and strategy in corporate policy. National governments which follow the Canadian policy of issuing "Guiding Principles for Good Corporate Behavior" can be expected to take a close look at corporate structure and strategy, especially with respect to the degree of conformity with national economic policy.

3. Report of the Task Force on the Structure of Canadian Industry (Ottawa: Queen's Printer, 1968).

4. See Charles P. Kindleberger, *American Business Abroad* (New Haven: Yale University Press, 1969), Lecture 6.

The Global Corporation

Intent in managing the "global" corporation can only be guessed at; there are few if any such firms. It is interesting, however, to speculate on the hypothetical possibility of such corporate independence of all national policies and of the focusing of managerial intention solely on corporate interests. How would it be organized and where would it operate with such freedom of strategy?

George W. Ball's "Cosmocorp"[5] would be formed under new international law that would "denationalize" the parent company. Noting the lack of phasing between the archaic political structures of the world, on the one hand, and on the other hand, the development of modern business structures, he underlines the need for central management in the multinational corporation that is not so restricted to the divergent interests of national partners that it loses its ability to pursue the true logic of the global economy. One way to rise above this deterrent, he suggests, is the establishment by treaty of an international companies law. The law would be administered by a supranational body, including representatives drawn from various companies. These representatives would exercise normal domiciliary supervision; but they would also enforce antimonopoly laws and establish guarantees for uncompensated appropriation.

The new international companies law, if properly drawn and enforced, could go far toward the realization of the "global" corporation envisaged by the Canadian Task Force. The law of the new treaty might place limitations on the restrictions that nation-states could impose on companies established under the treaty. Such limitations would presuppose operative standards; Ball suggests that one might be "the quantity of freedom needed to preserve the central principle of assuring the most economical and efficient use of world resources."[6] The drafting of such limitations would clearly require a series of international conferences in which representatives of multinational corporations and

5. George W. Ball, "Cosmocorp: The Importance of Being Stateless," in *World Business, Promise and Problems*, edited by Courtney C. Brown (New York: Macmillan, 1970), pp. 330-338.

6. *Ibid.*, p. 337.

other economic entities, as well as national representatives, would necessarily participate.

Such a supranational authority might be established in Geneva, or some other appropriate center of international activity. Each of the newly-created world companies, however, would have home countries in signatory nations as multinational corporations now do; but the laws of these countries could not infringe the overriding regulations of the organic treaty.

Ball's speculative Cosmocorp would become truly international not only through such legal arrangements but also through other measures: share ownership in the parent company would be spread through the world so that the company could not be regarded as the exclusive instrument of a particular nation; and there should be a gradual internationalizing of boards of directors and parent company managements. If these suggestions seem unduly speculative and unattainable goals, the further observations of this seasoned diplomat are worthy of note.

No world government is envisaged in the idea of Cosmocorp, nor is anything resembling a radically new world political system contemplated. The idea does not, in fact, introduce a proposal any more startling than what can already be seen on a smaller scale in the European Economic Community. There a common companies law for all Common Market countries is now being drafted. When it is adopted by the six-plus nations, the EEC will administer the law with a body of regulations applicable in all the member countries.

The inherent logic of Ball's proposal appears in his statement: "Freeing commerce from national interference through the creation of new world instrumentalities would inevitably, over time, stimulate mankind to close the gap between the archaic political structure of the world and visions of commerce vaulting beyond confining national boundaries to exploit the full promise of the world economy."[7]

The practical necessity for overcoming the "bad phasing" which Ball speaks of, is the point of Kindleberger's thesis that economic integration cannot be achieved by customs union alone; it requires "factor movements, and factor movements on

7. *Ibid.* p. 338.

an adequate scale to achieve or closely approach integration, requires institutions beyond those normal to factor markets."[8] To make substantial progress toward economic integration it will probably be necessary to develop corporations that are equally at home in the various political entities party to the integration attempt. Ideally, within EEC that would be a European corporation reconstituted under European charter or resulting from mergers "that would transcend national frontiers and would create truly European and not national decision-making entities."

Managerial intent, derived from the corporate purpose suitable to such companies, whether on the European Common Market model or on the larger model of Cosmocorp, would clearly shape both strategy and structure in these multinational corporations. This would be the case, too, if one were to go a step further and develop a model of a quasi-sovereign transnational corporation for development of the open seas beyond the national boundaries of sovereign states.

A Corporate Sovereign

A world-wide corporation, not operative within the territories of sovereign states, but only in and under the oceans, with headquarters on an island created for the purpose, and with authority drawn from contractual sources in the private sector, is a proposal[9] that transcends received doctrines of international law and practice. These operations would include the direction of any and all uses of the resources and the territories of the open seas, the stimulation of ocean research and technology, and the prevention of acts of pollution and piracy. For these and other purposes its ships, planes and satellite communication systems would patrol the seas, though not with any but defensive weapons.

This corporate sovereign might seek initially to establish its corporate personality through a charter granted by some nation willing to foster the plan, and then, by prior agreement, launch out on its own as a sovereign person through the stages of recognition by states and through a United Nations declaration endors-

8. C. P. Kindleberger, "European Integration and the International Corporation," in Courtney Brown (ed.), *op. cit.*, p. 99.

9. Richard Eells, "Corporate Sovereignty: A Charter for the Seven Seas," *Columbia Journal of World Business*, Vol. V, No. 4, July-August 1970.

ing its aims, activities, and organization as a sovereign entity. Capital necessary to establish the corporate sovereign as a going concern would be raised by subscription. Subscribers of equity capital would be sought only among educational, conservation-oriented, industrial and public bodies actively involved in ocean-ography and the use of ocean resources. A quota of stock would be allocated to each sovereign entity in the United Nations on the basis of its GNP, with a provision for variations in the quotas to favor the developing countries and in order to avoid domi-nance by the larger and more developed nations.

The corporation would be governed by a board of directors elected by the stockholders. It would be empowered originally, and assert sovereign power thereafter, to grant licenses to public and commercial organizations for the use of the resources and territory of the open seas. It would establish standards of proper use of the oceans, and would receive royalties for such use, trans-mitting the receipts after costs to the stockholders. The corpo-rate sovereign would deny and rescind licenses and royalties if its standards were not met. The sanction of denial would apply to the nation of a noncompliant or offending user, thus shifting enforcement to each nation. The corporate sovereign would pro-vide a consultative service, available on request, concerning oceanographic matters in national waters, and would leave to the future the question whether nations may assign to the corpora-tion certain functions in their own territorial waters.

Whether such a corporate sovereign would possess sov-ereignty as defined in Austinian or other traditional terms of jurisprudence and political theory is a moot point that is perhaps of less practical than abstract interest. The essential point is that there is no adequate and uniform law of the sea to which the multinational corporation can turn for the stimulation and pro-tection of truly transnational ocean ventures. Ocean ventures transcend the sovereign territories of nation-states and reach out in pioneering ways to a part of the world arena that is now rapidly opening up for development. So long as this situation persists and so long as nations delay the codification and enforce-ment of sea law to cover multinational corporate development of the oceans, ingenious enterprisers will devise and perfect plans like these for a corporate sovereign to fill the gap.

Toward A Global Political Economy

Corporate managers are likely to be more immediately responsive to the demands of home and host governments than to the more abstract norms of a world economy. These norms are formulated into no binding law and are enforceable by no global sovereign. It is different at the national level. The demands of "public interest" within a sovereign state, as declared by enforceable law, may be of a debatable content that managers would wish to see changed; but insofar as *national* public interest speaks through law backed by national sanctions and through public opinion that inevitably impinges on the making of corporate policy, no doubt exists in the managerial mind that corporate intent responds to the "public interest." Indeed, it is one of the greatest hazards of transnational business that managers must work in environments of disparate nationalistic conceptions of the public interest—each of which may be justifiable enough as expressions of the public interest within each of the several nations where business is carried on, but where no two or more of these public interest concepts are reducible to universal principles.

The common interest of all nations, the overarching general interest of mankind in a world political economy, is thus left in limbo. Even in the absence of a world government this global public interest is already seeking expression in enforceable law by many nations within whose boundaries the multinational corporation must carry on its business. Home and host governments can and do enforce nationalistic policies that run directly counter to the transnational interests of multinational corporations; and controversy of a bitter ideological tone rages over the universality of norms derived from such transnational corporate interests. A universal or global "public interest" assumes a world political economy with norms that are not parochial, national, regional— or corporate. Exclusive concern for nationalistic and particularistic barriers to transnational business clouds the search for global dimensions of political and economic policy. National governments are as guilty of myopic vision on this matter as corporate managers who neglect the pressures of extra-corporate global demands.

Despite the excessively pluralistic pattern of politics in the contemporary international system, there have been significant unifying demands of great importance to business that crosses international frontiers. At the highest level of human aspiration, these demands derive from the ancient religious and ethical norms, such as the Stoic ideals that were incorporated into Christian ethics. The recent ecological insight into the human condition, linked as it now clearly is with the more general condition of all life on this planet, has plainly exposed as never before the suicidal possibilities of technological progress out of phase with human organization. As mankind moves dangerously along the ecological, as well as nuclear, precipice, however, more and more thought has been devoted at policy making levels to the organizational response to universal demands for humane policies. The responses can be seen, among other things, in renewed efforts to transcend the excessively pluralistic and parochial, in both the economic and the political organization of the world.

Efforts in political organization range all the way from specialized conventions to federal structures. The primary example of federalism is the United States system dating from 1789, following the failure of confederation, under the Articles, to deal with trade wars between the states, but not succeeding with adequate national power to unify a national market until almost 150 years later. The business sytem required a continental market, the abolition of barriers to trade at state lines, uniform legislation in matters of industry and trade, and a free flow of the factors of production within the entire market. The defensive aspects of the federal system were well stated by Hamilton in *The Federalist*: "Let the thirteen states, bound together in a strict and indissoluble union, concur in erecting one great American system, superior to the control of all transatlantic force or influence, and able to dictate the terms of the connection between the old and the new world."

The Swiss federation is an interesting expression of a common interest among the European powers in the neutralization of that piece of territory. Switzerland had proclaimed her own neutrality after Napoleon's defeat; but then allied forces invaded France through Swiss territory. The eight great powers of Europe declared in 1815 that Switzerland was to ·be permanently neutralized in the "general interest" of Europe, and Switzerland acceded to the instrument of declaration, receiving a degree of security from external aggression that did not, however, save her from civil war in 1847 when the seven Roman Catholic cantons tried unsuccessfully to secede. The Swiss general interest was thereafter secured in a federal system.

The European Communities of today do indicate a substantial move toward expression of a European "general interest" that transcends the national public interest of the several nations in these communities. The European Atomic Energy Community (EURATOM), the European Coal and Steel Community, and the European Economic Community (EEC), although still less than federal in structure, do point to the possibility that after centuries of civil warfare within the European continent, there will eventually be an institutionalization of the continental public interest. It remains to be seen whether the price of that larger unity will be high—a new superpower that could impede further advances toward a global political economy.

There is certainly the brighter possibility: that a united Europe will be the necessary step toward the larger community that is envisaged by those who have striven for more than a century, laborious step by laborious step through international conventions, to get functional coordination among sovereign states of the world. Some of these steps have been taken because the inconveniences of noncooperation appeared at last to outweigh the advantages to be gained from such a negative policy. International river communities were among the first instances. The European Danube Commission (1856 and 1865) established an international administration that replaced national administrations. The Universal Postal Union (1874) offered such obvious advantages to members that "even the most narrow-minded guardians of national sovereignty have considered it advisable to surrender the untrammelled postal sovereignty of their countries in order to enjoy the benefits of treating the whole world, for postal purposes, as one single territory." [10] Concern for national health and fear of epidemics, which respect no political frontiers, have also brought unity of effort through international conventions that require functional surrender of sovereignty. However, the transformation of this disunited "system" into an interna-

10. Georg Schwarzenberger, *Power Politics: A Study of World Society* (New York: Praeger, 1964), p. 228.

162

tional community has not occurred, and will not occur, by means of a limited number and scale of functional agreements among the powers.

Yet the moves toward a world political economy have not been insubstantial; and for the multinational corporation these moves pose a dilemma: is it better to seek the safe havens of sovereign states—with suitable strategies vis-à-vis home and host governments—in pursuit of profit, or should this be only a defensive strategem pending an eventual institutionalization of the emergent world economy on a sound basis? The work toward such an international community geared to productive enterprise will not be subversive of the current international system, but it will directly oppose the economic nationalism which has barred progress toward freedom of world trade. Giant forces contend for supremacy in the struggle between economic nationalism and the kind of world political economy that multinational corporate enterprise requires. The experience of nations during the two World Wars shows these contending forces at work.

During the First World War, the Allied and Associated Powers were able to pool their economic resources—partly through wartime state control of economic activities within each nation, and partly through coordination at the inter-Allied level. While the war was on, there was even inter-Allied discussion of postwar economic reconstruction, but what planning there was reflected little vision of a world of trade liberated from nationalism. It reflected instead the fear that the Central Powers, in the case of a German victory, would dominate production and the markets of the world. This defensive position led after the war to economic nationalism, protectionism and discrimination, an allied answer that was inconsistent with the third of President Woodrow Wilson's Fourteen Points, namely, that all economic barriers to trade be removed "so far as possible," and that there be established "an equality of trade conditions among all the nations consenting to peace and associating themselves for its maintenance." The qualifying clause, "so far as possible," was a loophole for the United States as well as other Allied powers. The League Covenant (Article 23 e) provided for freedom of communications and of transit, and equitable treatment for the commerce of all members of the League but only "subject to and in accordance

with the provisions of international conventions existing or here-
after to be agreed upon." Even the wording of these texts indicates less than a determined effort to proceed to peace with the
same kind of international economic coordination that helped to
win the war.

Between the two World Wars, tariff and non-tariff barriers
multiplied during the depression of the 1930's. Protective trade
barriers developed into a maze of nationalistic laws: high tariff
protection, quota restrictions on imports, and exchange controls,
to name but the most notorious. These trade barriers threatened
to halt any possible development of a global economy, as they
seemed, in country after country, to become permanently fastened on the world. During the Second World War, however, two
things happened that might eventually lead to the dismantling
and outlawing of these nationalistic barriers while preserving the
essentials of the international system.

The first of these wartime and postwar moves had to do again
with inter-Allied efforts to win the war. A number of joint boards
for economic warfare were effective, but of greatest importance
was lend-lease. The lend-lease principle of a common "arsenal of
democracy" was established. Lend-lease meant the allocation of
common resources for allied strategy; material aid in the form of
airplanes, munitions, tools, food, and other commodities was
granted—not sold outright—to foreign countries whose defense
was deemed vital to the United States. The bilateral lend-lease
agreements specified that the terms and conditions of the benefits provided by the United States "shall be such as not to burden
commerce between the two countries, but to promote mutually
advantageous economic relations between them and the betterment of world-wide economic relations." The terms were to
"include provision for agreed action" between the two countries
"open to participation by all other countries of like mind," and
certain specified purposes:

> the expansion, by appropriate international and
> domestic measures, of production, employment,
> and the exchange and consumption of goods,
> "which are the material foundations of the liberty
> and welfare of all peoples";

the elimination of all forms of discriminatory treatment in international commerce;

the reduction of tariffs and other trade barriers.

In addition to these essentially wartime joint efforts, which to some extent transcended the old nationalistic and particularistic patterns, there were also remarkably fruitful joint efforts toward postwar economic cooperation: the Interim Commission for the Establishment of a Food and Agriculture Organization (FAO, 1943), now in the United Nations, the International Monetary Fund or IMF (1944), the International Bank for Reconstruction and Development or the World Bank (1944), and the International Civil Aviation Organization (1944), to name but a few. The Atlantic Charter, the lend-lease agreements, and these other substantial steps toward a world trading system were new; they had no parallel in and after the First World War. There was now clearly an effort toward establishing a postwar global economy based on nondiscrimination and a higher standard of living everywhere, through a full, fair, and free exchange of goods and services.

The Dumbarton Oaks proposals (1944), for example, followed by the San Francisco Conference of 1945, laid far more stress than had been the case during the First World War on the importance of international social and economic cooperation. The United Nations Charter reflects this, especially in the preamble statement that "higher standards of living, full employment, and conditions of economic and social progress" were to be among the objectives of United Nations. An Economic and Social Council (ECOSOC) was to rank as a "principal organ" of the United Nations; its main function was to coordinate the activities of the Specialized Agencies, which have wide international responsibilities in economic, social, cultural, educational, health, and related fields.

This wartime planning for a postwar and world-wide political economy is impressive in retrospect. It went very far beyond the experience of the First World War. Yet it must be seen now that the immense task facing statesmen at the time was beyond them; they were unable to complete a structure of functional internationalism—if, indeed, the term is allowable, if it is not self-denying in its nationalistic implications—in the postwar period for reasons that are clear enough now. Dean Acheson writes [11] informatively of political leaders' misconceptions of the world around them, both in anticipating postwar conditions and, then, in recognizing what they actually were when they came face to face with them. That was true of the degree of physical destruction, damage, and loss caused by the war; it was true as well of vast social dislocations that were undermining the continuance of great states and empires. Only slowly "did it dawn upon us that the whole world structure and order that we had inherited from the nineteenth century was gone and that the struggle to replace it would be directed from two bitterly opposed and ideologically irreconcilable power centers" in Washington and Moscow. Slowly they began to comprehend "the immensity of the task and the strength of the four horsemen—human fecundity, human ignorance, human pugnacity, and human stubbornness." [12]

Evidence of the failure to meet the exacting standards of world-oriented functional action, that we can all too easily supply in retrospect, can be seen in the history of Bretton Woods in 1944. At that conference, which achieved so much in launching the IMF and the World Bank, a crucial third agency, the International Trade Organization (ITO) never got off the ground. The purpose of the third agency was to expand world trade and employment, and to attack in particular the nationalistic tariff and quota barriers to trade. The vast powers of production in the world were to be brought into full play by an agreement on the principles of exchange and distribution which would permit trade, production, employment, and consumption all to expand together.

Not until November 1947 was an International Conference on Trade and Employment convened at Havana, under the sponsorship of the United Nations, to draft a charter for the projected ITO. The Havana Charter for ITO was completed in March 1948. The United States Congress refused to accept the Charter. The ITO never came into being. But, meanwhile, the governments which had formed the preparatory commission for the Havana Conference had agreed to sponsor negotiations aimed at lowering

11. Dean Acheson, *Present at the Creation* (New York: W. W. Norton, 1969).

12. *Ibid.*, pp. 725-729.

customs tariffs and reducing other trade restrictions among themselves, without waiting for the ITO to emerge.

The first tariff negotiating conference was held at Geneva in 1947, side by side with work of the committee that was preparing the ITO Charter. Tariff concessions resulting from these negotiations were written into a multilateral treaty called the General Agreement on Tariffs and Trade, or, more popularly, the GATT.

The General Agreement on Tariffs and Trade

The General Agreement, which was signed at Geneva on October 30, 1947, was originally accepted by twenty-three countries, and came into force on January 1, 1948; but it soon became evident that no acceptances of the ITO Charter—the Havana Charter—could be expected until the position of the United States towards the establishment of the ITO was made clear. With the indication in December, 1950 that the Charter would not be submitted again to the Congress, the attempt to establish the International Trade Organization was abandoned.

The GATT was originally intended as a stopgap arrangement pending the entry into force of the Havana Charter and the creation of the International Trade Organization, which would have been a Specialized Agency of the United Nations. But, as events have worked out, the GATT has stood alone since 1948 as the only international instrument which lays down rules of conduct for trade. These rules have been accepted by a high proportion of the leading trading nations.

As of June, 1970, eighty-seven countries had acceded to the GATT including seventy-seven "contracting parties," one which had acceded provisionally (Tunis), and nine countries to whose territories the GATT had been applied and were, as independent states, maintaining a de facto application of the GATT pending final decisions as to their future commercial policy. These nine were Algeria, Botswana, Cambodia, the Democratic Republic of the Congo, Lesotho, the Maldives, Mali, Singapore, and Gambia. In one way or another a large majority of the sovereign states of the international system are presumed to apply the GATT in their trading relations.

The GATT is thus a multilateral trade treaty between governments embodying reciprocal rights and obligations; it is not the formal organization that the ITO might have been. But in the agreement the term "Contracting Parties" (in capital letters) stands for the governments, which have fully acceded to the GATT, acting collectively. There is an administrative staff, or secretariat, headed by a Director-General, located in the Palais des Nations at Geneva. A Council of Representatives was established to undertake urgent, as well as routine, work between the usually annual sessions of the Contracting Parties. The Council meets five or six times a year but is not convened at regular intervals.

Four major principles are contained in the GATT.[13] These principles, not always lived up to by all the contracting parties, involve specific prohibitions against the restrictive pall which has settled over large parts of international trade and which could delay the emergence of a world-wide political economy, or even smother it, if trade is not opened up.

The first principle is that trade should be conducted on the basis of nondiscrimination. In particular, all contracting parties are bound by the most-favored-nation clause in the application and administration of import and export duties and charges.

The second general principle is that protection shall be afforded to domestic industries exclusively through the customs tariff and not through other commercial measures. Thus, the use of import quotas as a means of protection is prohibited. Import quotas may be used for certain other purposes—notably to redress a country's balance of payments—but the circumstances in which they may be used are very carefully defined, and there are elaborate procedures for consultations so as to ensure that quotas comply with conditions laid down and minimize any damage to the trade of other countries.

The third principle, inherent throughout the Agreement, is the concept of consultation aimed at avoiding damage to the trading interests of contracting parties.

Finally, the GATT provides a framework within which negotiations can be held for the reduction of tariffs and other barriers

13. The text of the General Agreement is published in *Basic Instruments and Selected Documents*, Volume IV: "Text of the General Agreement 1969" (Geneva, March 1969), available as Department of State Publication No. 8468 (Washington, D.C.: U.S. Government Printing Office, 1969).

to trade and a structure for embodying the results of such negotiations in a legal instrument. Thus, the importance of this code can be measured by the fact that it binds countries whose foreign trade represents 80 per cent of the total volume of world trade and whose interests are as diverse as their geographical location.

Fundamental in the entire plan of the GATT is the notion that maximum production and trade are possible only when trade is reasonably free to flow without discrimination to the best market wherever that may be, without running into tariff or non-tariff barriers and without the uneconomic channeling inherent in some bilateral arrangements. Multilateral tariff bargaining, as devised in 1947 and employed at subsequent conferences held under the GATT up to 1964, was a new development in cooperation between governments. The technique called for the holding of simultaneous bilateral negotiations between pairs of countries and the generalization of the resulting concessions among all the partners. A novel feature was the fact that governments, in determining the concessions they were prepared to offer, were able to take into account the *indirect* benefits they might expect to gain as a result of *all* the liberal pairs of negotiations.

While the GATT did not dispose of the preferences of one nation over another existing at the time, it did provide that these were not to be increased; and it further provided that countries could undertake negotiations to eliminate such preferences. The elimination of quantitative restrictions on trade—the fixing of quotas or amounts of specific commodities that may be exported or imported during a certain period—was an objective of the GATT as it was conceived in the Havana Charter.

The allowance of exceptions to the ban on non-tariff barriers, both in the Havana Charter and in the GATT, indicates that some countries were unwilling to be deprived of this restrictive method; they have continued to be unwilling, and there was by 1970 a strong trend away from the nonrestrictive principle. Balance of payments difficulties have been a primary cause. The GATT provides that quotas may be applied by a country "to the extent necessary (i) to forestall the imminent threat of, or to stop, a serious decline in monetary reserves, or (ii) in the case of a contracting party with very low monetary reserves, to achieve a reasonable rate of increase in its reserves." Consultation with the

International Monetary Fund is required if advantage is taken of these provisions; when the Fund determines that a country no longer needs to use the restrictions to protect its monetary reserves, right to resort to the exceptional clause is lost, and also the right to discriminate.

When the GATT was launched, the foreign economic policy of the United States—the leading power in the non-Communist world of multinational corporate action—was based on the fundamental premise that certain goals were sought: first, the maintenance of free and democratic institutions throughout the world through extensive support of free governments by economic as well as other means; second, the promotion of economic growth and rising standards of living abroad as well as at home, and especially in the less developed countries; third, the prevention of economic instability and disturbances that could lead to depression and unemployment abroad as well as at home; and, finally, the development of a high degree of cooperation among nations in a common effort to solve common problems. [14]

Subsidiary objectives of United States foreign economic policy included strengthening of the nation's balance-of-payments position: without a strong position, the United States would not be able to carry out its programs of foreign trade and of trade liberalization, nor could it develop the desired close relationships with nations of the Atlantic Community.

As the United States moved toward the end of the sixties, however, the global situation changed in many ways, occasioning a reassessment in Washington of the conditions and even the ends, of the global political economy and the implications for foreign policy. And, the impact of these changes on the structure, policies and strategies of multinational corporations could turn out to be extensive and profound. Much would depend upon general trends in the world economy, and, of course, the state of the economy in the United States, which accounted for almost half the world's output in its gross national product.

The combined trade balance of the world's industrial nations deteriorated in 1968 and 1969, and there was a sharp reduction in United States trade surplus in 1968, followed by further dete-

14. John Parke Young, *The International Economy*, Fourth ed. (New York: Ronald, 1963), pp. 313 and 497.

rioration in 1969. This occurred after the longest boom ever recorded in the United States; and shorter booms in Western Europe, Japan, and Canada had led to stiff further increases in output, employment, and incomes in 1969. The conditions of generally healthy trade expansion might have been expected to lead to a widespread relaxation of commercial policies; but this did not happen in many of the major countries.

Some of the causal factors are debatable, but others are clear. Overseas official spending, deficits in overall payments accounts, the war in Southeast Asia, a "game plan" in the United States that called for a flattening of economic growth, a disciplined fiscal and monetary policy, together with the expectation that without too much unemployment a GNP deflator of less than 3 per cent could be achieved by the end of 1971—these and other factors must be considered.

Whatever the cause, serious imbalances began in 1970 to be manifest: domestically, in strong price-cost pressures and, internationally, both in severe disturbances in the balance of payments of several of the major nations and in recurrent crises in the foreign exchange markets. A period of nationalistic restrictiveness threatened to intervene in what could be in the long run a more open world political economy. Standing, as we do, so close to the retrogressive trend it is impossible to say whether they are to be persistent and long-lasting.

Implications for Multinational Corporations

If the retrogressive trend deepens, and there develops a closed world of tightly insulated, nationalistic compartments, the multinational corporation will adapt as best it can to this highly unfavorable pluralism of ingrown political economies. If the retrogressive trend soon gives way to the more general movement toward a global political economy, the multinational corporation will respond to new opportunities for enterprise on a vast scale.

In either case, the structure of the multinational corporation will be a function of the structure of the political economy not only of the non-Communist world but also of the new international system together with all that this implies for trade. The multinational corporation may learn to live with and prosper in some parts of *both* the Communist and the non-Communist sectors of the globe.

The multinational corporation, in doing this, could turn out to be one of the more effective bonds that can tie together vital elements of the human race in the forthcoming ecological crisis of human fecundity versus economic productivity. At the political surface of inter-sovereign action, no such bonds may be acceptable, but at the level of enterprise they may be; indeed, these bonds may be grasped as the last hope for the requisite unified action by Man the Producer to save goods and services for Man. There may come the time when the great decisions of the day will be made neither by "parliaments and resolutions" nor by "blood and iron," but by those who can organize the world for life-sustaining production.

Projections of Multinational Corporate Structure

The best of the futurists reject the claims of macro-historians of the Spenglerian type that there are valid comprehensive theories and "explanations" of long-term trends, and that from these trends can surely be extrapolated the basis for policy in corporate entities. [15] Yet corporate policy makers need developmental constructs or models that will, as accurately as possible, locate the relevant local, regional, and global settings in which corporate action will be planned and carried out.

These projections will be of various kinds. Some will be of a sequential nature, specifying the chronological steps involved in corporate action in various arenas. The possible sequence of significant past, current, and future changes is an aid in viewing the future with impartiality and without dogmatic and doctrinaire blinders. Other projections will identify the relevant participants in the arenas of corporate action, both within the multinational corporate organization itself and in the total political-economic environment. Still other projections will relate participants in the world arena of corporate action to types of corporate organization and to steps in decision processes.

The postindustrial (or "post-mass-consumption") society in

15. See Herman Kahn and Anthony J. Wiener, *The Year 2000: A Framework for Speculation on the Next Thirty-Three Years* (New York: Macmillan, 1967), p. 27.

affluent parts of the world in one Bell-Kahn-Wiener projection [16] lists among possible developments a diminished role for the market as compared to the public sector and "social accounts"; the decline of business firms as the major sources of innovation; the reduction of most "economic activities" to a tertiary and quarternary (service-oriented) status as against their previously primary or secondary (production-oriented) status; widespread "cybernation"; the erosion of work-oriented, achievement-oriented, and advancement-oriented values in the middle class; a per capita income about fifty times the preindustrial; and the emergence of new dominant values—secular, sensate, humanist, perhaps self-indulgent. If one were to stop there and to try to project the future structure and functions of the multinational corporation given that context, the projection would look very different from one that took account of another table of possibilities: some possible causes of changes in the old nations that these authors designate as far from "surprise-free."

These possible causes, leading to very different projections for nations and corporations, include: invasion and war; civil strife and revolution; natural disaster; famine and pestilence; persecution and despotism; depression or economic stagnation; the development of doomsday or near-doomsday machines that are not very costly (adumbrating the MIRV's); the resurgence of communism or the revival of fascism; a racial, North-South, rich-poor, East-West, or other disruptive polarization of the world; an economically dynamic China; a politically dynamic United States, Soviet Union, Japan, West Germany, Brazil and other powers; new religious philosophies or other world-wide organizations; possible regional or other multinational organizations (their reference here was evidently not to multinational corporations); and the "psychologically upsetting impact of new techniques, ideas, philosophies, and the like." [17]

Then the Kahn-Wiener projection goes on to list the characteristics of a relatively "surprise-free" early twenty-first century: the rise of new great powers—perhaps Japan, China, a European complex, Brazil, Mexico, or India; new political and perhaps even

16. *Ibid.*, Table IX at p. 25.

17. *Ibid.*, Table VIII at p. 24.

"philosophical" issues; a levelling off or diminishing of some aspects of the basic, long-term, multifold trend, such as urbanization; the realization of the postindustrial and industrial worlds; probably no world government, but possibly success with population control, arms control, and relatively stable international security arrangements; but the presence of disruptive, irrational and ideological movements in certain of the world's industrializing areas; and yet, in the United States and in Western Europe "either a return to certain Hellenic or older European concepts of the good life, or an intensified alienation and search for identity, values, meaning, and purpose." This search would be made necessary and facilitated by an affluence and permissiveness without precedent in the postindustrial economy.

These projections were not predictions; they were part of a provocative study, intended as a context for speculations about large-scale, long-term changes. As such, they are apposite to our search for the future arena of multinational corporate action; but we cannot lean on them—any more than the authors did—as reliable guides to public and corporate policy without more investigation. There must be more research in depth; some of this research is pursued in the work cited, although none with specific reference to the multinational corporation, a term not to be found in the authors' index. Especially relevant are their discussions of: world-wide industrialization and modernization; the hundred technical innovations which are very likely in the last third of the twentieth century; the second wave of industrial revolutions; the ten "far-out possibilities" (including electric power availability at less than .03 mill per killowatt hour); comments on science and technology (including the "biological manipulation of man"); international politics in "the standard world" and in some "canonical variations" of this standard world (including more integrated and more inward-looking worlds, and projected worlds in great disarray); and of some "twenty-first century nightmares" (including nuclear war scenarios, business cycle worlds in economic stagnation and deep depression, new mass or elitist movements, social controls for the imposed order of a garrison state, and intense international anarchy.)

The speculations of these and other futurists are necessary grist for the mill of the multinational corporate manager of the future, who will make his sober way among the nightmares with respectful attention to all hypotheses that may bear upon long-range corporate planning.

The Structure of Decision

Hypotheses about the future of the multinational corporation, and about its present meaning, organization and decision processes, must rest not only on rigorous logic and quantified data but also on much that might be rejected by purists as impressionistic and non-quantifiable information and even prejudice. It would be unwise to reject such materials out of hand. Decisions on corporate as well as on public policy often rest on other than strictly rational grounds.

It is well known that reliance solely on the assumption of rational decision making can be grossly misleading in projecting corporate behavior, as distinguished from the projecting of individual behavior, in the economizing process of pure market theory. If one assumes, for example, that the price system is the sole means by which the individual man economizes, then all other means are ruled out in the market model; for purposes of hypothesis-building, it is admissible to assume that all men can calculate quantitatively and come to a decision about maximizing selected values, but it is dangerous, for policy purposes, to make the further assumption that all men fit this model of action. And it is to a high degree dangerous to assume that corporate decisions are made in accordance with this model. If the "self-interest role" is difficult to sustain realistically with respect to individuals acting in a market in which the price system alone controls decision-making, [18] it is even more difficult to square with the facts of corporate business life.

The managers of large firms cannot and do not act strictly in accordance with behavioral theory that rests exclusively upon an assumption of narrow self-interest defined in terms of a price system that operates largely through money rewards and penalties. Nor is that only because they are under pressure at times to act the part of "business statesmen" pursuing the interest of a larger moral code, say, some national or global "public good" or

18. Robert A. Dahl and Charles E. Lindblom, *Politics, Economics, and Welfare* (New York: Harper & Bros., 1953), pp. 225*ff.*

some religious conception of right action. It is doubtless true that indoctrinated concern for values of this kind does influence the decisions of managers. But far more important is the fact that, as governors of large organizations, managers are subject to valid pressures from all of the contributor-claimants in the corporate constellation of interests—stockholders, creditors, suppliers, employees of lesser rank (for they are themselves employees), consumers, and so on, not forgetting that governments may be among these contributor-claimants, too. There is the further important fact that corporate managers, like others in similar private governments and bureaucracies, have to carry out several, often conflicting, roles. One role is that of maximizer of profits and minimizer of losses for the corporation as though these were identical with personal gains and losses. As salaried managers, however, they are in a very different position from that of profit taking owner-operators; their personal rewards and deprivations do not depend directly upon the profits and losses of the enterprise. The profit and loss cues from the market for managerial decision compete with many internal and external cues of quite another kind. Some of these cues arrive from political sources that may invite—or deter—the disposition to gamble on opportunities that cannot be reduced to precise calculation. Others arrive from within the bureaucracy, and affect salary, promotions, and status in many forms, not excluding fraternal acceptance or rejection by other members of the team. Perhaps most important of all, in role influence on managerial decision, is the necessity one is under at critical times to resist deliberately some rational calculations in favor of the bold action that is expected of the man at the top. This is not to say that irrationality is a virtue in corporate decision-making—as in politics—but that it is sometimes not only an unavoidable but strategic necessity.

In the multinational corporation, it has been said that "profit maximization is a distant shimmering Nirvana, not a basic operational behavioral model,"[19] and that the foreign investment decision process, upon close inspection of actual cases, turns out to be something very different from that which is presented in widely accepted models. Thus, Aharoni rejects a number of clas-

19. Yair Aharoni, *The Foreign Investment Decision Process* (Boston: Harvard Business School, 1966), p. 259.

sical theories of the managerial firm in favor of revised positions. Among the revisionist positions he cites are Baumol's view that the managerial firm maximizes sales subject to the profit constraint; Rothschild's view that the entrepreneur's primary motive is long-term survival; Williamson's economics of discretionary behavior in which the management of a firm insulated from competition has "expense preference," especially in the systematic accumulation of staff and emoluments; and Becker's account that deals with management discretion as to discrimination and nepotism in the marketplace. [20]

In Aharoni's study of the foreign investment decision process—which is of primary concern to us because of direct cross-border investment that is essential to multinational corporate action in the world arena—considerable attention was given to the trend toward the abandonment of the traditional maximization assumption and the adoption instead of the concept of "satisficing." [21] In "satisficing"—not satisfying—decision-makers are willing to sacrifice some of the rewards of a maximization solution of an economic problem in order to reduce the pains that they are likely to incur in trying to find such a solution.

The idea of satisficing occurs, for example, in Herbert Simon's "bounded rationality." He states that the capacity of the human mind for formulating and solving complex problems is very small compared with the size of the problems whose solution is required for objectively rational behavior in the real world—"or even for a reasonable approximation to such objective rationality." [22] The goal of satisficing replaces the goal of maximizing, the result being a course of action that will yield results that are "good enough" in the circumstances.

20. Wm. J. Baumol, *Business Behavior, Value, and Growth* (New York: Macmillan, 1959); K. W. Rothschild, "Price Theory and Oligopoly," *Economic Journal*, Vol. 57, No. 227, September 1947, pp. 299-320; Oliver E. Williamson, *The Economics of Discretionary Behavior: Managerial Objectives in a Theory of the Firm* (Englewood Cliffs, N.J.: Prentice-Hall, 1964); Gary S. Becker, *The Economics of Discrimination* (Chicago: University of Chicago Press, 1957).

21. Introduced by Herbert A. Simon in his *Administrative Behavior*. See the second edition (New York: Macmillan, 1957), p. xxiv. Cf. Russel L. Ackoff, *A Concept of Corporate Planning* (New York: Wiley Interscience, 1970) for the additional concepts of optimizing and "adaptivizing."

22. Herbert A. Simon, *Models of Men* (New York: Wiley, 1957), p. 198.

The "economic man" of classical economic theory would never be satisfied with satisficing; he would instead fearlessly face the task of an exhaustive exploration of *all* possible alternatives and carry out to the last detail all of the rational implications of each alternative. Simon's "social man" is more realistic. He does not even know what all the alternatives are; his approach is to formulate the problem as best he can under the circumstances and then look for a satisficing solution among the most likely alternatives. The search may stop right there without going on to an elaborately rational consideration of other alternatives.

The implication of this for an organization such as the multinational corporation is that the real "administrative man" of organized business faces severe limits in applying strict rationality in decision-making, and the structure of decision in the organization should reflect the fact of satisficing. The implication for the multinational corporation, specifically, is that patterns of authority—such as centralization versus devolution—must reflect this insight. The corporate manager—at headquarters as well as in subsidiaries abroad—must be expected to do no more than to construct a model of the real situation in order to deal with it; it will not be realistic to assume that he will deal with the real world in all its complexity and with a full knowledge of *all* the alternatives. The multinational corporate manager behaves rationally only with respect to his own model, a model that is constructed on the basis of his own limited knowledge. While his model does depend upon the way he perceives, learns and thinks, there are inputs from the organization itself that may be more or less adequate, depending upon its intelligence operations and communication system.

The importance of an adequate intelligence input in the multinational corporation appears especially when key elements of risk depend on the cross-border character of the business, and on the difficulties that arise when decisions are to be made not by an individual but by a group of persons. If it is true that rational behavior is central to administration and that "the major normative problem of a theory of organization is to find ways for increasing the rationality of behavior within organization,"[23] then the problem in the multinational corporation is especially

23. Donald W. Taylor, "Decision Making and Problem Solving" in *Handbook of Organizations*, edited by James G. March (Chicago: Rand McNally, 1965), p. 63.

challenging. The need to know more than the goals of an adaptive organism, such as the multinational corporation, and to go on to an understanding of its internal structure and adaptive mechanisms in order to predict short-run behavior, has been emphasized by students of administrative behavior. [24] The principle can be turned around: in the multinational corporation, one expects to find in successful examples an adaptive mechanism organized as a "coalition" [25] of the managers, the workers, the stockholders, the suppliers, the customers, the lawyers, the tax collectors, the regulatory agencies, and all the rest, [26] that can operate as a goal-achieving organism.

This idea of a "coalition" as a model for the multinational corporation has been criticized by Aharoni on the ground that it avoids explicit recognition of the environment, that it excludes social processes and commitments. [27] It is argued that decision can be better explained as a social process in which circumstances may "keep the final decision-maker from understanding the nature of the commitment he is making," or, alternatively, as a "process of the accretion of commitments and not as a highly intellectual, highly deliberate process." [28] Aharoni looks for "a basic framework that provides an effective way for explaining and predicting business organizations' behavior under uncertainty." Uncertainty, information, and commitment belong, in his opinion, in any realistic investment theory, and by inference to other kinds of decisions as well. The coalition model, revised in the light of Aharoni's critique, would recognize the environment explicitly for decisions on an entire range of internal and external corporate relationships. [29]

24. H. A. Simon, *Administrative Behavior*, 2nd ed., p. 221.

25. James G. March, "The Business Firm as a Political Coalition," *Journal of Politics*, Vol. 24, 1962, pp. 662-678.

26. R. M. Cyert and James G. March, *A Behavioral Theory of the Firm* (Prentice-Hall, 1963), p. 63.

27. Aharoni, *op. cit.*, p. 272.

28. *Loc. cit.*

29. Described in Aharoni, *op. cit.*, Ch. 11. He agrees with the Cyert and March four relational concepts of quasi-resolution of conflict: uncertainty, avoidance, problemistic search, and organizational learning, and also with their argument that latent conflict of goals exists and the further position that goals are an independent restraint to action. But in addition to their solutions—acceptable-level decision rules and sequential attention to goals—he draws attention to the "dynamic bargaining process" and leadership influence as two additional variables in permitting the organization to settle conflicts.

As multinational corporations adapt their organizational structure to the pluralistic structure of the political economies of the world, they not only exhibit a high degree of realism, but they also—often unconsciously—make their own contribution toward a *restructuring* of that arena. This unending search for adaptive corporate structures may prove to be far more responsive to the basic needs of mankind than are the political structures that hang on with the weight of tradition.

A general treatment of organizational structure as a kind of business strategy was undertaken in the pioneering work of Alfred Chandler,[30] who began his study with the idea that one could find new truths for business history by examining the way in which *different* enterprises have carried out the *same* activity—such as manufacturing, marketing, procurement of supplies, finance, or administration—as distinguished from examining the way a *single* firm carried on *all* of these activities.

This comparative method was pursued by Chandler in detail with respect to four companies: Du Pont, General Motors, Standard Oil Company (New Jersey), and Sears, Roebuck and Co., and in less detailed analysis in many others. Administration, in his conception, included executive action and orders as well as the decisions taken in coordinating, appraising, and planning the work of enterprise and in allocating its resources. He concluded that "different organizational forms result from different types of growth" and that this thesis would be stated more precisely "if planning and carrying out of such growth is considered a *strategy*" and "the organization devised to administer these enlarged activities and resources" is considered as a *structure*.[31] Structure follows strategy, and several basic strategies combine to form the more complex types of structure.

Strategies, in this sense, included for Chandler such things as expansion of the volume of business, leading to the creation of an administrative office to handle one function in one local area; growth through geographical dispersion, leading to the need for a departmental structure and headquarters to administer several

30. Alfred D. Chandler, Jr., *Strategy and Structure: Chapters in the History of American Industrial Enterprise* (Garden City, N.Y.: Doubleday, Anchor Books, 1966). First published by the M.I.T. Press in 1962.

31. *Ibid.*, pp. 15-16.

field units; and the move into new functions through strategies of vertical integration and diversification. Although new strategies, resulting in part from innovative decisions, create new administrative needs, he found that executives often clung inefficiently to old structures.

The new administrative needs grew from new strategies, which, in turn, were responses to opportunities arising from population changes, a rise in national income and from technological innovation. Sometimes executives were aware enough of these opportunities, but, because of undue concentration on everyday tactical matters, they neglected to respond with structure to fit new strategy. The difference lay in the outlook of the executives: their past training and education, their awareness of the total and changing environment, their positions in the firm—all were relevant factors. Ability to *institutionalize* strategies was also a very significant factor, once awareness of opportunities and the need to innovate structure were present.

This *institutionalizing* competence, whether in business or in other sectors of human activity, is a rare and precious quality. It is more urgently needed in transitional decades, when old epochs die as the new are born. In churches, universities, corporations, labor unions, and the public governments of the world arena it is everywhere the same—the old structures too often stand in the way of new strategies responsive to new needs. The study of Ford's expansion into a vast transnational business, by Wilkins and Hill,[32] is an outstanding example of both the potentialities and the limitations of contemporary work in this field. Their study does not place Ford in the world arena, but it is the first full-length history of the activities of an American company which early became a multinational enterprise. From a mere exporter of cars, the Ford Motor Company soon became the founder of large concerns abroad that imported and assembled the American output; then, the converter of these concerns into factories turning out complete cars, trucks, and tractors on the American model; and, finally, the owner of larger plants that made and sold vehicles of completely foreign design—often for export to the United States.

32. Mira Wilkins and Frank Ernest Hill, *American Business Abroad* (Detroit: Wayne State University Press, 1964).

The Wilkins-Hill study tells of the obstacles to the strategies that produced this large structure: alien prejudice and condescension; waves of nationalism expressed in tariff walls; unfair taxes; quota restrictions; governmental decrees; special requirements due to geography, climate, and unpredictable variations in taste, and all the vicissitudes of hot war and cold war. The study shows how Ford's experience overseas reflected a wide range of national demands, and how the company responded over decades to a long series of world changes.

The next fifty years of multinational corporate strategy and structure will similarly reflect new demands and world changes. The study of Ford shows vividly how the foreign trade of the United States stood in sharp contrast with her foreign policy after the First World War. Politically opposed to "foreign entanglements," Americans as investors and traders, nevertheless, welcomed expanding trade possibilities. Before the war, the United States had been an international debtor. After the war, it suddenly became the world's greatest creditor nation.

In 1920, American exports rose to $8 billion, an all-time high not again to be reached for more than twenty years, in 1943. American overseas investments mounted. Among the firms that enlarged their facilities abroad were Standard Oil, Eastman Kodak, United States Shoe Machinery, International Business Machines, and the Ford Motor Company. During 1919 Ford's foreign and domestic sales rose to more than a million units, a feat never before achieved by any motorcar manufacturer. [33]

Ford, however, was not the first American multinational corporation, as Mira Wilkins has shown in her more recent historical study of this institution. [34] But before the First World War, foreign business was peripheral to domestic investment with a few exceptions such as Standard Oil (N.J.), Singer, International Harvester, and New York Life. Direct foreign investment by American firms had already become substantial by 1914, and not just for the extractive industries and utilities. By 1914, American direct foreign investment, as a percentage of GNP, was as big as it was to be in 1966; and the process had started as early

33. *Ibid.*, p. 89.

34. Mira Wilkins, *The Emergence of Multinational Enterprise: American Business Abroad from the Colonial Era to 1914* (Cambridge: Harvard University Press, 1970).

as the colonial period. The Wilkins study shows how structure and strategy varied to cope with host-country governmental attitudes and actions.

The adaptive organizational structure of multinational corporations has been described by some observers as increasingly involved with national governments as well as with supranational agencies. This involvement has developed in three ways. First, there has been the growing influence of legislation to prevent companies from getting too much power in any particular national economy. Second, there has been the converse situation in which some national governments have built up multinational corporations on their territories through state sponsorship of research and state-assisted mergers. Finally, there has been the operation abroad of state-owned enterprises such as airlines, the Soviet bank, British Petroleum, and British Steel Corporation. At the level of supranational organizations, the involvement is only germinal but might eventually lead to the establishment by the United Nations and by regional communities of facilities for registering and incorporating companies.[35] Thus, some sort of involvement with national or supranational governments may be the general rule for many large multinational corporations for a long time to come.

35. Michael Z. Brooke and H. Lee Remmers, *The Strategy of Multinational Enterprise* (London: Longmans Group Ltd., 1970), p. 296.

Chapter VII

CORPORATE STRATEGIES AT THE HIGHEST LEVEL

Policy has been defined as "strategic moves that direct an organization's critical resources toward perceived opportunities in a changing environment."[1] As applied to the multinational corporation, this refers to strategic moves, made in general at the highest level within a corporate group, which direct the group's critical resources toward opportunities that corporate policy-makers perceive in the changing environment of the world arena —opportunities to pursue the chosen goals of the group most effectively.

We shall examine multinational corporate strategy in this sense, noting in particular *the several types of strategic moves* open to corporate policy makers in a global arena in which there are many kinds of protagonists. The chief protagonists in that arena are, of course, sovereign states. The strategic moves at the top level of national policy-making direct the critical resources of sovereign states toward opportunities that political, military, and other leaders perceive as relevant to national goals. As we shall see, there are significant parallels between the types of strategic moves made by sovereign protagonists and those made by multinational corporations. But more than this, we shall see that there are significant interrelationships between national and corporate strategic moves.

Conceptions of Strategy

The widespread contemporary use of the word "strategy" in describing all kinds of competitive situations, indicates that this is too pregnant and power-laden a word to be left exclusively to the military. We speak of strategy in game theory and in com-

1. Raymond A. Bauer and Kenneth J. Gergen (eds.), *The Study of Policy Formation* (New York: The Free Press, 1968), p. 2.

merce. And as Cervantes reminds us, "Love and War [being] the same thing . . . stratagems and policy are as allowable in the one as in the other." Yet it is true that only in very recent times has there been any extensive literature[2] on the nature of strategy which "concerns the elusive nature of the thread of opposition and conflict that runs through the various relationships of men, from the striking of a bargain to the dread clash of war."[3] The military reference is important because the corporate protagonist in the world arena has always to consider at least indirect reliance on the use of force as a critical resource.

Strategia, in the Greek, referred to generalship as the science and art of military command exercised to meet the enemy in combat under advantageous conditions. Much later, Mahan regarded contact in battle between adversaries as the distinctive element in tactics, while those who had to plan the basic dispositions of strength in a campaign or war faced strategic problems. Sir Edward Hamley wrote that "the theatre of war is the province of strategy, the field of battle is the province of tactics." Tactics, then, as a more limited form of action, refers to the science and art of disposing and maneuvering troops, ships, or airplanes in action or in the presence of the enemy, so as to use in action the resulting dispositions. As the range and capabilities of weapons, and entire weapons systems, have mounted spectacularly, the line of demarcation between tactics and strategy becomes less certain as a matter of military doctrine—and indeed as a matter of high policy in governments.

The "critical" engagement in the nuclear missile age could last but a few minutes; and the locus of engagement might have no geographic site, such as the traditional theatre of war, but rather a space-oriented trajectory for counterforce (indeed, e.g., of counter-city) directed MIRV's with first-strike capability. One "tactical" move of this kind by an officer in a lower echelon could determine the outcome of the war. The definition of strat-

2. See Edward Mead Earle (ed.), *Makers of Modern Strategy: Military Thought from Machiavelli to Hitler* (Princeton: Princeton University Press, 1943), and Bernard Brodie, "Strategy," *International Encyclopedia of the Social Sciences*, Vol. 15, pp. 281-288.

3. John McDonald, *Strategy in Poker, Business and War* (New York: W.W. Norton, 1950), p. 11.

egy must be changed with technological change. That fact is reflected in a definition used in an Air Force dictionary:

1. The art or science of using such factors as time, space, geography, politics, and trends of events, together with available or potential power, to achieve a previously conceived objective.

2. The use of these factors to create advantageous conditions for meeting the enemy in combat, either to compel surrender or to achieve some other objective; the process of working out an operation so as to strengthen a nation or force, or to lessen the effects of defeat, in its ultimate position.[4]

Strategy and the military conception of it have undergone revolutionary change during and after World War II.[5] The bomber airplane, as Brodie[6] has pointed out, had already taken war beyond the battlefield; but nuclear weapons and the weapons systems based upon them, guaranteed that "strategic bombing," variously interpreted, would thereafter be of vital importance not only in redefining the theatre of war but also in redirecting top policy on the modes of warfare and the preparations for it. The strategy of force, in policy making at the highest levels of national governments, had to be reconsidered because of reactions against the use of nuclear weapons as possibly suicidal for all adversaries, thus leading to a new body of doctrine on limited war as deliberate restraint, and on "massive retaliation."

This new kind of warfare led to skyrocketing costs for the rapid technological advance toward ever larger and more complex weapon systems. It called upon the services of more and more of the manpower of the nation, especially of its scientists and technicians, who probed deeply into esoteric fields that might never have been explored save for the urgency of national defense needs. The heavy reliance on science and technology led far

4. W. A. Heflin (ed.), *The United States Air Force Dictionary*, Air University Press (Washington: U.S. Government Printing Office, 1956), p. 494.

5. *Ibid.*, pp. 327 and 340.

6. Brodie, *op. cit.*, and *Strategy in the Missile Age* (Princeton: Princeton University Press, 1959), Ch. 4.

beyond the "hard," physical sciences and engineering and into the social sciences. During World War II, for example, economists were used for target selection in strategic bombing and for a whole range of problems in economic warfare. Anthropologists were called upon for hard-to-get information about enemy and occupied areas. Political scientists pushed out new frontiers in comparative government, in international relations, in military government and overseas administration, in political communications, in public law, and in many other disciplines.

Tragic wartime lessons in national unpreparedness in many disciplines, in meeting the research and long lead time requirements for new weapons, and in numerous hitherto unrelated areas, led to general postwar revision of strategic doctrine in the direction of greater comprehensiveness. We were face to face with the century of total war, with its demands for the total reach of strategic thinking, if a nation were to survive. In military strategy alone the new dimensions were impressive. The nuclear missile age makes great demands on political sophistication at the strategic level. Deterrence becomes a matter not merely of bigger and better weapons, but even more importantly of better thinking about the political constraints on the strategy of force. Experts on the threats to peace in the entire world arena—on the moves of the Soviet superpower in Europe, in the Far East, and in the eastern Mediterranean; the rise of a Communist China; on the decolonization of large parts of Africa, Asia, and the western Pacific, followed by the rise of a score of new states in the international system, many of which remain unaligned, poor, and a threat to the international economy; on the possible emergence of new powers such as Japan and a united Europe—sit nearer to the President, as master strategist, than those across the river in the Pentagon or up the street in the State Department. The older strategies of force and diplomacy had to be coordinated at a higher level, together with the newer strategies of international economics and international communication.

National strategy, in short, had become a complex of specialized *strategies*, only one of which—the military—had a widely-recognized body of doctrine before World War II. During the war, it was said that "strategy is the art of controlling and utilizing the resources of a nation—or a coalition of nations—including its armed forces, to the end that its vital interests shall be effectively promoted and secured against enemies, actual, potential, or threatened."[7] It was recognized that chapters on the economic foundations of military power had long before been written by Adam Smith, Alexander Hamilton, Friedrich List, and others,[8] and the emergence of the civilian as strategist had been underlined in studies of Churchill, Lloyd George, and Clemenceau,[9] as well as the geopoliticians Ratzel, Mackinder, Kjellén, and Hanshofer. And during the war, there were further developments in psychological warfare, which had already been used in World War I.

But, by the end of World War II, these several approaches to warfare had not been welded into a single and comprehensive policy science that interrelated the several strategies and showed that in combination they applied to peace as well as to war, and to all protagonists in the world arena—including multinational corporations. The command of all kinds of resources by all kinds of collectivities—some antedating the modern state—for dealing with adverse natural conditions, as well as with human adversaries, has always required strategic capabilities that combine the use of force with the skillful use of other critical resources. The contemporary policy sciences now notice all these strategic uses by policy makers in private-sector as well as public-sector collectivities. The outmoding of strategic doctrine as exclusively military is thus due not only to changes in the nature of warfare, but also to slowly maturing social theory about conflict resolution in the world arena.

At the level of national strategy, terms such as the "cold war" are invented to straddle the apparently conflicting facts that indicate, on the one hand, the antagonistic, and, on the other, the cooperative, aspects of state interaction, East and West. Conflict, short of nuclear exchange (and usually, since 1945, short even of the immediate threat of "conventional" war between the two major contenders in the East-West confrontation of interests, since the actual military conflicts have been

7. Earle, *op. cit.*, p. viii.

8. *Ibid.*, Ch. 6.

9. *Ibid.*, Ch. 12.

between proxies of these principals), proceeds concurrently with probings for a community of interests—especially in the avoidance of nuclear mutual destruction. Conflict, as one writer has put it, "is never fully separated from cooperation nor cooperation from conflict"; and indeed, "different periods of history combine the two in varying measures," the difference between the states of peace and war lying "merely in the degree to which one of these elements predominates." When international issues are tackled predominantly by negotiation and force is used only marginally, there is "peace," while the open use of violence to settle these issues means "war." As for "cold war," it is neither peace nor war: "hostile relations predominate, but not to the exclusion of negotiations, and the use of violence remains circumscribed." [10]

Under the circumstances of a "cold war," the range of strategies used by the contestants is as broad as possible, whereas in a "hot war," the major emphasis is on military strategy, although even then not to the exclusion of other kinds of strategy. In "peace" there is talk of "negotiation from strength," and properly so since military capabilities are always in the background to assure the diplomats and to provide stability to the situation. [11] Nor can one make realistic, sharp distinctions in this context between nuclear and conventional capabilities: the art of deterrence is too little comprehended to rule out decisively the "conventional" instruments of national policy as determinative factors in much state interaction; of course, the use of economic, technological, and ideological instruments of policy may, in fact, have become more important in strategic decision than military capabilities.

The appropriate combined use of all these instruments of policy in national strategy is the hallmark of statesmanship. The political leader of today cannot be judged alone by the nobility and acceptability of his objectives; the use of balanced strategies for reaching acceptable goals is at least of equal importance, especially in view of the potentially devastating use or non-use of

10. Joseph Frankel, *International Relations* (New York: Oxford University Press, 1964), pp. 146-7.

11. Raymond Aron, *Peace and War: A Theory of International Relations*, trans. from the French by Richard Howard and Annette Baker Fox (Garden City, N.Y.: Doubleday, 1966), p. 24.

certain instruments of policy. The non-use of massively destructive nuclear weapons is a case in point; so also is the use of economic and technological instruments, such as development in non-industrial regions of the earth and ecological measures to assure human survival and health.

The new emphasis upon science—including the behavioral and social sciences—and technology in the strategic thinking, at the highest level, of all the protagonists in the world arena now places heavy demands on a nation's intellectual resources; at the same time, it makes strategic dogma at that level unprecedentedly vulnerable to challenge. This can be clearly seen in the output of "think-tanks" like the RAND Corporation, the Hudson Institute, and other autonomous, nonprofit research institutions, where independently-minded people devote their specialized capabilities to national security problems. When security problems are handed to them from Washington, the resultant research memorandums are not in the nature of obsequious replies to technical inquiries; assumptions of public policy makers that are considered invalid or faulty are often challenged and refuted with demonstrations that use new analytical and research tools—the results are often received at the policy centers of the Pentagon and elsewhere with silent indulgence. Research and analysis of security problems has now spread, and will increasingly spread, to other intellectual institutions, because public policy makers— both at national and local levels—find it increasingly necessary to rely upon *outside* intellectual resources for inputs to strategic decision processes.

The net result is that strategic thinking is being constantly and rapidly enriched *both for private-sector and public agencies*, including the multinational corporation. This means that dubious assumptions about multinational corporate strategy will be increasingly challenged by thinkers from these intellectual institutions. The long-run outcome will be good for everyone, although the immediate effect will probably be disturbing to many.

The Range of Strategies

The use of the term "national strategy" to distinguish it from the more traditional military strategy indicates an important step toward a more comprehensive understanding of the structure of the modern world. With the application of game theory to power relationships, war, and business, we begin to get a new perspective. The literature on national strategy is but the first chapter of a coming body of doctrine concerning strategy for every important collectivity in the various arenas of power, national, regional, international, and transnational. Books are beginning to appear on corporate strategy, [12] and we may expect a proliferation of books and articles that will consider one by one the range of strategies that are used—or are prescribed for use—by many different kinds of organizations. The strategies of transnational, or so-called universal political parties already have been reduced to revolutionary doctrine. The universal churches and communities of the faithful have long practiced—and sometimes reduced to writing—their own strategies. That is true also of the labor unions. The blacks, the young, the alienated, the hippies, and others with more transient existence, practice less matured strategies.

All these organizations may be regarded as engaged in the formulation and execution of policy defined as the invention or assessment of alternative courses of action or inaction and involving a special kind of thinking that is necessary because of discrepancies between the events that do happen and events that are preferred (values). [13]

National Strategies

Strategy is perhaps best observed by looking closely at the types of strategic instruments that states obviously employ: military, diplomatic, economic, and communicational (or psychological and ideological). [14] Each of these suggests parallel or related strategies in managing the affairs of multinational companies. Perhaps it is fair, also, to say that there is a legal strategy [15] that is distinct from diplomacy, and that this might very well be designated a fifth type of strategic move applicable to multina-

---

12. E.g., H. Igor Ansoff, *Corporate Strategy* (New York: Penguin, 1968).

13. H. D. Lasswell, "The Scientific Study of International Relations," *The Year Book of World Affairs, 1958* (London: The London Institute of World Affairs, 1958), p. 3.

14. Wm. T. R. Fox and Annette Baker Fox, "International Relations: Modes of State Action," *International Encyclopedia of Social Sciences*, Vol. 8, pp. 56-58.

15. *Ibid.*

tional corporations both in their relations with each other and with sovereign states. And, by extending the argument, international organization may be regarded as a sixth type; the parallel in multinational corporations would be not bigger and better cartels, but an intermix of private-corporate with public-international organizations.

International organizations have become the instruments of nation-state policy only in the past two centuries. They have rapidly proliferated in the twentieth. In the 1960's, the United States was a member of more than 400 international organizations. This proliferation of public international organizations is a stage in the gradual movement toward a global system of orderly government, but one marked by a functional method of attacking international problems of many kinds, rather than the holistic approach to world government that is vainly urged by impatient reformers. It is further arguable that *international* organization at the level of public governments, as an instrument of state policy, will not succeed in the long run without complementary *transnational* organization on functional lines in the private-sector. The International Labor Organization is an example of the intermix of the two approaches; labor unions, employer organizations, and governments all have representation in the ILO. Similarly, one might expect the rise of future regional and worldwide organizations in which multinational corporations would have representation. If that turns out to be so, then it would clearly be the case of international organization as an instrument of multinational corporate policy. The management of that instrument would require the development of an international organizational strategy that would be as specialized as the other strategies we are considering here. In this connection, it is well to note that national governments today maintain corps of specialists for international organizational work, which is not the same as traditional diplomacy.

Corporate Strategies

The national strategies outlined above provide a point of departure for a discussion of parallel strategies of multinational corporations as minor actors in the current world arena. Multinational corporate managers of the future will have to be prepared to govern their firms as more than business enterprises that have "gone international." The large-scale multinational corporations will emerge as major actors in a mature international system. The corporate strategies that managers of these corporate entities must master will be different in degree, but not in kind, from those which are today practiced by national leaders. Table I shows these strategies in parallel with national strategies.

Table I

National and Corporate Strategies

Strategy	National	Corporate
FORCE	Threat and use of military force and police.	Threat and use of force by private police and guards.
DIPLOMACY	The use of diplomatic and other representatives of sovereign states for negotiation and bargaining.	The use of corporate representatives for negotiation and for quasi-political and non-economic bargaining with external entities.
ECONOMICS	The use of governmental economic measures to promote national and allied interests, and to affect hostile interests adversely.	The use of corporate economic measures to promote corporate and allied interests and to obtain economic advantage over competitors; "business strategy" in the narrow sense.
COMMUNICATION	The use of the media of communication to promote national interests abroad.	The use of the media of communication to promote corporate interests in relations with other entities.

These parallels will be challenged by those who resist the idea that multinational corporations are quasi-public entities with responsibilities that go beyond conventional business responsibilities. Yet when one tries to match corporate power with corporate responsibility in transnational business—noting the fact that corporate power in the world arena has to be commensurate with the hazards as well as the opportunities there—it seems obvious that strategy must match both power and responsibility in the large-scale multinational corporations.

Current conceptions of corporate strategy adhere in general to the more conventional understanding of "business strategy." In the most comprehensive sense, strategy is "a course of action designed to manage *base values* for the achievement of policy objectives," [16] where the base values at the disposal of sanctioners include authority, military power, wealth, skills, enlightenment, rectitude, well-being, loyalty, and other bases for influencing the behavior of states, other collectivities, and persons. Business strategy, usually, refers to but one of these base values: the control over wealth sources and processes.

Force

The long continued use of armed forces by states suggests that physical and other forms of violence (e.g., chemical and biological techniques of warfare and police action) will not soon —if ever—be dispensed with as instruments of national policy, both in the world arena and domestically. The substantial figures for police, for prison personnel, for special guards, for investigators armed with the ultimate sanction in any nation, together with statistics of arrests, imprisonments, punishments and executions, to say nothing of the oppressive burden of foreign defense, all indicate the ubiquitousness of this sanction.

There are, of course, limitations in the use of force as a strategy. Popular governments cannot coerce effectively unless violators are relatively few in number and lack support and sympathy among the population at large; a coerced majority, that can still vote, will not tolerate coercion very long. Even in dictatorial governments, where voting is impossible or meaningless, the rulers have to be systematically attentive in applying the entire spectrum of instruments of coercion—"a centralized and disciplined police system, a secret police, a compliant judiciary,

16. M. S. McDougal and F. P. Feliciano, *Law and Minimum World Public Order* (New Haven: Yale University Press, 1961), p. 309, italics added.

military and bureaucratic establishments ready to obey . . . when duty requires the coercion of large numbers of fellow citizens." [17] The demand for "law and order" is never met completely. Totalitarian governments never get total submission.

The strategy of force has always been regarded as indispensable to organized society—and, as a corollary, indispensable to all who live in an organized society—except by state-skeptics of the extreme anarchist position. [18] The anarchists' "half hatred of society, half love of mankind," [19] leaves them vulnerable to those who do not hate social organization enough to deny themselves coercive strategy. The anarchists and extreme individualists always concede in the end to organized collectivities that can command the *ultima ratio*. The anarchist's denial of the legitimacy of all forms of coercion of man by man still stands, however, as a challenge to their critics, notably when the latter naively argue that the state alone may use force while all others use noncoercive sanctions. The point is relevant to any realistic view of multinational corporate strategy, which must include the strategy of force.

The private guard of a corporation is not an anomaly. In the world arena, something like a private armed force becomes a necessity for corporate survival in some situations. And corporate managers, like everyone else, must rely on the indirect use of public force when it can be legitimately engaged in the defense of their property and their organizational capabilities.

The governance of society, in all of its pluralistic complexity, necessitates widely distributed foci of power to govern men and widely divergent kinds of authority-structures to take care of man's many-faceted nature. Family groupings, churches, educational institutions and productive entities in the economy, all possess to some degree the force-capability as an instrument of local and particular organization policy. Whether it is regarded in law as "devolved," or otherwise derived from state authority, or original, whether inherent in an organization or only permitted,

---

17. Robert A. Dahl, *Modern Political Analysis* (Prentice-Hall, 1963), p. 76.

18. Wm. E. Hocking, *Man and the State* (Yale University Press, 1926), Chs. 7 and 25; Paul Avrich, *The Russian Anarchists* (Princeton University Press, 1967); Irving L. Horowitz (ed.), *The Anarchists* (Dell, Laurel Editions, 1965).

19. Barbara Tuchman, *The Proud Tower* (New York: Macmillan, 1965).

the use of the forcible instrument of policy is evident in almost every organization.

The major user of force, of course, in our era is the nation-state. Its tendency to monopolize both the right to, and the actual use of, force is growing. The flow of this trend is in the direction of national capitals; it is not toward local and particularistic governmental centers, nor toward a universal world government. In these circumstances, multinational companies must look to national governments (whether in home or host countries) for the use of force, on their behalf, as an instrument of corporate policy. Company police forces play little or no part in the strategic decisions of such companies but play rather tactical and subordinate local, protective, and security roles in defense of certain installations.

The essential problem in the strategy of force is the effective use and control of organized violence in defending and advancing the basic aims of policy. Since the sixteenth century in the West, the problem has been one primarily for nation-states and not for lesser entities, and as such it has focussed on the art and science of war. As the Western state system has spread throughout the world, the problem has developed into the problem of the control of war as an institution.[20] This exclusive focus upon the conduct of war by nation-states can mislead the student of multinational corporate policy.

War, though it is sometimes hopefully said to be on the way out as an instrument of national policy, is, of course, a major instrument that will not soon be dispensed with by nation-states. The use of force, by a state that has no other effective means of enforcing in its favor a rule of law that is being disobeyed by another state, or as a means of altering an adverse rule, is to be expected in the absence of a more comprehensive structure of authority for the settlement of such controversies.

20. Cf. Quincy Wright, *A Study of War*. Second edition (Chicago: University of Chicago Press, 1965); Raymond Aron, *op. cit.*; Klaus Knorr, *On the Uses of Military Power in the Nuclear Age* (Princton University Press, 1966); Herman Kahn and Anthony J. Wiener, *The Year 2000* (Macmillan, 1967), Ch. 7: "Some Possibilities of Nuclear War"; Daniel Bell (ed.), *Toward the Year 2000* (Houghton Mifflin, 1968), pp. 277-296: "Violence" by James Q. Wilson; Carl Kaysen, "Military Strategy, Military Forces, and Arms Control" in *Agenda for the Nation*, edited by Kermit Gordon (Brookings, 1968); and Albert Lepawsky *et al.*, *The Search for World Order* (New York: Appleton-Century-Crofts, 1971).

For these reasons, the strategy of force is generally studied as the instrument of national and alliance policies, and implemented through the armies, navies, air forces and police organizations of nations. Historical perspective, reaching back at least into the later European Middle Ages, and projective thinking into a possible post-national era, are requisites for a proper assessment of the role of force in multinational corporate strategy.

There is a swing of the pendulum in serious thought about the art and science of war between offense and defense. Permanent fortifications, for example, are emphasized in periods when the defensive is predominant. When the offensive governed thought on the art of war "permanent fortifications were by-passed or blasted and their place taken by field fortifications."[21]

The race between attack and defense goes on throughout military history, and it seems to be a persistent element in strategic thought on the use of organized force. Permanent fortifications, such as medieval castle strongholds of local lords, became anachronistic after gunpowder had been introduced in the thirteenth century and then applied through the technological advances of the next two centuries to projectiles and heavier cannons. The private castle had lost its defensive capability by 1500, and even fortified towns fell in such numbers in Italy before Charles V's forces that a new defense system obviously was needed. In our own times, the vulnerability of fortress guns to strong siege howitzers, and more recently, the vulnerability of a *Festung Europa* to offensive assault as well as the dubious durability of even a superstate's nuclear capabilities as against an enemy's missiles, all point to the continuing seesaw between offense and defense.

As time passed, trade seems to have worked against a defense strategy and to ally itself rather with offense and attack. The parochialism of the lonely castle and the fortified town gradually gave way to the more expansive requirements of commerce on land and sea. Nationalistic kings, at the opening of the modern period, overcame with their offensive armies not only the narrowly local defense systems but also forced through the idea of open seas for world trade.

21. W. H. Baumer, "Fortification," in *Encyclopaedia Britannica* (1958).

We moderns smile a little at the castle-builders, but the political economy of castle-building has never been adequately studied, particularly in relation to our contemporary defense structures. One wonders whether, given our continued reliance upon the strategy of force, we stand in principle on different economic grounds than the castle-builders. Castle fortresses must have absorbed appalling percentages of an overlord's "gross feudal product"; but was the percentage larger than ours today? One wonders if we do not still live in the castle, ruinously for a political economy pointed toward the welfare of more than a few.

The problem is accentuated in the age of nuclear missiles, not so much because of the cost of producing the nuclear missiles (the cost has been vastly reduced in two decades) but rather because the permanent and field fortifications required in defense are so costly. Indeed, it may be that not even the most advanced and costly modern versions of the castle (such as shelters for men and weapons) will ever succeed against nuclear weapons. Escalate the defense, and the offense moves up at an equal or greater rate—at astronomical expense, incalculable and possibly insupportable by any contemporary national economy.

The strategy of force has indeed become so expensive that the tendency is for the ordinary knights to seek the protection of the great overlords of our times—the superstates. Since the rise of modern nation-states, economic venturers have sought the protection of these successors of feudal authority. A prevalent doctrine has it that businessmen use the state apparatus simply as the "executive committee" for their exploitative purposes.

Theories of imperialism thus underline the backing in the world arena of trading companies and modern corporations by the swords of sovereigns. Yet the question is: Who was using whom for what? Was the sovereign sword the instrument of "private enterprise"? Was the king using men of commerce to enhance national power? Or were both sides impelled not only by their will and imagination, but as well by changes in science, technics, and the economy, changes that brought into play the strategic uses of force first on one side and then on the other, at times defensively and at other times with offense as the dominant thought?

The rapid growth of a money economy at the end of the Middle Ages worked a basic change in the agricultural foundations of medieval society and on the art of warfare as well. Cities and wealthy overlords took advantage of the money economy to build regularly paid professional armies for protracted services, as distinguished from the relatively short-term feudal forces of knights whose service obligations were personal and limited. New classes of freemen were drawn into the service of city-states and then national kings, men who were less bound by older military traditions and more readily adaptable to new forms of weapons and fighting. [22] A renaissance in the art of warfare, dependent upon a changed economy as well as military technology, in the sixteenth century served the new "capitalists."

Feudalism was giving way to the National State, but a historian of economic analysis writes that the warrior classes who had ruled the feudal organism did not easily give way. They ruled on for centuries, often forcing the bourgeoisie to submit, except in the Netherlands. The prince personified state and nation. The new sovereign nation-states were militarily aggressive because of their social structure, but not—as Marxist theory later on would have it—because of capitalist elements in this structure. In the early centuries of the new nationalism, the nation-states were aggressive because of the persistence of aristocratic rule, the access to easily disposable wealth, and the breakdown of the supranational powers of the medieval Church and Empire. The object of policy for sovereigns was the wealth and power of the state. The political economy of nations was an economy planned with a view to war; but not necessarily, nor principally, for the advantage of the new capitalist class. [23]

Even if it were conceded that the picture changed in the late nineteenth and early twentieth centuries, to the advantage of the more politically skillful capitalists of our time, it remains to be proved that this advantage was sought by, and accrued to, "capitalists" in general, using any acceptable definition of that term. Yet it is true that a vicarious strategy of force, an indirect use of force by non-state protagonists who persuade public governments to intervene on their behalf, has always been an instrument of

22. Felix Gilbert, "Machiavelli," in Earle (ed.), *op. cit.*, pp. 3-25.

23. Joseph A. Schumpeter, *Capitalism, Socialism, and Democracy* (Harper & Bros., 1942), Ch. 12, and his *History of Economic Analysis* (New York: Oxford University Press, 1954), pp. 144*ff*.

policy in many kinds of private organizations. The business corporation is no exception to this rule, and, indeed, its very existence and powers as a legal, corporate entity depend upon the existence of the state in the background and upon the rule of *ultima ratio regum*. Resort to the courts, to say nothing of armies, is a reliance upon this ultimate power of organized force, though the immediate reliance is on the rule of law.

In the contemporary world arena, where primary reliance upon legislation, adjudication, and executive power at the supranational level cannot possibly be justified in the management of multinational companies, it is to be expected that the power of nations will be relied upon instead. The multinational company naturally turns to its home state, but not necessarily in the first instance. While the reliance upon either a home or host state may not, except in extreme cases, call forth direct use of force on behalf of the company or against others, the strategy of force can never be absent from consideration in corporate policy. To ask for or accept the support of one nation's military and police protection can lead to hostility on the part of other nations and a loss of esteem in critical sectors of public opinion. Frequently, a decision at the highest corporate level is necessary to balance the many involved considerations.

The vulnerability of multinational corporations is comparable with that of early American companies which sought to do business within a national market beyond the state of their domestic jurisdiction. Many decades passed after the adoption of the Constitution of 1787 before a "foreign corporation," i.e., one seeking to do business in other than its home state, could look to federal power as its protector against discriminatory state power. The making of the national and continental market was importantly a matter of judicial interpretation of the appropriate clauses of that Constitution by the United States Supreme Court so as to provide corporate access to federal courts, together with protection of the commerce, due process, and equal protection clauses. Not until after the Civil War (a major war of the nineteenth century) was there final denial of authority in states of the Union to assert a coercive strategy against American multistate corporations—the early counterparts of our twentieth-century multinational companies. Both have sought larger markets under the handicap of an inadequate structure of authority in these markets and subject to the ultimate power of expulsion in parochial areas of these markets. The parochial nationalism of today, however, has at its command far more force as a sanction than the states of the Union ever had. The problem of the multi-national corporation is to make strategic moves that sometimes rely upon national force and at other times deftly avoid doing so.

Multinational corporations, like other participants in world affairs, are in some cases closely involved with national efforts to strengthen military sanctions—as in the military-industrial-sci-entific complex—and in other cases quite uninvolved with that complex and desirous of maintaining in the United States as neutral a status as possible. They seek simply to survive and to be profitable producers in a very turbulent and dangerous arena. When the United States, for example, was about to announce a decision, during the Arab-Israeli hostilities, on whether to send more Phantom jets to Israel, Aramco, the American company in Saudi Arabia, is reported to have asked both the White House and the State Department for one week's advance notice if the decision would be for immediate compliance with the Israeli request; that would give the company time to evacuate all American personnel.[24]

During the Arab-Israeli six-day war in 1967, about 55 percent of the normal oil flow was shut off with the closing of the Suez Canal and the oil pipelines. Persian Gulf oil was used by American forces in Southeast Asia, and it fueled American and NATO forces in Western Europe. Any drastic change in the pattern of supply would have had serious consequences not only for defense but also for America's balance of payments. Up to 80 percent of Western Europe's oil came from Arab countries; West Germany, for example, got 60 percent from Libya and 20 percent from Persian Gulf sources. More than 90 percent of Japan's petroleum came from the Middle East. A cutoff of five weeks could have closed down Japanese industry.

In this crisis, as in others, many nations and industries have had a stake in the outcome of the threats of force, and the potential impact on a particular multinational corporation has

24. See the column by Marquis Childs, United Features Syndicate, on September 23, 1970: "U.S. Fears Action by Israel on SAMs."

always to be weighed, in the light of all available information at the highest level of corporate policy. Nor is a multinational corporation always a mere bystander in these crises. It may constitute a ponderable factor in the calculus of force in national chancellories. It must therefore be prepared for the consequences. The assessment of fluid patterns of force in international politics demands of multinational corporate policy makers an astute judgment of trends in world affairs, as free as possible from ideological prejudice.

The strategy of force is thus a major, but often undiscerned and unacknowledged, element in the strategy of multinational corporations. It would continue to be so even under a world law enforceable by a single authority, just as today domestic corporate policy relies upon the ultimate sanctions available to national governments. To obscure this fact is to overlook basic elements of corporate action vis-à-vis governments.

A basic and long-term problem of multinational corporate policy is how a given firm can work toward those conditions which minimize the need for coercive force in domestic and international arenas. The institutional arrangements[25] required to optimize peaceful adjustment of conflicts are of primary importance. The systematic exploration of institutional possibilities to reduce the costs of conflict is now no mere academic exercise for the multinational corporation, exposed as it is to the escalating dangers of the world arena. Creativity in managerial analysis and skills is nowhere more urgently required than in this baffling area of corporate strategy. It is a seriously neglected area, even in most of the largest companies.

Diplomacy

Bismarck, the *Blut und Eisen* chancellor, declared in a famous speech in 1862 that it was "not by speeches and decisions of majorities that the greatest problems of the times [are] decided—that was the mistake of 1848-49—but by blood and iron." The theme is often repeated. Swinburne's stanza proclaimed that

25. See, e.g., Steven J. Brams, "The Search for Structural Order in the International System: Some Models and Preliminary Results," *International Studies Quarterly*, Vol. 13, No. 2, June 1969; "The Fifty Years' Crisis: International Society from Versailles to Vietnam," *International Journal*, Vol. 24, No. 4, Autumn 1969.

it is "Not with dreams, but with blood and with iron, shall a nation be moulded to last."

The choice is not between sanguinary conflict and pusillanimous dreaming but among a range of strategies that do not foreswear any. For corporations as well as nations, these strategies must be appropriately chosen, interrelated, and timed. Diplomacy may be regarded as the master strategy in that it determines the proper mix both in a well-run state and in a well-run multinational corporation, where corporate strategies, like the product mix, ought to be decided at the highest level of policy making.

What is diplomacy? Like the strategy of force, it is a neglected art and science in multinational corporate policy where the strategies of economics and communication tend to get most of the attention. One reason it is neglected is that it is too often identified exclusively with state action at a misconceived level of striped-pants social activity. Embassies are now often heavily staffed with personnel who have no negotiatory functions at all, and this tends further to mislead observers about the essential diplomatist function of a chief of mission and his deputies.

Modern diplomacy, from the sixteenth century on, has been the method in common use for communication between governments of sovereign states. The function of the diplomat is the guarding of the interests of his government in negotiations with the government of the country to which he is accredited. The conventions and usages of diplomacy that have proliferated over the centuries, while grounded essentially on principles of international law concerning the privileges of sovereigns, when regarded superficially tend to obscure the negotiatory essence of diplomatic action. The negotiatory skill of the successful diplomat is not merely the skill of the trader. At the negotiating table, he may win a compromise simply by wearing the opposition down, persistently, and even long-windedly elaborating his case with endless patience and even mien. The manner can be as important as the substance of diplomacy.

Multinational companies have corporate governments that are required to undertake at least quasi-diplomatic functions in the world arena. But the softening of the "quasi-" seems uncalled for if one makes the appropriate distinction in terms. The diplomatist strategy broadly conceived is not, nor can it be, the exclusive function of sovereigns and their plenipotentiaries, although diplomacy may be.

"Diplomacy" comes through the French language from a Greek word *diploma* (literally, a doubling) for the doubled or folded sheet used by the Romans in antiquity to denote, at first, a passport or license to travel by the public post and, later, any imperial grant of privileges. By extension, the humanists of the Renaissance applied *diploma* not only to the acts of kings but also more generally to privileges granted by great personages, while the study of documents of the middle ages in general was referred to as *res diplomatica*—a term later translated simply as "diplomatics": the science of the critical study of official as opposed to literary sources of history, i.e., of charters, acts, treaties, contracts, judicial records, rolls, chartularies, registers and like documents. These documents embrace both public and private deeds. With such an etymology, "diplomacy" runs into difficulty today as a sign referring only to the acts and deeds of sovereign states.

It is sometimes said that the diplomat is the mere civil front for force, one who uses negotiation as a means of securing the best advantage for his nation short of violence, minimizing so far as possible the frictions and the resentment of potential adversaries. But diplomacy is not merely war in its nonviolent stages (even conceding for the sake of argument the Hobbesian dictum that the state of war is the natural state of relations among nations). Nor is it simply a more or less covert, coercive operation with pressures in the offing; indeed, nonsovereign negotiators do not have the requisite force capabilities in reserves and neither do the mini-states that have sprung up since World War II. They do have, however, certain other kinds of power to rely upon in negotiation: economic, technological, moral or, generally, some strategic position stemming from such things as geographic location and prestige. As soon as one admits the possibility of other reserves than force in the diplomatic process, then negotiation, that stands at the core of this process, can be thought of in all inter-group relationships including the external affairs of multinational companies with governments of states, with multinational public organizations, with labor unions, with other companies, and so on.

Diplomacy as negotiation cannot usefully be thought of as bargaining alone, although bargaining is frequently its essence. Bargaining will involve the *quid pro quo*, often of economic value, in the absence of all threat of force. But the negotiators may have nothing to trade, nothing to extort, only the desire to find common interests and common courses of action. The art of persuasion enters here as essential to diplomacy, calling upon men of letters rather than men at arms, an attribute of the diplomat well understood among the Italians of Machiavelli's day and in our own by those who understand the breadth and depth of communication as both an art and a science. Negotiatory techniques today make heavy demands upon "letters and science" in this broad sense, as well as upon the substantive fields of the natural and social sciences and the humanities. The dimensions of contemporary efforts in this respect can be seen in the work of ECOSOC and UNESCO, for example, but equally in the interrelations of nonsovereign private international organizations and in the external relations of multinational companies.

These external company relationships do not fall entirely under the heading of the vicarious uses of force and bargaining for economic advantage. Thus, in the ecological struggle for environmental advantage, multinational companies have much in common with other kinds of organizations: for example, with respect to the physical environment in the problems of soil erosion, of water and air pollution, of global telecommunication and of mastery of outer space; with respect to the biological environment in the problems of population control, epidemiology, the development of new agricultural resources, etc. Among interorganizational relationships of all kinds, multinational companies seek through their own species of diplomatic action certain common interests with others so as to expedite common courses of mutually advantageous action through corporate policy.

It is not usual to refer to such external company relationships as involving the practice of corporate diplomacy; yet in the best-run multinational companies, it is now recognized as a necessity to retain and train specialized personnel for precisely such managerial functions. Nor can external relations of multinational companies be subsumed usefully under traditional public relations categories. The corporate "image," like the image of a nation that is fashioned through pomp and ceremony as well as showing the iron fist, has to be deliberately cultivated, but that is not the essence of corporate external relations, especially in the world arena.

Nor are these external relationships essentially "business relationships" in the narrowly economic sense of that term. In some instances, the negotiations carried on by corporate envoys are hardly different in kind from those carried on by regularly accredited diplomatic plenipotentiaries. The resultant corporate agreements are not folded, sealed and deposited in the same way, nor do they become elements of international public law; they do, however, sometimes affect the governance of substantial areas of human affairs, and this may go on for years as part of the operative structure of authority in essential markets. International cartels are a case in point.

The representatives of corporations do not have the "right of legation," that is the right of a sovereign state to send and receive diplomatic envoys. [26] The diplomatic agents of sovereigns never include representatives of private organizations, nor even of most public organizations. The supposition, sometimes encountered in discussions of multinational corporations, that these organizations might eventually rise to the status of quasi-public governments in transnational law, runs against the hard fact that a rigid classification of diplomatic agents is adhered to by foreign offices. Diplomatic status does not extend to the representatives of companies, however rich and powerful, or however essential to the maintenance of public order on a world basis they may be.

The reason for their exclusion is that they fit none of the theories of diplomatic immunity. They cannot claim diplomatic status on the basis of extraterritoriality, nor on the basis of representation. A foreign corporation clearly comes completely within the jurisdiction of the host state. The corporation's offi-

---

26. See Green H. Hackworth, *Digest of International Law* (1940-44), Vol. IV, p. 393; Manley O. Hudson, *International Legislation* (1919-45), Vol. IV, p. 2388; Raoul Genet, *Traité de Diplomatie et de Droit Diplomatique* (1931), Vol. II, pp. 5-76; Herbert W. Briggs, *The Law of Nations: Cases, Documents, and Notes*, Second edition (Appleton-Century-Crofts, Inc., 1952), Ch. X.

cials represent no sovereign.[27] A *functional* conception of organizational representation as expounded by Briggs is akin to the doctrine of Grotius, that an ambassador ought to be free from all compulsion, and emphasizes "the necessity of insuring free communication between States."[28] There is a question of communication among vitally important organizations in the world arena, and particularly among those upon which an emergent world order might be based. The world of 140-odd sovereign states neither exhausts the list of such vital organizations, nor does it include more than a few that will eventually bear the burdens of economic and military sanctions requisite to a world order under law. Some of the larger multinational companies today far outstrip most of the sovereign states in economic capabilities and, therefore, constitute one kind of organization whose representatives must be heard with respect.

A theory of corporate diplomacy is already implicit in the general theory of the "diplomatist's" function as elaborated in revisionist views of the fundamental character of international relations. In the Yale school of thought on international law, for example, it has been stressed that any organized group—state, corporation, or other—has functionally specialized subgroups, among which one finds within the leadership subgroup, in addition to subgroups specialized to intelligence, advisory, morale, propaganda and other functions, a "diplomatist division" that is specialized "in power relations (negotiation and agreement) with

27. Lawrence Preuss has observed that the theory which bases diplomatic privileges and immunities upon the representative character of the diplomat "equates the immunities of the agent with those of the sending State itself," and that such agents were originally the representatives of a sovereign Prince who could not subject themselves to the jurisdiction of a receiving state for "acts performed within the scope of their official functions as determined by their national law and within limits set by international law." This theory of the immunity of agents of sovereign princes came to be applied to agents of sovereign states. Preuss observes further, however, that the theory is inadequate as the sole legal basis for diplomatic immunities "in that it explains only those exemptions concerning official acts which diplomatic agents enjoy in common with other State officials, such as consuls" and "leaves unexplained those immunities which they possess with reference to acts performed in a private capacity." Preuss, "Capacity for Legation and the Theoretical Basis of Diplomatic Immunities," *New York University Law Quarterly Review*, Vol. 10, pp. 170-187.

28. Briggs, *op. cit.*, pp. 762-3. He cites the view of Preuss: "As the foundation of diplomatic immunities, the theory *ne impediatur legatis* or the interest of function is now predominant, having supplanted the fiction of exterritoriality as the theoretical basis of diplomatic privileges and immunities. It shares the field with the representation theory, without being excluded by it."

other groups, rather than the manipulation of symbols, violence, or goods and services."[29] A special case of the "diplomatist division" is the foreign service of a nation-state. The diplomatist division of a multinational corporation would be a parallel external affairs service. Like the foreign service of a nation-state, the diplomatist division of a multinational corporation would engage in the continuing direct interplay of offer, counteroffer, acceptance and rejection. A diplomat is a diplomatist with formal status, having the duty to negotiate persistently. A multinational corporate external representative will likewise negotiate persistently and with respect to power relations.

There is much more to the "diplomatist" function in both states and corporations than formal representation. The diplomat, as a diplomatist with formal status is part of a "diplomatist division" of a nation-state, and this larger division includes more than a diplomatic corps; it includes many kinds of mediators, arbitrators, conciliators, specialized negotiators, and administrators. On the darker side, it also includes "fixers" whose moves, if exposed, would be counter-productive. There is also the spy, the saboteur, and the *agent provocateur* in national diplomatist divisions which may or may not find a place in the multinational corporation.[30]

Negotiation may refer to power practices where the outcome is not coercively determined as it would be if the purpose were "unconditional surrender" and submission. The function of the diplomatist division of corporations, as well as states, is "to protect and expand values by means of negotiation," and while the term has been applied in recent times, for the most part, to the conduct of external relations of states, "there is also internal diplomacy, the process by which the individuals and group spokesmen of society come to terms with one another by various forms of negotiation."[31]

The sweep of functions in the "diplomatist division" of states and corporations, wide as it is, must not be interpreted to include

29. H. D. Lasswell and A. Kaplan, *Power and Society* (New Haven: Yale University Press, 1950), p. 193.

30. *Ibid.*

31. H. D. Lasswell and Myres S. McDougal, "Legal Education and Public Policy," 52 *Yale Law Journal*, 203-295, at 276.

the separately defined strategies of force, the use of economic resources, and communicational strategy. The multinational corporate negotiator may engage collaterally in economic bargaining, but the diplomatist function ought not to be confused with the strategic use of economic resources, which requires personnel specialized to this latter function. The negotiatory function overlaps but is distinct and requires highly specialized training in its own right. Some of that training will parallel the professional training of diplomats, especially in the study of international law and politics and of the historic practice of diplomacy as a key to the underlying principles if not to the contemporary usages that a multinational corporate representative will adopt in the world arena.

The core diplomatic skills have been defined as negotiation, analysis, persuasion, reporting, and languages. In the State Department's own self-appraisal, *Diplomacy for the '70s*, it was charged that the Department and the Foreign Service had "languished as creative organs, busily and even happily chewing on the cud of daily routine, while other departments, Defense, CIA, the White House staff, made important innovative contributions to foreign policy." These words will ring a bell in not a few multinational corporate diplomatist divisions.

Not that multinational corporations have much to learn from the diplomatist divisions of nation-states. It is probably the other way around. Some of the large multinational corporations are models of the way to run complex transnational operations efficiently. They have introduced modern techniques of communication that are better than those of most governments, which rely still on the slower and outdated system of diplomatic reporting. They do not have large standing bureaucracies, with divisive elements that yield to no single superior; the Secretary of State tends to become a relatively remote head of an increasingly irrelevant bureaucracy instead of the President's extension in foreign affairs, and the pattern runs similarly in other countries. At the highest level of multinational corporate policy making, there is generally a top-level policy staff that permits the president of the corporate group to focus consistently on all of the interactive internal and external policy alternatives, and thus to frame politically significant choices for action in the world arena. The bureaucracy of the nation-state is, of course, in the unenviable position of having to deal with a far more complicated situation.

In the earlier industrial age, international politics involved the interaction essentially of nation-states, most of which operated as more or less self-contained autarchic units on a world scene with relatively few protagonists. Since the Second World War, there has been a revolution in communications, in the international economy, in the nature of weapons technology, in the flow of all kinds of non-state activities across frontiers. The result has been to downgrade the importance and autonomy of the nation-state. The fusion of the domestic political process with the international process at many levels means that there is a new "metropolitan politics" that profoundly affects the external affairs of states. There is a "global metropolitan process which is messy, overlapping, unclear and influenced simultaneously by many conflicting constituencies, both domestic and foreign" while the world has become "more congested, more intimate, yet also fragmented and differentiated."[32] In this situation, the multinational corporation has been able to stick to its main task of profitable production, moving into the global arena with singleness of purpose, relatively free of the multitudinous tasks that fall on political shoulders in nation-states. As the multinational corporation rises, however, to the status of a major protagonist in the international system, it begins to take on more tasks—with resultant expansion of strategies.

The diplomatist's strategy in the nation and in the corporation has tended to become similar. On both sides, there have been and will be changes in structure and strategy. One veteran diplomat has warned against confusing diplomacy with "management" since "one cannot 'manage' foreigners as one can [manage] subordinates in a business firm, government department, or secretariat of an international organization"; and since they cannot be managed, there can be no "management" of the "interacting" relations which evolve from dealings with them, for these are often subtle relations that are influenced by "factors of history and psychology, not to say national sensitivity, over which we

32. Zbigniew Brzezinski, "The Diplomat is an Anachronism," *The Washington Post*, July 5, 1970.

have little or no control, and by conditions we cannot contrive into or out of existence." [33]

Economics

We turn now to the best known of corporate strategies—economic measures, notably the skillful handling of goods and prices. The economic strategy we will consider here is more nearly the "business strategy" that is now coming to the focus of attention in literature on the modern corporation.

For Dean H. Igor Ansoff, for example, "business strategy" consists of "a set of management guidelines" which specify a firm's product-market position, together with certain other matters: the directions of growth and change sought by a firm; the ways and means it engages in competition, enters new markets, and organizes its resources; and the strengths it seeks to exploit as well as the weaknesses it tries to avoid. [34] The strategic problem of the firm, understood as the problem of the relationship between the firm and its environment, was until recently little noticed, and was even left outside the domain of microeconomic theory. Ansoff proposes to include strategy, giving it his own working definition. The strategic decision area is located in the management process, together with two other decision areas: administrative and operational. The "strategic decision area," while concerned with environmental relationships, does not extend very far out into the world arena as we have been considering it.

Ansoff specifies as a strategic decision problem, for instance, the selection of product-market mix which optimizes the firm's return-on-investment potential. Key decisions include the objectives and goals; diversification, expansion, administrative and finance strategy; and growth method, as well as timing of growth. Key characteristics of strategic problems are that decisions are centralized, they have to be made in partial ignorance, they are non-repetitive, and are not self-regenerative.

Ansoff's models show how strategic decisions fit into serial and parallel decision-making. He presents a careful account of the

33. Smith Simpson, "The Nature and Dimensions of Diplomacy," *Annals* of the American Academy of Political and Social Science, Vol. 380 (November, 1968), pp. 135-144.

34. H. I. Ansoff, *Business Strategy* (Penguin, 1969).

nature and types of "strategic change"—"a shift in the product- or service-mix produced by the firm and/or the markets to which it is offered."[35] A key step in this shift is discovery of a product-mix idea. His two basic types of strategic change—expansion and diversification—are discussed in terms of various kinds of "diversification strategy" and of "expansion strategy."

There is now a decided trend toward more attention to the other three strategies, although they are generally still relatively minor in importance compared with the strategy of economics. This assumption of major and even dominant significance for economic strategy may be attacked on the ground that the multinational corporation is on the way to becoming far more than enterprise. Regarded as an emergent major protagonist in world affairs, the multinational corporation necessarily devotes more and more attention to the strategies of force, diplomacy, and communication; in the long run, the multinational corporation may become a master strategist in the latter two fields. It can never compete with the nation-state in the strategy of force, but its influence on the limitation of nuclear warfare may turn out to be substantial because of statesmanship at corporate helms expressing a corporate interest in preserving vast transnational productive mechanisms. And, the world's need for these mechanisms will increase as the pressure of population mounts, together with rising expectations throughout the world.

With a mounting responsibility to supply needs in a world faced with want, multinational corporations will inevitably be the foci for the accretion of power requisite to discharge the responsibility. The long-term result will be the appearance on the world scene of new centers of power that will leave far behind the significance of "powers" now listed among the sovereign states of the international system.

The nature of this new power, arising in economic strategy but at length transcending that strategy, has been foreshadowed in some accounts of multinational corporate strategy, although the transcendent character of the new strategy is seldom stated with clarity. "The power of the multinational corporation,"

35. H. I. Ansoff, "Toward a Strategic Theory of the Firm," in Ansoff (ed.), *Business Strategy*, cited, at p. 21.

writes Fayerweather, "stems from the resources and political strength of the parent country which are variously distributed among the multinational corporation, other companies, and the government";[36] he goes on to say that the basic power is reinforced by other countries with multinational corporations. Then he points to the fact that corporations have the power to withhold resource transmission at the precommitment stage, and even at later stages when the degree and continuity of resource flow can be to some extent controlled by a firm. Also the "collective willingness" or unwillingness of multinational corporations to transfer resources to a country, depending upon assessments of the investment climate there, is a source of corporate power.

A further source of corporate power is governmental foreign aid from developed countries, when that aid is qualified by demands that multinational corporations be given fair treatment as defined by legislators and administrators who, in turn, are not immune to corporate persuasive capabilities. The mix of corporate and home-government powers is obvious here; but one should not underestimate the prime source of the power involved—it is economic. This is true not only with respect to multinational corporations in the less developed countries but also to those in countries which are highly industrialized. The governments of developed countries hesitate to discriminate against the foreign subsidiaries of other developed countries for fear of retaliation against the investments of nationals abroad. In general, there is such a seamless web of cross-border economic relationships among practically all nations today that the vaunted power of sovereigns can often be held at bay by nonsovereign entities.

36. John Fayerweather, *International Business Management: A Conceptual Framework* (McGraw-Hill, 1969), p. 115. The entire chapter, on the mutuality of interests between the multinational firm and host nations in processes of transmission of resources and innovations in host societies, is a substantial contribution to the literature on economic strategy. Cf. Howe Martyn, *International Business* (Macmillan, 1964); Richard D. Robinson, *International Business Policy* (Holt, Rinehard and Winston, 1964); Raymond Vernon, *Manager in the International Economy* (Prentice-Hall, 1968), Ch. 10: "Strategic Issues in International Investment"; Peter Gabriel, "Investment in the LDC," *Columbia Journal of World Business*, Summer 1966; and in Courtney Brown (ed.), *World Business: Promise and Problems* (Macmillan, 1970), articles by Howard V. Perlmutter, "The Tortuous Evolution of the Multinational Corporation," Donald M. Kendall, "Corporate Ownership: The Multinational Dimension," and I. A. Litvak and C. J. Maule, "Guidelines for the Multinational Corporation."

The global economic strategy of the multinational corporation can be considered in two ways: first, as a business strategy in terms of costs and benefits; secondly, as an economic strategy with the accruement of benefits to society as a whole as well as to multinational corporations.

The global strategy of economics—as distinguished from the more limited "business strategy"—is today a common concern of all peoples, nations, and entities, including corporate entities engaged in business enterprise. The core of this strategy of economics is the design and execution of courses of action—by whatever collectivity—for the management of such basic values as wealth, skills, enlightenment, and authority, for the achievement of a policy objective of a specific kind: the most efficient use of the earth's resources for the use of man in a symbiotic relationship with others in the biosphere. This production and flow of goods and services, directed by pricing, rationing, administration, and otherwise, will always be in the hands of economic strategists, public or private or both.

The strategy of economics with global objectives may or may not be consistent with business strategy in multinational corporations. On the other hand, a global strategy of economics may not be conceivable without multinational corporations or their equivalent. There will be, in any case, persistent problems of business strategy, such as the capital-formation question in the face of unification-fragmentation forces[37] and the need to resolve "world," "national," "corporate," and other interests.

Communication

Communication is not an incidental or peripheral strategy. It is in some respects central to all the others and it applies to the actions of all participants in the world arena. The world's news services would find it difficult to rival the information-gathering techniques of the shipowners and bankers. Their knowledge of world affairs is truly phenomenal, their interest in daily events is all-encompassing: "An election in India can be as significant to a shipowner (anticipating a grain haul there from Canada, perhaps) as the nationalization of an oil field. A minor amendment to

37. See Fayerweather, *International Business Management*, cited above, pp. 133*ff.*

little-known legislation in any of a hundred national capitals is known to the last detail if it affects the shipowners."[38]

The political implications of the information revolution are hardly yet fathomable. Used by nations, the strategy of communication is sometimes referred to in the policy sciences as the ideological, or psychological, strategy. It is a strategy concerned with ideas and with changing men's minds; not necessarily with dogmatic ideas, or ideas of the visionary-theorizing-doctrinal brand, but more comprehensively with the use of all media, signs and symbols[39] for the purpose of attaining desired goals.

Communicational strategy is used by nations in the world arena along with the other types of strategy—military, diplomatic, and economic—to further national interests and to achieve the goals of national policy. There is a parallel to national uses of communication in multinational corporate strategy. We are dealing here not with an analogous situation but rather with an identical process used by both public- and private-sector organs as a major policy instrument.

The skills of management, in business enterprises of whatever size, include the skills in the manipulative use of symbols which can modify human response. There is a language of power in the politics of private as well as public sectors of society: the language of registering and modifying decision; "a battle cry, verdict and sentence, statute, ordinance, rule, oath of office, controversial news, comment and debate."[40] The skills involved are no

---

38. "The Billionaire Sea Lords: How They Rule the Oceans," *Forbes*, August 1, 1970, pp. 20-23.

39. For a general introduction to communicational strategy in this broad sense: Charles W. Morris, *Foundations of the Theory of Signs* (University of Chicago Press, 1938), a pioneer work on semiotic; and Lyman Bryson (ed.), *The Communication of Ideas* (Harper & Bros., 1948). On ideology as the term is used in the sociology of knowledge, see Karl Mannheim, *Ideology and Utopia* (New York: Harcourt, Brace & Co., 1936, later as a Harvest Book paperback). On ideology as an instrument of Communist policy: Zbigniew K. Brzezinski (ed.), *Ideology and Power in Soviet Politics* (New York: Frederick A. Praeger, 1966); Paul E. Sigmund, *The Ideologies of Developing Nations* (New York: Frederick A. Praeger, 1962); E. Lane, *Political Ideology* (New York: The Free Press/Macmillan Co., 1967); and Andrew Gyorgy and G. Blackwood, *Ideologies in World Affairs* (Waltham, Mass.: Blaisdell Pub. Co., 1967).

40. H. D. Lasswell, Nathan Leites and Associates, *Language of Politics: Studies in Quantitative Semantics* (New York: George W. Stewart, 1949), Ch. I. Cf. H. D. Lasswell, Daniel Lerner, and Ithiel de Sola Pool, *The Comparative Study of Symbols: An Introduction*, Hoover Institute Studies (Stanford, Calif.: Stanford University Press, 1952) and Daniel Lerner, "The Coercive Ideologists in Perspective," in Lasswell and Lerner (eds.), *World Revolutionary Elites*, Ch. 7.

longer statable in the banal talk about "making friends and influencing people"; there is now a formidable science of linguistics, a range of professional skills based on the systematic use of the semiotician's signs and symbols.

The basic literature on communicational strategy has to date concentrated almost entirely on international and cross-cultural communication at political levels[41] and with reference to mass communication media.[42]

In a careful study of international political communication, Davison has distinguished four broad categories of "ideas in international traffic," two of the official (state) type and two non-official:

1. Official communications that are intended to influence foreign audiences, for example, those of the U.S. Information Agency.

41. See W. Phillips Davison, *International Political Communication* (New York: Frederick A. Praeger, 1965); John W. Henderson, *The United States Information Agency* (Praeger, 1969); H. D. Duncan, *Communication and Social Control* (New York: Bedminster Press, 1962); Karl W. Deutch, *The Nerves of Government: Models of Political Communication and Control* (New York: The Free Press, 1963, and with a new introduction, 1966). Bibliographies: Bruce Lannes Smith and Chitra M. Smith, *International Communication and Political Opinion: A Guide to the Literature*. Prepared for The RAND Corporation by the Bureau of Social Science Research, Washington, D.C. (Princeton: Princeton University Press, 1956); Bruce Lannes Smith, Harold D. Lasswell, and Ralph D. Casey, *Propaganda, Communication, and Public Opinion: A Comprehensive Reference Guide* (Princeton: Princeton University Press, 1946). On communication data: Bruce M. Russett *et al.*, *World Handbook of Political and Social Indicators* (New Haven: Yale University Press, 1964), pp. 105-137. See also Bernard Berelson and Morris Janowitz (eds.), *Reader in Public Opinion and Communication*, Enlarged Edition (Glencoe, Ill.: The Free Press, 1953); Daniel Lerner (ed.), *Propaganda in War and Crisis* (New York: George D. Stewart, Publishers, Inc., 1951); William E. Daugherty in collaboration with Morris Janowitz, *A Psychological Warfare Casebook*. Published for Operations Research Office (Baltimore: John Hopkins University Press, 1958); A. L. George, *Propaganda Analysis* (Evanston, Ill.: Row, Peterson, 1959); J. J. Kirkpatrick (ed.), *The Strategy of Deception: A Study in Worldwide Communist Tactics* (New York: Farrar, Straus & Co., 1963); S. M. Faber and R. H. L. Wilson (eds.), *Man and Civilization: Control of the Mind* (New York: McGraw-Hill, 1961); H. D. Duncan, *Communication and Social Order* (Totowa, N.J.: Bedminster Press, 1962).

42. Wilbur Schramm (ed.), *The Process and Effects of Mass Communication* (Urbana: University of Illinois Press, 1954); W. Schramm, *Mass Media and National Development: The Role of Information in Developing Countries* (Stanford, Calif.: Stanford University Press, and Paris: UNESCO, 1964); W. Schramm (ed.), *The Science of Human Communication: New Directions and New Findings in Communication Research* (New York: Basic Books, 1963); F.I.C. Yu, *Mass Persuasion in Communist China* (New York: Frederick A. Praeger, 1964); Lucian W. Pye, *Communications and Political Development* (Princeton: Princeton University Press, 1963).

2. Official communications that are not intended to exert a political influence abroad, such as those of the U.S. Armed Forces Radio and Telegraph Network overseas.

3. Private communications that are intended to have a political influence on foreign audiences, such as those of groups working to promote international understanding.

4. Private communications that do not have a political purpose, such as those of international news services or business enterprises with interests abroad.[43]

Davison's four categories are not distinct and mutually exclusive. The sources, purposes, and effects of communications[44] are not always clear. A business message, intended only as a private commercial transaction, may have widespread and serious political repercussions. There may be mixed motives in the private communications of a multinational company, which must try, among other things, to adapt to or create a favorable political and social environment abroad for business survival and growth. Where do the transmitted ideas come from: the desk of a manager strictly concerned with business matters, or indirectly from some government department concerned with such matters as gold flows and balance of payments? Limitation of corporate communicational strategy to communications that have a strictly business impact would exclude some of the most significant strategic patterns of multinational corporate management, those which might be designated as quasi-political because they are designed for the "language of power." It is a language that multinational corporate managers learn to use as defenders of the enterprises they represent.

In terms of Davison's four categories, the essential question for the corporate strategist of communications is how to use both public and private communication to advance the policies of a multinational company. This quest breaks down into several tasks:

---

43. Davison, *op. cit.*, p. 10.

44. Davison's use of "communication" in the singular to designate the whole *process* by which meaning is transferred, and "communications" in the plural to refer to the messages themselves, is adopted here.

1. The most effective uses of the communication *process* for company policy purposes—

    (a) *internally*, in the interrelationships of company components and interpersonal relationships; and

    (b) *externally*, in the interplay of company and external sources of messages.

2. The communications as *messages* designed to achieve company policy objectives in—

    (a) *internal*, and

    (b) *external* relationships.

The effective use of symbols is essential in military, diplomatic, and economic strategy. The policy objectives may be the same but the strategic means differ even though they are used complementarily toward common ends of policy. The task of corporate communicational strategy is to use both public and private communication more effectively to advance corporate policies. Preconceptions about "propaganda" have to be laid aside and realistic evaluations must be made of the political effects that all media—newspapers, radio, TV, films, the movement of capital, goods, services, and persons, and other means of cross-border communication—can achieve.

Systematic study has to be made of the network of channels that carry the flow of ideas throughout the world, of the effectiveness of the use of mass media, of alternative means available for achieving the desired results in the "battle of ideas" in the world arena, of the conditions that must affect policy decisions on corporate communication as a strategy under widely varying situations, and of general recommendations regarding the use of communication in harmony with other corporate strategies for the pursuit of corporate goals.

The international communication network has become a rapidly expanding complex of public and private persons, organizations, media, and cross-border interrelationships. Governments often seek assistance from private-sector entities for purposes that entail collaborative efforts in economic, diplomatic, military and communicational strategy. The converse is true, too, with much reliance on ways of keeping multinational corporate managers fully informed about United States foreign policy and communicational strategy, for example.

The interplay of government and private-sector organizations in this field is fraught with some danger. This is evident in the press exposure of covert government intelligence work that has subjected some nongovernmental organizations to ridicule and worse. These private-sector groups, including multinational companies, may elect to bar too close an association with intelligence-gathering and other agencies of their home governments. Finding the proper pattern of coaction between multinational companies and governments will lay a heavy responsibility on the shoulders of corporate components specialized to the communicational process. They will always have to weigh the dangers of associating their communicational strategy too closely—if at all—with the ideological strategy of home and host governments.

A similar caveat applies to the intelligence function of managers in multinational corporate headquarters and in subsidiaries abroad. Communicational strategy involves the input of information as well as the output of messages to the external world. The input is essentially an intelligence function that can be compared with the intelligence function in national governments.[45] Like national intelligence, corporate intelligence rests basically on nonclassified information, that is to say, on papers not stamped as confidential or secret by some government; the intelligence function must not be conceived of as an essentially arcane and secretive operation. In some part, it is so, and must be so, given the adversary relationships that prevail both in the international system and market competition; but to equate the intelligence function with espionage is seriously to distort the problem of information input.

The transnational flow of unclassified information is of incalculable dimensions. It goes on at governmental as well as at nongovernmental levels, in war and in peace, in ceaseless streams that

---

45. Major works are: Harry Howe Ransom, *The Intelligence Establishment* (Harvard University Press, 1970), an outgrowth and revision of *Central Intelligence and National Security* (1958); Sherman Kent, *Strategic Intelligence for American World Policy* (Princeton University Press, 1951); Roger Hilsman, *Strategic Intelligence and National Decisions* (The Free Press of Glencoe, 1956).

are only partly and momentarily hindered by hostilities between nations. This communicational flow is, in fact, one of the most vital—and by the general public vastly underestimated—bonds that are already preparing the way for a global community. The inchoate world order depends upon strengthening these communicational bonds, just as it depends upon the bonds of trade, long forged by cross-border enterprises. The information centers of these enterprises have been called, with much justification, "management's hidden asset." [46]

The information centers of multinational corporations are not, of course, mere libraries that collect documents and file papers. Unwritten as well as written communications must also be handled. In 1970, more than 200 countries and territories were within reach of 97 percent of the world's telephones. Satellite systems have vastly increased the capability of communications systems. Documents can be transmitted by facsimile signals. Corporate personnel can move with ease throughout the world. There are numerous sources of governmental as well as private-sector information that are often untapped as corporate communicational input. The problems of acquisition, organization, analysis and synthesis, maintenance and storage, retrieval and dissemination of information in the large multinational corporation, are all of fundamental importance in communicational strategy, but there are special problems as to use.

The output side of communication, as a strategy, is not a matter of advertising, speechifying, and "effective" letter-writing. The communicational strategist has to make a systematic study of all manner of output, including nonverbal as well as verbal messages that are sent out by whatever component or person in a multinational corporation. There are productive and counterproductive ways of communicating in all functional aspects of an enterprise, from supply to sales.

46. Morton E. Melzer, *The Information Center: Management's Hidden Asset* (American Management Association, 1967). A practical book with reference to many important and scattered sources of information, an account of the systems approach to information, organizing the information center, establishing the scope of its services with attention to qualitative and quantitative growth patterns, automation, costs and budgets, and the "Sigma approach" as a summarizing informational function. Cf. Richard C. Fahringer, "Potentials for Worldwide Management Information Systems," and Robert C. King, "Administering an International Computer."

There is a vast difference between interpersonal communication and mass communication, which is aimed at majorities or large minorities; both have little known consequences for multinational corporate policy. If the mass media can increase sales, it must be remembered also that the Bedouin on his camel hears through his transistor radio that he is part of a nation and shares its problems and aspirations.[47] Multinational corporations may hope to strengthen transnational economic bonds through trade that is enormously abetted by electronics; but divisive nationalism is abetted in the same way. Technological advances will provide in the future cheaper broadband transmission and a potentiality to provide complicated, cheap, and reliable terminal equipment through microelectronics; multinational corporations will make use of these advances for their own strategies, but so will all the other protagonists in the world arena.

The protagonist that will come out ahead in the future uses of communicational strategy is likely to be the one that first understands the social, economic and political implications of a sound theory of communication—a broad, coherent and useful theory of the process that includes all physical means of communications and will lead to many new signals and uses for these signals. The trend, technologically, is toward "the generalization of communication, in the sense that human nerves have a generalized transmission function that is utilized in all our senses and powers."[48] The environment provided by the new technics of information transmission will be as different from the present one as this one differs from the pretelephone world. Advanced circuitry will produce more than the "nonlinear" revolution of McLuhan.

It will not necessarily produce the psychological and cultural basis for a world community. It may cement the old parochialism, or merely help to create a new parochialism at the national or regional level, or in racial or other terms. The growth of transnational business in the multinational corporation will depend upon communicational transcending of boundaries that foster

47. John R. Pierce, "Communication" in Daniel Bell (ed.), *Toward the Year 2000*, pp. 297-309.
48. *Ibid.*, p. 309.

parochialism. In particular, multinational corporations will require communications media that cannot be blocked by autarchic nation-states; they will also need means to decide for themselves what messages to transmit, notably the mapping in men's minds of possible transnational relationships of a global reach. Parochially-minded political elites will try to block this effort, yet such an effort is indispensable to world trade.

Chapter VIII

THE ROLE OF GLOBAL CORPORATIONS

The multinational corporation is a major social institution whose significance will be fully understood only with the passage of time. Yet even now it is possible to discern some salient points, notably the evolution of a new form of corporate enterprise at the transnational level, and the role of the multinational corporation in shaping a new global economy as the present anachronistic international system fades into history.

The historic significance of the multinational corporation is an interesting chapter in the development of business institutions. The modern corporation is a response not only to technological change but also to changing concepts of property, of the managerial function in organizations that separate control and ownership, and of corporate personality in relation to public and private polity. In the United States, for example, the development of constitutional protection of the rights of "persons" has been closely related to the rise of the modern corporation; and the free movement of capital across frontiers of the States of the Union has been facilitated by an important body of constitutional interpretation concerning the federal system.

The corporation has become the dominant form of business organization not only because of its utility in the profitable production of goods and services, but also because businessmen can, by its use, develop a species of private-sector polity within the constitutional structure of the public polity of the nation. Without the corporate form of private government in business enterprise it is difficult to see how most of the great national companies could have grown up to serve a national market. There is a symbiotic relationship between these public and private polities that is an essential characteristic of contemporary capitalism in its several forms. In the United States, this symbiosis can be expounded partly in terms of United States constitutional development and partly as a matter of economics; but the whole story demands the discipline of political economy.

In the United States, as in other nations of the non-Communist world of the "West" (now including Japan and other eastern hemisphere countries), the corporation is an integral part of a *national* economy that expands the "corporate domain" beyond previously restrictive local jurisdictions, and businessmen now seek a *transnational* corporate domain. With this search occurring on a large scale, especially since the Second World War, we enter the era of the multinational corporation which crosses national frontiers to do business in the face of enormous odds inherent in an international system of sovereign entities that stand guard at their frontiers. The world arena is dominated in law—and, in the case of the superpowers, in fact—by those who govern these sovereign entities. Their foreign affairs are *inter-national*; if each sovereign state were completely authoritarian and totalitarian, there would be no cross-border activities except at sovereign command or by sovereign permission. Cross-border business would, in that case, be entirely inter-national and completely governed by the public polities of the nations involved.

The transnational activity of the multinational corporation is a very different thing. There is a clear distinction between "international economics" and "international business." The distinction is too often overlooked, with consequent confusion of thought about the meaning and future role of the multinational corporation. Transnational activity embraces all movement of things, persons, ideas and vibrations across official national frontiers. It comprises both the official activities of states in the international system and all non-state activities.

There may have been a time when the greater part, or at any rate the most significant part, of transnational activities was official, but the acts of governments in their foreign relations can hardly be said to account for most transnational action today. Even those which claim the power to control all the domestic and foreign activities of their subjects, with unprecedented instruments of policy at their command, must accept the fact that non-state entities—using the same instruments—now compete successfully with the sovereign state for influence in the world arena. They are able to do so because many of these nonsovereign entities are more powerful than states, and, more importantly, because some nonsovereign entities respond to human demands that sovereign states cannot meet at the exclusively official level of international relations.

The present international system is simply not adequate to deal with many of the problems that businessmen face when they establish business operations in several sovereign states. There is no overarching structure of supranational authority, comparable with the national authority of home and host governments, to prescribe uniform and enforceable "laws merchant." There is no single source of power to establish a multinational corporate entity with a legal personality of its own. The multinational corporation is an ingenious institutional device—or better, a complex of devices—to overcome the severe handicaps of balkanization in the present international system of scores of sovereign states (ever increasing in number) that yield to no supranational body.

The multinational corporate enterprise strongly energizes the move toward a viable global economy to supersede a dangerously sick non-system of international economics that is frustrated by our outdated international political system. Ours is an age of "creative destruction," to borrow from Schumpeter, in which new ways must be found to live with the consequences of the various revolutions of our time.

Multinational corporate strategy is not always above reproach from given ethical points of view. The goal values of companies— as of churches, political parties, and other transnational organizations—vary. It cannot be said that all of these aim toward the creative purpose of shaping a new global economy under the living law of a world order. On the contrary, the very idea of a world order is anathema to many. Nor are multinational corporations as a whole now bent on making a world order in which they will play an integral and constructive organic part. Some of them are opportunists who find the anarchy of the world arena highly advantageous for short-term rewards.

Others, however, are there for the long pull, and that means the assumption of those institutional responsibilities that must be shouldered by citizens of the world. Still others, doubtful about any world-wide political-economic system for the near future, make their contribution by efforts aiming at regional unity, as in the Common Market. Among the more skeptical are multinational corporate managers who see their best chance for the survival of their business in cleaving closely to the national policies of home and host governments, but at the same time using all the influence at their command to negotiate for optimum conditions in every jurisdiction.

The negotiatory capability of a multinational corporation vis-à-vis sovereign states is sometimes considerable. Corporate negotiators, backed up by economic power and communicational techniques, as well as the forces at the disposal of governments, may not meet the international jurist's criteria of "actors" in the international system; they are not among the sovereign makers of treaties and international law, but they are decidedly among the makers of an emergent transnational system. The multinational corporation is, in fact, often so potent and independent an activator of transnational movements in goods, services, personnel, credit instruments, and the like, that the elites of sovereign states become jealous and fearful of its power.

What is to be the precise role of the multinational corporation in the emergent system? Will it be just another sovereign state, a corporate sovereign, with the reduced authority that all actors in the international system must suffer if the world is to be saved from suicidal destruction? Or will it take its place alongside other transnational institutions—religious, scientific, artistic, educational, ethnic, and so on—that may work out a system of collaboration with the present major and sovereign actors? The international system of sovereign states could in this latter way be transformed through functionally specialized supranational organizations that would provide a substantial framework for a global economy; the beginnings can already be seen in such institutions as the World Bank and the International Monetary Fund, to be followed in time by an updated Bretton Woods agreement, and new functionally defined regional organizations.

It is not improbable that this will be the answer to the major problem of multinational corporate action in the world arena today: how to establish a secure transnational "corporate domain" for a transnational business. The answer to this problem will not be found alone in the restructuring of the international political system. Required is the simultaneous restructuring of the business corporation itself; but the potentiality for constructive change in the corporation probably exceeds that of the modern state.

The corporation is an ancient and adaptable device for getting things done. As a device for getting the world's work done on the scale of large regional and even global undertakings, we can already see its potentialities. These potentialities will be fully realized, however, to the extent that the manager of a multinational company thinks of his organization as more than an opportunistic measure for survival in a hazardous world arena. Conceptualization of multinational enterprise as a building block in a future world-wide economy is the necessary ingredient.

The present multinational corporation must be thought of as the modern corporation in a transitional stage of development. What the next developed form will look like is still problematical. It may well be true, as Erich Jantsch has said,[1] that the eventual world corporation cannot be national, nor even multinational in the sense that it is a mere agglomeration of national corporations; nor can it be Western or Eastern in its orientation, for it must be "transcultural" in all its policies and practices. He proposes that as an institution of the future—if that is what it is to be—the world corporation must adapt to a total "mankind-oriented" approach in policy, in organization, in strategies.

In seeking answers to this question of transitional forms, the serious student of corporate action in the world arena will lean heavily on some of the newer disciplines for aid in analysis and forecasting. The futurists' hypotheses are provocative. "Total system dynamics" may provide a useful intellectual tool for extracting the central issues. Vickers' global frame of reference is a case in point:[2] *ecology*—the relations between ourselves and the total physical environment; *economy*—the relationships among men's activities as producers and consumers; *politics*—the relationships among men and groups in terms of power; and *appreciation*—referring to systems of values and norms, not excluding

1. Erich Jantsch, "The 'World Corporation': The Total Commitment," *Columbia Journal of World Business*, May-June 1971, pp. 5.-12.

2. Geoffrey Vickers, *Freedom in a Rocking Boat: Changing Values in an Unstable Society* (London: The Penguin Press, 1970).

esthetic standards and goals. There are other ways to classify the required subject matter of corporate managerial work ahead; all must go beyond the traditional boundaries that hold managerial thinking within the narrow confines of business economics.

The more far-sighted multinational corporate managers are already transcending these boundaries. This was evident in a recent conference of international business leaders with Professor Arnold Toynbee in London. They had come together to discuss the implications for multinational corporations of Toynbee's observations on "the reluctant death of national sovereignty." For Toynbee, national sovereignty persists today as an unworkable concept. It limits our ability to protect ourselves and our environment, when national governments can do nothing by themselves, for example, to stop the poisonous transnational flow of pollutants: air and water know no national boundaries. Only a world authority, it is now clear, can deal with ecological problems.[3]

The multinational corporation needs and must have peace; it requires open trade routes by air and by sea, and the freedom to move goods, money, and people across frontiers, without interruption.[4] This was the view of Orville Freeman, president of Business International, Inc. He regarded the multinational corporation as something new and of notable magnitude in its reach for "a global shopping center"; the assets of these corporations had already exceeded the gross wealth of any nation of the world except the United States—and this "in but a few years under very great handicaps, having to jump over the host of national boundaries and impediments."

Eldridge Haines, the founder and former chairman of Business International, Inc., observed at this conference that the multinational corporation was still an evolving institution. The companies in this category are trying "to internationalize the

3. "Will Businessmen Unite The World?", *Center Report: A Center Occasional Paper*, Vol. IV, No. 2, April 1971, published by the Center for the Study of Democratic Institutions, Santa Barbara, California.

4. Cf. Sanford Rose, "Capital Is Something That Doesn't Like a Wall," *Fortune*, February 1971: "The program to limit the flow of dollars into overseas investments has confused and infuriated U.S. business without achieving its aim of cutting the balance-of-payments deficits," he wrote, concerning the futility of the U.S. Foreign Direct Investments Program of 1968. Irresistible capital flows occur in other currencies as well.

ownership" and the boards of directors, to share the rewards of success so that the profit would not go to industries in one particular country, and to "give assurances to people in various parts of the world that their interests are being weighed when big decisions are being taken at the summit." He also saw a growing awareness of, and action to implement, the "international social responsibilities of a multinational corporation."

The role of the multinational corporation in the development of a viable, world-wide political economy is now being given serious consideration by scholars, businessmen, and statesmen. The concept of an international government of the oceans, for example, has become the concern of a wide variety of interests, governmental as well as commercial, expressed in terms of a global equity in the exploitation of the ocean's resources for the benefit of all and with due regard for conservation and preservation of the environment. Neil Jacoby has proposed a model ocean regime that includes both regulatory and operating functions, with the corporate form constituting an appropriate means for planning and carrying out operations established by an ocean regime.[5] As time goes on, the uses and functions of the multinational corporation will undoubtedly be expanded in response to man's effort to bring order into the world arena and to avoid the precipitous decline into the chaos that Professor Toynbee fears.

Given the harsh dialectics of Order vs. Freedom, East vs. West, Capitalism vs. Communism, etc., so characteristic of our century, it would be rash to predict the corporate goals of tomorrow. But if the multinational corporation establishes its function as an indispensable means of getting much of the world's work done in this age of crises, there will be time enough to ponder its eventual role in a global political economy. Current attacks on "the corporation" notwithstanding, the utility of this organizational instrument in the hazardous world arena will not be seriously questioned. That the goals and values of its managers may be questioned is an entirely different issue that should never be confused with the merits of the multinational corporation as a social institution.

5. See Neil H. Jacoby, "Corporate Enterprises in an Ocean Regime," *Columbia Journal of World Business*, March-April 1971; and Richard Eells, "Corporate Sovereignty: A Charter for the Seven Seas," *ibid.*, July-August 1970.

*   *   *

The theme of this book can be stated in the following propositions:

> The modern corporation, already recognized as a major social institution within most industrialized nations, is now rapidly becoming a transnational institution of major importance in the world political economy; its organization transcends political frontiers in order to enter a global marketplace.

> Widely known as the *multinational corporation* because of its organizational spread into many different countries, the modern corporation conducts its transnational or cross-border activities in characteristic patterns that derive to a large extent from the peculiarly pluralistic structure of the so-called "international system."

> While multinational corporations—especially those which are based in the United States—have proliferated since World War II and now comprise some of the largest business enterprises in the world, the terminology for describing this development has not yet sufficiently stabilized to permit one to state categorically what statistical universe is properly designated by the term: "multinational corporation"; the *definition* of this term (and its equivalents) has become more than an exercise in semantics and now enters the realm of public policy making discourse.

> The new role of the modern corporation as a major institution in the world is evident in contemporary debate about public policy at national and international levels where *the significance of the multinational corporation for the political economy of nations, regions, and the world as a whole* is being probed with still unforeseeable results for corporate as well as for public policy.

230

The organization, procedure, and strategy of multinational corporations, together with their *functions* in the world's political economy, are all *related to the present patterns and future trends in the international political system, and in international economics.* The multinational corporation is also related to other transnational activities—social, educational, scientific, ethnic, religious, and so on; so-called "international business" does not exist in a social vacuum or a sector apart, and the multinational corporation especially— as an organizational form that has proved to be well-nigh indispensable for getting much of the world's work done.

Of major significance here is *the search for congruence*: for political boundaries in the international system that will be congruent (or at least not incongruent) with "corporate domains" of indispensable multinational firms in an ecologically sound worldwide political economy or aggregate of regional political economies; present organizational and procedural patterns in multinational corporations exhibit attempts to leap across frontiers in the absence of such congruence and to counter sovereign states' strategies with corporate strategies of appropriate ingenuity and power.

While men struggle with the problem of a world order under law to supersede the anachronistic international system, the *multinational corporation of today and tomorrow must perforce devise its own corporate strategies* not only for survival and profitable enterprise in the world arena of strongly contending forces, but also for adapting their transnational organizations to rapidly changing conditions in that arena, anticipating where possible new global structures of political economy within which the multinational corporation can play an organic part.

Epilogue

THE DEVELOPING CRITICISM OF
THE GLOBAL CORPORATION

In 1971 when this book was written, there was every reason to believe that the global corporation was on the brink of achieving a new status on the world stage. Many straws were in the wind: the enormous growth of foreign direct investment in the 1960s and early 1970s; the rapidly escalating demands and expectations of people around the world for the goods and services that large, well-managed companies could provide; the continued presence or threat of tariff barriers in the nation-states of the world; the willingness of these same nation-states to encourage the entrance of American (and other) capital, technology, and management skills; the failure of the nation-states in or out of the United Nations to work out procedures for regulating such companies; and much more—all this made it appear that multinational companies were about to achieve a new autonomy or a kind of quasi-sovereignty in the world arena.

It was the enormous size of these companies and the economic—and, consequently, social, political, and psychological—power that these companies commanded that made a new role seem so likely. To appreciate this one must only consider how large multinational corporate operations have become. Thus, by 1973, according to the estimates of the Council on Economic Development, the Gross World Product was valued at $3 trillion, of which some $450 billion, or 15 percent, was produced by multinational corporations. The sheer size of some of these companies is made clear when one considers that the gross sales of General Motors in 1969 were larger than the Gross National Product of all but twenty-two of the countries of the world.[1] And this multi-national part of the world economy has been growing at a rate of 10 percent per year. This is a faster growth rate than that of many nations, and some economists speculate that, before the close of the century, some three hundred giant, multinational businesses will produce more than half of the world's goods and services.

Since this book was first published, multinational corporations have continued to grow, but their size and power have more and more been subjected to criticism from many sources. Of course, there had been a developing literature of examination and criticism during the 1960s, but concern was limited to a relatively small group. Thus, a special census was taken of the operations of multinational corporations for the calendar year of 1966 by the Bureau of Economic Analysis of the U.S. Department of Commerce, and this has proven to be an important measure of these companies. The census covered all known U.S.–based multinational corporations, including some 3,400 U.S. parent companies and about 23,000 foreign affiliates. This census has subsequently been supplemented by a sample survey of the operations of multinational corporations for the calendar year 1970, covering 298 U.S. parent companies with about 5,200 foreign affiliates. These studies documented the phenomenal growth of the U.S. multinational corporation, but still this growth was not a matter of widespread interest and concern.

Then, in 1972, Jack Anderson revealed that ITT had considered giving a million dollars to the CIA to prevent Dr. Salvador Allende Gossens from becoming President of Chile, and this more than any other event called attention to multinational companies and opened a period of intense scrutiny and criticism of whatever attributes of sovereignty—or quasi-sovereignty—these companies had accumulated.[2]

1. U.S., Congress, Senate, Committee on Finance, Subcommittee on International Trade, *The Multinational Corporation and the World Economy,* Staff Report, February 26, 1973 (Washington, D.C.: Government Printing Office, 1973), p. 8.
2. U.S., Congress, Senate, Committee on Foreign Relations, Subcommittee on Multinational Corporations, *Multinational Corporations and United States Foreign Policy,* Parts 1 and 2, Hearings on the International Telephone and Telegraph Company and Chile, 1970–71 (Washington, D.C.: Government Printing Office, 1973).

In March of 1972, the Office of International Investment in the Bureau of International Commerce of the U.S. Department of Commerce published three studies in the first volume of a projected three-volume work on U.S. multinational corporations entitled *The Multinational Corporation: Studies on U.S. Foreign Investment.*[3] The first study, "Policy Aspects of Foreign Investment by U.S. Multinational Corporations" provides "a survey of the role and significance of the multinational corporations and discusses the interaction of the multinational corporation, government and labor, in the areas of employment, technology transfers, investment controls, and the balance of payments." The second study, "U.S. Multinational Enterprises and the U.S. Economy" presents "a summary and extrapolation of the conclusions drawn from nine case and industry studies." The third study, "Trends in Direct Investment Abroad by U.S. Multinational Corporations, 1960–1970," provides "a statistical analysis of the main elements of the growth in U.S. foreign direct investment during the decade of the 1960s."

Then, in April of 1973, the Commerce Department published the second volume, *Why Industry Invests Abroad: Summary of Findings,* which examines "the factors that have motivated U.S. business to establish production facilities abroad. . . . It does so by assaying the factors that motivated 76 U.S. companies in 15 industrial categories to undertake investments outside the United States." Volume 3 of the study will "provide statistical data and analyses of the financial, trade and employment effects of a selected sample of U.S. multinational corporations."

As a result of the revelations about ITT's contemplated political activities, Chile secured unanimous passage on July 28, 1972, in the United Nations Economic and Social Council, of resolution 1721 (LIII) requesting

> . . . the Secretary-General, in consultation with Governments, to appoint from the public and private sectors and on a broad geographi-

---

3. U.S., Department of Commerce, *The Multinational Corporation: Studies on U.S. Foreign Investment,* Vol. 1 – Part I. Policy Aspects of Foreign Investment by U.S. Multinational Corporations; Part II. U.S. Multinational Enterprises and the U.S. Economy; Part III. Trends in Direct Investments Abroad by U.S. Multinational Corporations – 1960 to 1970 (March 1972); Vol. II – *Why Industry Invests Abroad: Summary of Findings* (April 1973); Vol. III – to be published.

cal basis a study group of eminent persons intimately acquainted with international economic, trade and social problems and related international relations, to study the role of multinational corporations and their impact on the process of development, especially that of the developing countries, and also their implications for international relations, to formulate conclusions which may possibly be used by Governments in making their sovereign decisions regarding national policy in this respect, and to submit recommendations for appropriate international action, the study group to consist of not less than 14 nor more than 20 persons.[4]

To facilitate the work of the Group of Eminent Persons, the Department of Economic and Social Affairs of the United Nations Secretariat prepared a report, *Multinational Corporations in World Development,* published in 1973. The Introduction to this report summarizes a point of view that has now achieved some prominence:

> In the past quarter of a century the world has witnessed the dramatic development of the multinational corporation into a major phenomenon in international economic relations. Its size and geographic spread, the multiplicity of its activities, its command and generation of resources around the world and the use of such resources to further its own objectives, rival in terms of scope and implications traditional economic exchanges among nations.
> . . . Multinational corporations, which are depicted in some quarters as key instruments for maximizing world welfare, are seen in others as dangerous agents of imperialism.
> The political and social dimensions of the problem of multinational corporations are only too apparent. The United Nations' present involvement in the subject was in fact prompted by incidents involving certain multinational corporations. The concern and excitement occasioned by those incidents testifies that the general public is no longer willing to stand by passively. The degree of uncertainty that exists regarding the way in which the power of the multinational corporations may be exercised and what the reactions and consequences are likely to be is no longer acceptable. Despite the considerable and transnational power which multinational corporations possess they, unlike governments, are not directly accountable for their policies to a broadly based electorate. Nor, unlike purely nation-

4. United Nations, Economic and Social Council, Resolution 1721 (LIII), cited in United Nations, Department of Economic and Social Affairs, ST/ECA/190, Sales No. E.73.II.A.11, *Multinational Corporations in World Development* (New York: United Nations, 1973), pp. 106–7.

al firms, are the multinational corporations subject to control and regulation by a single authority which can aim at ensuring a maximum degree of harmony between their operations and the public interest. The question at issue, therefore, is whether a set of institutions and devices can be worked out which will guide the multinational corporations' exercise of power and introduce some form of accountability to the international community into their activities.

The multinational corporations have developed distinct advantages which can be put to the service of world development. Their ability to tap financial, physical and human resources around the world and to combine them in economically feasible and commercially profitable activities, their capacity to develop new technology and skills and their productive and managerial ability to translate resources into specific outputs have proven to be outstanding. . . . At the same time, the power concentrated in their hands and their actual or potential use of it, their ability to shape demand patterns and values and to influence the lives of people and policies of governments, as well as their impact on the international division of labor, have raised concern about their role in world affairs. This concern is probably heightened by the fact that there is no systematic process of monitoring their activities and discussing them in an appropriate forum.

The important contribution that such firms can make to world welfare needs to be understood in the context of the objectives that they pursue. While their operations are often global, their interests are corporate. Their size and spread imply increased productive efficiency and reduction of risks, both of which have positive effects from the point of view of the allocation of resources. Yet, their predominance can often create monopolistic structures which reduce world efficiency and may displace or prevent alternative activities. The concentration of multinational corporations on the production and promotion of certain types of products and services not only influences consumption patterns but, in developing countries, often responds mainly to the demand of small segments of the population.

The divergence in objectives between nation-states and multinational corporations, compounded by social and cultural factors, often creates tensions. Multinational corporations, through the variety of options available to them, can encroach at times upon national sovereignty by undermining the ability of nation-states to pursue their national and international objectives. Moreover, there are conflicts of interest regarding participation in decision-making and the equitable division of benefits between multinational corporations and host as well as home countries.[5]

5. United Nations, Department of Economic and Social Affairs, ST/ECA/190, Sales No. E.73.II.A.11, *Multinational Corporations in World Development* (New York: United Nations, 1973), pp. 1–3.

The final report of the Group of Eminent Persons, *The Impact of Multinational Corporations on Development and on International Relations,* puts the problem this way:

> Home countries are concerned about the undesirable effects that foreign investment by multinational corporations may have on domestic employment and the balance of payments, and about the capacity of such corporations to alter the normal play of competition. Host countries are concerned about the ownership and control of key economic sectors by foreign enterprises, the excessive cost to the domestic economy which their operations may entail, the extent to which they may encroach upon political sovereignty and their possible adverse influence on socio-cultural values. Labour interests are concerned about the impact of multinational corporations on employment and workers' welfare and on the bargaining strength of trade unions. Consumer interests are concerned about the appropriateness, quality and price of goods produced by multinational corporations. The multinational corporations themselves are concerned about the possible nationalization or expropriation of their assets without adequate compensation and about restrictive, unclear and frequently changing government policies.[6]

In addition to these United Nations and U.S. Commerce Department studies, the U.S. Tariff Commission has done an extensive study of "the implications of multinational firms on the patterns of world trade and investment and on United States trade and labor." This study was done at the request of the U.S. Senate Finance Committee and was published by that Committee in February of 1973.[7] This study was based on the data mentioned above which was gathered by the Bureau of Economic Analysis of the Department of Commerce.

Another result of the revelations about the ITT plans in Chile was the formation by the Senate Foreign Relations Committee of a subcommittee on multinational corporations. This subcommittee has held hearings on the ITT affair, the Overseas Private

---

6. United Nations, Department of Economic and Social Affairs, E/5500/ Rev. 1, ST/ESA/6, Sales No. E.74.II.A.5, *The Impact of Multinational Corporations on Development and on International Relations,* Report of the Group of Eminent Persons to Study the Impact of Multinational Corporations on Development and on International Relations (New York: United Nations, 1974), p. 26.
7. U.S., Congress, Senate, Committee on Finance, *Implications of Multinational Firms for World Trade and Investment and for U.S. Trade and Labor* (Washington, D.C.: Government Printing Office, 1973).

Investment Corporation (OPIC), and the policies of the U.S. government toward the International Petroleum Cartel and the creation of the Iranian Consortium.[8] Further studies are planned.

Besides these U.S. government studies, there has been a virtual rash of similar investigations carried out by the governments of many nations of the world. Important among these have been the semi-official "Watkins Report" in Canada, *Foreign Ownership and the Structure of Canadian Industry,* Report of the Task Force on the Structure of Canadian Industry, and *The Impact of Foreign Direct Investment on the United Kingdom,* an outside research project sponsored by the Economic Services Division of the Board of Trade, now the Department of Trade and Industry, by M. D. Steuer and others.[9]

And in the United States interest in multinational corporations has gone beyond studies; legislation has been introduced in the Congress which would increase considerably the taxation of profits from foreign investment by U.S. corporations, freeze foreign trade at the average levels of 1965–69 through the imposition of import quotas, and give the President power to prohibit the transfer abroad of U.S. capital or technology which, in the judgment of the President, would create unemployment in the United States.

From all of this evidence—and there is much more—it is quite clear that the multinational corporation has now become a major subject of concern around the world. Although it has many defenders, it also has many detractors and much of the literature concerning the multinational corporation is critical. The criticisms are directed to almost every aspect of the multinational corporation so that to look at them is a fairly adequate way of reviewing

8. U.S. Congress, Senate, Committee on Foreign Relations, Subcommittee on Multinational Corporations, *Multinational Corporations and United States Foreign Policy,* Parts 1 and 2, Hearings on the International Telephone and Telegraph Company and Chile, 1970–71, and Part 3, Hearings on the Overseas Private Investment Corporation (OPIC); *The International Petroleum Cartel, the Iranian Consortium, and U.S. National Security;* et al.
9. Privy Council Office, *Foreign Ownership and the Structure of Canadian Industry,* Report of the Task Force on the Structure of Canadian Industry (Ottawa, 1968); M. D. Steurer et al., Her Majesty's Department of Trade and Industry, *The Impact of Foreign Direct Investment on the United Kingdom* (London: Her Majesty's Stationery Office, 1973).

the current state and likely future of this new institution on the world stage.

Of the criticisms that are made of multinational corporations we will focus here upon those which are particularly germane to their multinational character. That is, multinational corporations are composed of divisions within many nations, and these divisions are thereby subject to the same kind of criticisms that any national or purely local corporation is subject to by virtue of being a business corporation. A local subsidiary of General Motors is subject to attack for its local hiring practices just like any corporation. To the degree that such matters are purely local or national, they are not our concern here; rather our concern is with the international or multinational aspects and implications of the activities of these companies.

First, we will examine those criticisms of the multinational corporation that concern its relations to nation-states or other groups, i.e., criticisms that concern essentially the external relationships of the multinational corporation. Then we will turn to a group of criticisms that, although they have external consequences, bear mainly on the way in which the multinational corporation is run internally.

The Quasi-Sovereignty of the Multinational Corporation

It is widely believed today that the large multinational corporations are more-or-less independent power centers, and, as such, compete improperly, if not unethically, with the nation-states. Consider the following from the recent United Nations report on this subject, *Multinational Corporations in World Development* (1973):

> . . . the manifold operations of foreign-based multinational corporations and their pervasive influence on the host country may be regarded as a challenge to national sovereignty. The challenge has, moreover, economic, social, political and cultural dimensions which are frequently inseparable from one another. The tensions and conflicts thus generated are, likewise, the result of complex interaction between many agents in many areas.

239

> Frequently, the multinational corporation is perceived as capable of circumventing or subverting national objectives and policies.[10]

Again, in London, in 1973, Her Majesty's Department of Trade and Industry issued a report entitled, *The Impact of Foreign Direct Investment in the United Kingdom,* with an entire chapter devoted to the problem of the multinational corporation and national sovereignty. This report puts it thus: "Both the advocates and opponents of the international corporation seem to agree that in some way inward investment restricts the national sovereignty of the recipient nation. . . [and that] economic control/ownership by foreigners has political consequences. . . ."[11]

The relative independence of the multinational corporation is stressed again and again, in report after report. These corporations are particularly seen as independent with respect to the host countries, especially the less-developed host countries. With respect to the developed host countries, where the largest amount of foreign direct investment is located, the problem of the independence or quasi-sovereignty of the multinational corporation is perhaps not so severe, and this for several reasons. First, the developed countries are experienced and knowledgeable and do not feel as threatened as the underdeveloped countries by the size and power of the large multinational corporations. Second, these countries are the ones that have their own multinational corporations seeking entrance to, or already in, the country from which the entering multinational is likely to come—so there is a certain complementarity. On the other hand, when multinational corporations enter a developed country to establish a manufacturing facility, it is often, but by no means always, the case that it could easily go right across the border to an adjoining country, and this can give the multinational corporations a certain negotiating advantage.

The multinational corporation entering an economically underdeveloped country, however, possesses great negotiating power relative to that country. If the multinational company seeks rare natural resources and *cannot* go some place else for them, then, of course, the negotiating power of the country is greater. The oil ex-

10. United Nations, *Multinational Corporations in World Development,* p. 46.
11. M. D. Steurer et al., *The Impact of Foreign Direct Investment,* p. 161.

porting countries of the world are good examples of this. But this is one of the few advantages possessed by the underdeveloped countries in dealing with large multinational firms. In general, such countries are eager for any economic development and feel driven to offer the best possible conditions to such companies. But this state of need, or dependence, is the source of deep disquiet for the leaders of the underdeveloped countries, if we can judge from their votes and comments in the United Nations. As much as they need the economic development promised by the entrance of multinational companies, they harbor resentment at their dependent condition and fear that they can never bargain on an equal basis, that if they fail to please, they will simply be cut off with nothing.

On the other hand, the multinational corporation is seen as independent of its home country. It seems anxious to avoid taxation at home; it is accused of "exporting" jobs from its home country; it is accused of almost giving away the American patrimony, represented here by our scientific and technological advances which have been achieved by the investment of American money—frequently government tax money invested in research—it is accused of moving its enormous liquid assets around among currencies in ways which have been disruptive to the stability of the dollar; and it has been accused of pursuing economic goals not in accord with home nation needs and planning.

If all of these charges of independence do not add up to a charge that the multinational corporation has managed to become a new sovereign force on the world stage, they at least suggest a "quasi-sovereignty" and more independence than many political leaders in many nations have been willing to accept. Because of this we have seen in recent years around the world more and more efforts to restrict the freedom of these new giants on the international scene. In the United States, the Burke-Hartke bill would increase taxes on the profits from foreign investment by U.S. corporations and impose other restrictions. In other countries, there has been a marked increase in nationalization and expropriation. In many countries, certain sectors of the economy have been reserved for national corporations, that is, corporations with home bases in other countries have been excluded from certain sectors of these nation's economies. The governments of members of OPEC are moving toward complete control of the facilities in their own territories. In Canada, a Foreign Investment Review Act has been seriously considered. The regulation of foreign investment is being considered in Australia, and in Mexico there is now a requirement for the regulation of new foreign investment. Similar controls have recently been enacted in other Latin American countries.

A Comparison with the East India Company

As we reflect on the charges of the growing power or quasi-sovereignty of the multinational corporations, it is interesting to look back in history to the East India Company, which for a long time represented sovereignty of Great Britain in India.

The story of the East India Company is a fascinating one, although the details of its history are generally unknown today among businessmen, even among many scholars in the field of business theory. The East India Company engaged in commercial business in our twentieth century sense of the term "business," namely, trading, selling, shipping, and making a profit for its stockholders. A brief review of its history will allow us to see some interesting similarities—and contrasts—with the modern multinational corporation and some of the anticipations about its future.

The first bookkeeping entry of the East India Company was made in 1599, some 376 years ago. From a trading company it developed into the government's administrator of life in India. Indeed, the East India Company was the political authority in India until 1858. One of the most important features in its development was its contribution to the extra-national expansion of the British Empire.

This remarkable company had a remarkable organization. At its prime, it had its own army, its own navy (the Bombay Marine), and its own coinage. Its army was sizeable; its navy small but effective; and the Company backed and guaranteed its own coinage. Moreover, the Company gave the maharajahs their status and their power. The Company organized, managed, and policed an entire subcontinent, while maintaining profitable commercial relationships with a wide area of the globe.

Now before we compare the East India Company's administrative and governmental tasks in India to the real, and the possible, quasi-sovereignty of the multinational corporations of today, we must point out certain differences between the two. As Neil H. Jacoby has written in *Corporate Power and Social Responsibility:*

> . . . [these] trading companies . . . [including the East India Company] were forerunners, but not true prototypes of today's multinational corporations. They were essentially trading rather than manufacturing organizations, with comparatively little fixed investment. And they operated within the colonial territories or spheres of influence of their own nations rather than under the jurisdiction of foreign sovereign states.[12]

And this is true; the East India Company did not have a large direct investment in India. A large direct investment in a foreign country is one of the widely accepted criteria today for multinational corporations. And it is true that while the East India Company was in business in India, India was not a foreign country with its own tariff walls—it was a part of the British Empire. Of course, the British Empire was a large and diverse conglomeration and had many of the characteristics within itself of a world market. What was produced in India was traded in a very wide commercial universe.

Having recognized this point, the crucial point here, however, does not have to do with the "multinationality" of the East India Company, but rather with the fact that it exercised sovereignty on behalf of the British Empire, within the borders of India. It was this exercise of sovereignty that generates the interesting comparison with what some have spotted as certain trends in the modern multinational corporation.

The point we wish to make here is the following: in the case of the East India Company, the British government called upon a private company to exercise sovereignty on its behalf in a portion of the British Empire. Rather than sending in its own army and developing its own administrative structure in India, the government deemed it more efficient to have a private company run the affairs of India.

By contrast, the multinational corporation of today is recognized by some to have acquired *some* of the attributes of sovereignty

12. Neil H. Jacoby, *Corporate Power and Social Responsibility* (New York: Macmillan, 1973), p. 96.

—what we are calling here quasi-sovereignty—on the world stage. Some have even predicted the replacement of the nation-state by the multinational corporation—a position to which I cannot subscribe. The contrast, of course, is that whatever quasi-sovereignty the multinational corporation may have achieved—or drifted into—it has certainly not been at the urging of any nation-state. Indeed, the nation-states today seem, as they awaken to the recognition of how much independence the multinational corporations have achieved, inclined to take steps to limit that development.

Now, while we are not likely to see any national government turn to a private company to exercise the full scope of its sovereignty over some part of its territory, we have seen lesser applications of this notion as when the federal government turned to private companies to run various special activities, such as atomic energy development, or even something as prosaic as small townships turning to private companies for garbage disposal. At one point a number of years ago, the Greek government considered hiring Litton Industries to run certain sectors of its economy. Although the phenomenon is not frequent, occasionally governmental bodies recognize that the organizational structure of private companies is much more efficient in accomplishing certain work than the bureaucracy of public government. So, the notion that the more authority oriented managements of private companies are more effective in producing results than politically dominated—although sometimes just as authoritarian—government bureaucracies, remains in the background as a basis for calling upon the private corporation—and, indeed, the private multinational corporation with vast financial and managerial resources—to execute large public goals in the future.

Finally, there is another sense in which multinational corporations "exercise sovereignty" on behalf of their home nations, i.e., a multinational corporation frequently does, in fact, if not in law, exercise the effective sovereignty of its home nation in foreign countries where the multinational corporation has offices. For example, it can—unfortunately—be argued that ITT and the copper companies were—in the eyes of the world—the real representatives of the United States in Chile, the State Department diplomats and advisors serving simply as the official and graceful "front" for our commercial interests which really carried the full weight of American sovereignty. That the Chairman of the Board of ITT considered reversing the political decision of the Chilean people was revealing; he apparently did not doubt that he represented the sovereign power of the United States in Chile. Had he had any serious doubts, he would hardly have considered offering the Central Intelligence Agency $1 million of his firm's money to carry out its purposes. Of course, such power is never officially in the hands of the multinational corporations, but it drifts there over time. When the matter becomes public or a real crisis threatens, the state reasserts its sovereign role—at least for a while.

It is not yet clear how the issue of the growing power and autonomy, or quasi-sovereignty, of the multinational corporation will be resolved. A number of proposals have been made about the establishment of world chartering agencies and the adoption of a code of ethics for multinational corporations. Some have proposed that the laws regulating and taxing the profits of multinational corporations in the various countries be brought into harmony. For the time being it appears that there will be a fairly swift series of national moves to restrict the operations of these companies in various ways. Whether international regulation will then follow is at this point unclear. In any event, the power, independence, and quasi-sovereignty of the multinational corporation will remain one of the major issues on the world's agenda.

The Lack of Concern for Social Justice

There is a widespread belief that the large multinational corporation lacks a real concern for social justice, that, indeed, its whole modus operandi is based upon exploiting the cheapest labor and natural resources—or both—that it can find, without fair recompense to the mass of the people, at the same time leaving former employees in its home country to survive as best they can. This is done, it is argued, to supply a relatively small part of the world with an unnecessarily high level of material existence, i.e., robbing the poor to satiate the rich.

That corporations in general—not just multinational corporations—are in pursuit of profit to the exclusion of every other social or even economic value is certainly not a new criticism. Nor is it an easy charge to evaluate. On the one hand, the entrance of a large multinational corporation into a poor part of the world is bound to bring some economic development to that area. Presumably this is a benefit to the people of the area. On the other hand, the introduction of the work ethic and the way of life of modern industrial capitalism into an economically underdeveloped country and a nonmodern social world can have a disruptive effect on the people, their culture, and their established institutions. On the scale of ultimate social values, these effects may completely offset any gains achieved economically. Of course, some say that economic development is beneficial no matter what, and that the price of a few year's of social disruption is small compared to the long-term economic benefit. This argument points to the United States as an example of the benefits to be gained by a continual revolution in life styles to achieve ever higher levels of industrial existence and comsumption. Others think that this is an irresponsible disruption of a society, that, particularly today, the small economic gain will be temporary and will be more than offset by the destruction of social mores that have proved their value over many centuries.

To many, then, the perceived lack of concern with social justice is among the most serious threats posed by the growth and strength of the multinational corporations. The counter-offensive is seen in more and more efforts to regulate direct investment abroad, even by more cases of expropriation and nationalization. The example of the OPEC nations, who control a scarce resource needed by the industrialized world where most of the multinational corporations have their home bases, has not been lost on many of the poor and underdeveloped nations of the world, and it would appear that their example will be followed unless the multinational corporations make concerted efforts to avoid exploitation of labor and resources.

Environment

Another major problem confronting the multinational corporation stems from the awakened sensitivity of people in all nations, but especially in the industrialized nations, to both local and global problems of the environment. The multinational corporation is more and more being confronted with criticism with respect to both kinds of problems. Local environmental problems are those whose main effects are felt within a limited geographical area—noise pollution, strip mining, congestion, trash, garbage, and industrial waste disposal, etc. Since multinational corporations have plants in many localities throughout the globe, they must cope with a wide variety of different criticisms about the environmental effects of their activities. In this connection, the laxity of laws and restrictions on the environmental effects of industrial processes in some countries can make it attractive for multinational corporations to move polluting operations from jurisdictions that have severe restrictions to those that have light or no restrictions, to jurisdictions that have been characterized as "pollution havens." Indeed, some underdeveloped countries have occasionally suggested that for the sake of some economic development they would be glad to have a little, or even a great deal of, pollution.[13]

In addition to local environmental problems, there are environmental problems that are global in their effects. Since many multinational corporations are large enough for their activities to have global consequences, such corporations come in for a fair share of criticism for these planet-wide environmental problems. Examples are provided by the petroleum and automobile industries, both of which are dominated by multinational corporations. These industries are held responsible for the dramatic increase in certain pollutants, which are having, and are expected to continue to have, unpredictable and perhaps grave consequences on the weather and food production around the world. Chemical companies continue to push DDT on the world market despite dire warnings of the long-term consequences on all life, and especially the food resources of the ocean. To these and other criticisms, the response of multinational corporations has been slow and complaining, and this footdragging has only gone to inflame public opinion not only against the responsible companies but also against the whole business community.

13. Richard J. Barnet and Ronald E. Müller, *Global Reach: The Power of the Multinational Corporations* (New York: Simon and Schuster, 1974), p. 345.

Multinational Corporate Intelligence Systems

Another problem concerns what can be called "corporate intelligence" on the world level. Following World War II, several organizations were formed in the United States that openly offered corporate intelligence services; the general public is still largely unaware of such organizations. They are staffed by men who have shifted from intelligence work in the federal government to intelligence activities in the private sector. In recent years, an increasing number of big corporations, especially multinational corporations, have either established private intelligence units or have hired intelligence consultants from the intelligence community of the United States government. The basic purpose has been to protect corporate secrets. But this is not a perfect universe and one would have to assume that some corporations would use an intelligence organization to acquire another company's secrets in our highly competitive society.

Recently, Mr. Tad Szulc, a distinguished and reliable former correspondent for the *New York Times* has written that "this emerging industrial-intelligence complex is more pernicious than the military-industrial complex about which Eisenhower warned when he left the White House."

Let us take two examples: oil companies and international banks. A number of international oil companies and a number of international banks have highly developed professional intelligence units that may indeed rival some government intelligence services. The interest of the oil companies, of course, is to know what competitors are doing or planning in the search for new sources of oil, in making international arrangements, in arriving at marketing decisions, and so on. It is alleged by the oil-producing countries in the Middle East that the international oil companies' intelligence operations even penetrate the governments of those countries. And, some of the international banks in the Middle East have developed the most detailed dossiers on the key people in each of the countries, and they carry on an intense day-to-day analysis of money flows and political power shifts, as well as long-range economic forecasts.

Then there is the matter of one corporation infiltrating another corporation. Infiltration seems to be the latest intelligence technique adopted by corporations from government operations. While an acceptable justification can be given for the intelligence activities of a government on the grounds that the security of the nation requires them, such grounds are not available to corporations. As the details of these operations become more and more known to the public, there will no doubt be strong criticism of multinational corporations for assuming this intelligence attribute of sovereignty. Restrictions by governments on these activities seem a likely response in the future.

The Cultural Education of Multinational Corporate Officers

Although the multinational corporation has become a world institution it has frequently carried with it a definitely parochial point of view. This limited point of view in the minds of the corporate officers who represent a multinational corporation around the world has been the source of much misunderstanding and subsequent criticism of the institution of the multinational corporation. It poses for these companies the necessity of providing for their personnel rather thorough programs of education in the cultures of the world. Many corporate officers are really unaware that they are viewed by the educated around the world as the unwelcome agents of cultural imperialism forcing the goals and tastes of the American culture into old and traditional cultures. That this can be accomplished, more or less, with the money and power that the companies wield is not in doubt, but it raises a fester that will likely be a source of trouble for these corporations many years into the future.

Granted that it is difficult to orient corporate officers who have grown up within the confines of one culture to the realization that the habits, traditions, and attitudes of peoples around the world from other nations, cultures, and religions are as profoundly meaningful to them as the habits, traditions, and attitudes of corporate officers are to themselves. But the position into which the American multinational corporation has propelled itself will require that, no matter the difficulty, its survival and acceptance in the future will be more and more dependent upon a sensitive perception and appropriate response to the cultures of other people.

Conclusion

In my estimation, these five problems are deeply serious ones for the multinational corporation, even though several of them are not at the forefront of current discussion. Indeed, two decades ago who would have thought that there was such a problem as the quasi-sovereignty of the multinational corporation? We were assured that there could be no conflict between these corporations and the nation-states because corporations were chartered by nation-states and were subject to their laws; Q.E.D., there was no problem about their sovereignty or quasi-sovereignty. But, obviously problems were implicit and have developed, for the nation-states are now moving to restrict and regulate the power, independence, and economic strength of the multinational corporations.

Nor are those discussed above the only problems confronting the multinational corporations. There are, of course, many others, some of which affect these companies on a world scale and others of which affect them in their home countries as well as in each of the countries where they have affiliates.

For most of the problems confronting the multinational corporation no clear solution lies ready at hand. Each of these problems has been studied, but before anything like a solution to them is achieved many more years of research and experimentation must go on. As each partial solution is effected with the goal in mind of benefiting either the corporation or the nation-state, the other will take compensating measures and new problems will replace the old.

However, no problem is solvable prior to an adequate diagnosis. In a world where there are so many problems—in a world which, by its nature, is so problematical—to identify which problem it is that we want to focus our attention on—and to define its scope—is itself a large step. In concluding this epilogue we might note that neither the university community, the business community, nor the legal profession has taken very seriously the need to come up with an adequate theory of the firm. Such a theory must adequately relate the goals of the corporation to the goals of the nation-states and the world as a whole, as well as make clear what the actual social, economic, and psychological basis of the business firm really is in the latter part of the twentieth century. Such a theory must include among other things an examination of the issues of corporate social responsibility and business ethics. Thus far only fragments of a real theory of the firm have appeared, and they have been largely economic fragments.

Even though business has supported the educational community in the areas of science and technology, as well as in the social sciences and law, this support has not been massive. In the areas of management and economic research, especially concerning the problems we have discussed, there has been only modest support. What the corporations have not realized is that the development of an adequate theory of the firm—and particularly the multinational firm—would be most advantageous to them. The example of antitrust is a propos. When a big corporation is sued by the government, it spends millions for its legal defense. The argument should be considered that perhaps the legal defense could have been made more effective if scholarly work had already been carried out for some time in law and business schools concerning the theory of the firm. For instance, studies in depth should have been done on the anticipated effects of proposed antitrust policies on the vitality of the nation.

The solution of all of these problems to a considerable degree, then, waits upon the development of an adequate theory of the firm; and the development of an adequate theory of the firm waits upon the business community, the university community, and the legal community. The problems mentioned above will not simply go away.

Index

RICHARD EELLS is the Director and Editor of the Program for Studies of the Modern Corporation, and an Adjunct Professor of Business at the Graduate School of Business, Columbia University. Previously, he held the Guggenheim Chair of Aeronautics at the Library of Congress and later was Manager of Public Policy Research for the General Electric Company. He has received various scholarly awards, including research grants from the Alfred P. Sloan Foundation and the Rockefeller Foundation. In 1971, he was appointed a Visiting Fellow to The Center for the Study of Democratic Institutions, Santa Barbara. He lectures frequently both in the United States and abroad. He serves as an advisor and consultant to a number of corporations and research organizations and is a trustee of several foundations.

THE HONORABLE GEORGE W. BALL is a Senior Managing Director of Lehman Brothers, Incorporated and Chairman, Lehman Brothers International, Ltd. Mr. Ball was Director of the United States Strategic Bombing Survey, London, 1942-44 and for a number of years engaged in the practice of law in Washington, D.C. He was Under Secretary of State for Economic Affairs in 1961 and Under Secretary of State, 1961-66. In 1968, he served as the United States Permanent Representative to the United Nations. Mr. Ball is a trustee of the American Assembly, Columbia University and has received the Legion of Honor (France) and the Medal of Freedom (United States). He has served as a director of several multinational corporations.